Portland

Second Edition

by Linda Nygaard
Dining chapter by Susan Wickstrom

John Muir Publications

Acknowledgments

Thanks to Portland historians and writers Terence O'Donnell and E. Kimbark McColl, whose exemplary work chronicles Portland's colorful history and spiced-up flavor from its beginnings through today. Thanks also to Deborah Wakefield, Paula Fasano, Bette Sinclair, Ken Hoyt, Joe Cronin, Susan Sokol Blosser, and Jo Ostgarden for their unerring faith and helpful enthusiasm. Jennifer, Ryan, and Lucas, your help truly saved the day!

Dedication

This one's for you, Maren, because you are sorely missed in Portland.

John Muir Publications, P.O. Box 613, Santa Fe, New Mexico 87504

Copyright © 1998, 1996 by John Muir Publications
Cover and maps copyright © 1998 by John Muir Publications
All rights reserved.

Printed in the United States of America.
Second edition. First printing September 1998.

ISBN: 1-56261-412-6
ISSN: 1088-3614

Editor: Sarah Baldwin
Graphics Editor: Heather Pool
Production: Nikki Rooker
Design: Janine Lehmann
Cover Design: Suzanne Rush
Typesetter: Melissa Tandysh
Map Production: Julie Felton
Printer: Publishers Press
Front Cover Photo: © Leo de Wys, Inc./Jim Domke—*Portlandia*
Back Cover Photo: © Larry Geddis—Portland and Mt. Hood from the Washington Park
 Rose Garden

Distributed to the book trade by
Publishers Group West
Berkeley, California

CONTENTS

How to Use This Book   **v**

1 Welcome to Portland   **1**
River City 2 • Portland History 2 • The People of Portland 4 • Portland's Neighborhoods 7 • Portland's Weather 16 • Portland Style 17 • When to Visit Portland 18 • Calendar of Events 20 • Business and Economy 26

2 Getting Around the City   **29**
The Lay of the Land 29 • Tri Met: Public Transportation 30 • Driving in Portland 32 • Parking 34 • Bicycling in Portland 35 • Taxi Service 36 • Other Transportation Services 36 • Portland International Airport 38 • Other Area Airports 41 • Train and Bus Travel 42

3 Where to Stay   **43**
Downtown 45 • Southwest 49 • Northwest 52 • Northeast 53 • Southeast 56

4 Where to Eat   **58**
Downtown 60 • Southwest 70 • Northwest 72 • Northeast 76 • Southeast 78

5 Microbreweries   **84**

6 Sights and Attractions   **92**
Downtown 92 • Southwest 106 • Northwest 107 • Northeast 108 • Southeast 109 • City Tours 110 • Day Spas 112

7 Kids' Stuff   **114**
Greater Portland 114 • Outside Portland 119

8 Museums and Galleries   **121**
Museums 121 • Art Galleries 124

9 Parks and Gardens   **131**

10 Shopping   **137**
Shopping Districts 137 • Books and Magazines 147 • Department Stores 149 • Portland Area Malls 150 • Factory Outlets 151

11 Sports and Recreation   **152**
Recreational Activities 152 • Spectator Sports 157 • Professional Sports 158

12 Performing Arts   **160**
Performing Arts Venues 160 • Classical Music and Opera 167 • Dance 167 • Theater 167 • More Performance Art 168

13 Nightlife 172

Dance Clubs 172 • Jazz Clubs 173 • Rock and Blues Clubs 174 •
Country Music Clubs 175 • Celtic Sounds 176 • Other Good
Places 177• Comedy Clubs 178 • Notable Movie Theaters 178

14 Day Trips from Portland 182

The Columbia River Gorge 182 • Astoria 183 • Montagne de Niege
187 • The River with No Shore 190 • The Willamette Valley 191 • Wine
Country 193

Appendix: City•Smart Basics 197

Index 202

MAP CONTENTS

Portland Zones vi

2 Getting Around the City
Fareless Square 33
Portland International Airport 41

3 Where to Stay
Downtown Portland 44
Greater Portland 50

4 Where to Eat
Downtown Portland 61
Greater Portland 68

5 Microbreweries
Portland Microbreweries 86

6 Sights and Attractions
Downtown Portland 94
Greater Portland 104

14 Day Trips
Portland Region 184

HOW TO USE THIS BOOK

Whether you're a visitor, a new resident, or a native of the "Jewel of the Northwest," you'll find *City•Smart Guidebook: Portland* indispensable. Written by Portland resident Linda Nygaard, with a dining chapter by Susan Wickstrom, this book gives you an insider's view of the best Portland has to offer.

This book presents Portland in five geographic zones. The zone divisions are listed at the bottom of this page and are shown on the map on the following pages. Look for a zone designation in each listing. You'll also find maps of downtown and greater Portland in Chapters 3, 4, 5, and 6 to help you locate the accommodations, restaurants, microbreweries, and sights covered in those chapters.

Example:

PORTLAND ART MUSEUM
1219 SW Park
226-2811   **DT**

Zone abbreviation = DT

Portland Zones

Downtown (DT)
The area bounded on the west and south by the I-405 loop, on the east by the Willamette River, and on the north by Lovejoy Street to the Broadway Bridge. Includes Old Town, Chinatown, and Portland Center for the Performing Arts.

Southwest (SW)
The area south of Burnside Street and west of I-405 and the Willamette River. Includes Civic Stadium and Washington Park.

Northwest (NW)
The area north of Burnside Street and the Broadway Bridge and west of Williams Avenue. Includes North Portland, Nob Hill, and Forest Park.

Northeast (NE)
The area north of Burnside Street and east of Williams Avenue. Includes Memorial Coliseum, the Rose Garden, the Convention Center, and the Lloyd Center.

Southeast (SE)
The area south of Burnside Street and east of the Willamette River. Includes the Oregon Museum of Science and Industry, Reed College, and Oaks Amusement Park.

GREATER PORTLAND ZONES

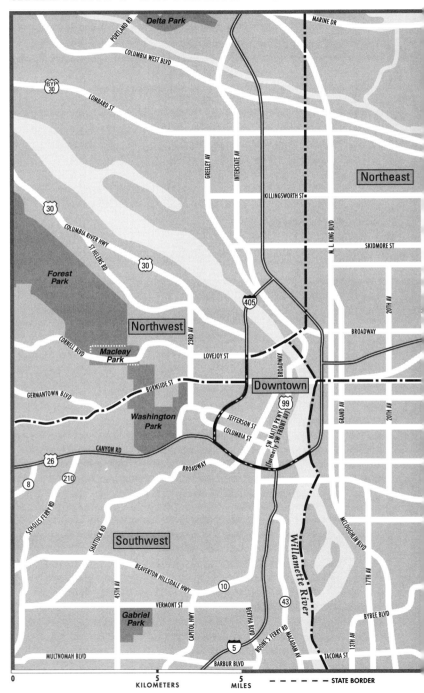

0   5 KILOMETERS   5 MILES   – – – – STATE BORDER

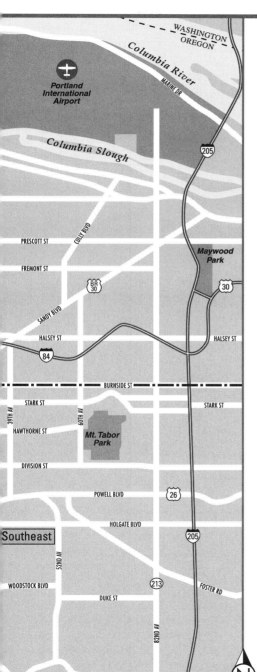

PORTLAND ZONES

Downtown (DT)
The area bounded on the west and south by the I-405 loop, on the east by the Willamette River, and on the north by Lovejoy Street to the Broadway Bridge.

Southwest (SW)
The area south of Burnside Street and west of I-405 and the Willamette River.

Northwest (NE)
The area north of Burnside Street and the Broadway Bridge and west of Williams Avenue.

Northeast (NE)
The area north of Burnside Street and east of Williams Avenue.

Southeast (SE)
The area south of Burnside Street and east of the Willamette River.

1

WELCOME TO PORTLAND

Portland has been called everything from urban and cosmopolitan to quaint and old-fashioned. Either way you look at it, you're right. The "Jewel of the Pacific Northwest" blends spicy big-city flavor with small town tradition. Nestled between the Cascade and Coast Mountains and surrounded by ancient fir forests, Portland has a thriving economy and a lively cultural scene. Inspired city planners managed to create a sophisticated city that is in harmony with its natural environment. Urban growth boundaries are fiercely protected, making housing costs rise but keeping the landscape intact. As a result, Portland moves at a slower pace than most cities of its size, and the people tend to be a bit more friendly than the average city dwellers.

Portland is an eclectic city. The Willamette River, running right through the city, creates natural division between the very different east and west sides. On the Westside, you'll find the city's center. Office buildings, upscale shopping, banks, and a busy transit mall give this side of the river a big-city feel. It's the glitzy side of life in Portland. Bankers, lawyers, real estate developers, and restaurateurs thrive there. New hotels, parking garages, and office buildings (like the new Federal Building, referred to as the "*Palace* of Justice" by some locals) are continually changing the Westside's landscape.

If the Westside defines Portland's financial core, the Eastside defines its heart and soul. Though the Eastside has its affluent residents, most are working artists, writers, musicians, shopkeepers, and entrepreneurial types. Neighborhood streets are narrow, and you'll find community gardens tucked in beside urban parks and in business sectors. The shops, businesses, and people have a palpable Eastside flavor. Celtic music, Ethiopian restaurants, restored vintage movie theaters, and tiny art galleries can be found all over this area. Street fairs abound in the summer. Shops often display their wares on the sidewalk. And you're guaranteed to find more than one "double take" opportunity if people-watching is your game.

Portland is a city for explorers. On any given afternoon, you'll be able to find a unique art form right on the street. Cobblestone streets carry trolley cars and horse carriages, pedestrians and bicyclists. Bridges lead to restored vintage architecture, and walking paths wind around the city, through the parks, and along the busy river. Although there's no shortage of things to do in Portland, you would be remiss if you didn't take a couple of hours on a sunny afternoon (yes, the sun does shine in Portland sometimes) to sit and observe. There's almost always something worth seeing wherever you find yourself in Portland.

River City

The Willamette River, the longest north-flowing river in the United States, plays an integral part in defining Portland's charisma. Home to houseboats, pleasure boats, barges, racing sculls, tugboats, and fishing vessels, the Willamette flows through the center of Portland, dividing the city into east and west.

While it's true that other cities can boast more bridges, none can claim more pride in them than Portland, and none can showcase such a variety of pedestrian-friendly bridges in such a small area. Portlanders are so proud of their bridges that they have organized the Willamette Light Brigade, a citizen volunteer group devoted to raising funds and inspiration for illuminating River City's bridges. Headed by Paddy Tillett, who hails from London and is one of Portland's most respected architects, the Willamette Light Brigade seeks to light every bridge on the Willamette River, using a different design for each. Plans are innovative and larger than life—one even calls for a neon salmon jumping over a bridge.

Portland History

The Lewis and Clark Expedition landed in the Portland area in 1805, some 40 years before Portland officially became a city. Clark's handwritten

TRIVIA

Portland is well known as a city with a clean and abundant water supply. Bull Run, Portland's water source, was so named after some cattle ran from a pioneer wagon train. Bull Run provides fresh, clean water to Portland through a gravity flow system, the oldest such system in the United States.

TRIVIA

Multnomah County's Central Library, 801 SW 10th Ave., is worth a visit. The early 1900s building was recently renovated and is full of Portland history and art. Tours are available on Wednesday at 2:30 and Saturday at 11:30. Just show up in the lobby and you'll be guided through an amazing experience.

journal records impressions of an Indian village that sat near present-day Portland International Airport. In the early 1800s fur traders like John Jacob Astor, ship captains like John McLoughlin, and other pioneer settlers came to establish trade, agriculture, and new roots. Most of the early settlers came from New England and New York, many arriving via the Oregon Trail between 1841 and 1860.

Legend has it that near the end of the Oregon Trail, pioneers were forced to make a choice to go north to Oregon or south to California. At the fork in the road were two handpainted signs. One, with an arrow pointing south to California, was a crude drawing of a gold nugget and a pickaxe. The other was a lettered sign that said "Oregon," with an arrow pointing north. It is said that those who could read came to Oregon.

The naming of Portland—also known as The City of Roses, Bridgetown, Rip City, River City, Stumptown, and many other pet names—is another favorite city tale. This one, however, is known to be true.

In 1845, a few years before Portland became part of a federal territory, two of its early settlers agreed to toss a coin to name the city, which at that time was little more than forested dreams. Francis Pettygrove, a Maine-born entrepreneur, and Asa Lovejoy, a Boston lawyer, each wanted to name the new city after their own favorite East Coast cities. Lovejoy thought Boston would be a good choice; Pettygrove wanted Portland. It's obvious who won the coin toss. Today, that coin can be seen on display at the Oregon History Center.

1993 Oregon Trail Celebration

Oregon Tourism Commission

By 1880 Portland's population had grown to nearly 20,000, with most residents living on the west side of the river. By 1900 Portland had boomed to a whopping 95,000 people. Today, the Portland metro area boasts a population of nearly 2 million, making it the 25th largest

TRIVIA

The highest elevation in Portland is 1,073 feet, at Council Crest.

metropolitan area in the United States. By comparison, Oregon's total population is 3 million, 45 percent of whom live in Portland.

The People of Portland

The city's residents are as diverse as its terrain. Portland's history is peopled with shanghaied sailors, timber barons, land tycoons, and suffragists. Something of its colorful history remains in the city today. Portlanders tend to be independent thinkers, a bit "off the wall" according to some, voracious readers, and tenacious in their environmental beliefs.

It's not uncommon to hear a foreign language or two spoken on the streets or to see a conservative business man standing next to a purple-haired, nose-ringed artist at the stoplight. At the local coffeehouses, you'll hear musicians wax poetically at a table adjacent to bankers talking about real estate values. Lunchtime brings people to the parks with a sack lunch and, often, a laptop computer or a sketch pad.

Portlanders love their downtown at night, too. Unlike many American cities, where nighttime draws the shades down on activity, Portland leaves

The Portland Mounted Patrol

The Portland Mounted Patrol Unit, a community policing effort started in 1979, has become one of Portland's favorite icons. According to Sergeant David Poole, the horses are "mediators by nature"; people often want to take pictures of them and their riders, or stop to chat or ask a question. The Mounted Patrol is eminently approachable, and visitors are encouraged to seek them out if assistance of any kind is needed. The patrol nearly met its demise in 1985 as a result of budget cuts. But Portland citizens rallied on their behalf, making such a fuss that the city rearranged the funding priorities and the Mounted Patrol continues to thrive today. You'll see them riding in pairs throughout the downtown area, and occasionally on the Eastside.

the lights on and the shades up. The city scene seems to flow like the river, changing from daytime business attire into diverse evening dress. Classic theater, grunge rock, swank restaurants, and poetry readings are just some of the things that beckon Portlanders downtown after dark.

Music plays a big part in the Portland scene. Tom Grant and Curtis Salgado are two local boys who made it big in the jazz and blues scene. International strains waft through the air on any given night. An evening walk downtown is like a lesson in cultural geography—music from Africa, the Caribbean, East India, and Greece can be heard within an easy stroll. Alternative rock and grunge notes can be heard, too, emanating from little-known clubs where little-known bands have been known to turn into big-name sensations.

Whether a visitor's taste runs toward sidewalk music or a symphony under the stars, a lazy afternoon in the park or five-star meal after sundown, a brisk bustle through the financial district or a stop at a riverside espresso cart, Portland will satisfy.

Portland's Neighborhoods

Good citizens are the riches of a city.
— C. E. S. Wood

As Charles Erskine Scott Wood, one of Portland's earliest attorneys (known to his friends as C.E.S.), noted in the 1800s, the people of the city are its finest resource. In Portland, community and neighborhood planning have always come first. Always. Urban sprawl is not a problem here. Urban growth boundaries are fiercely maintained and ardently guarded. For that reason, Portland remains one of the few cities in America with distinct neighborhoods, in which history is honored and growth is viewed with a cautious eye. According to some cities' standards, most of Portland's neighborhoods could be considered "close-in," since they are, for the most part, within a relatively easy 20- to 25-minute drive.

Through the pages of history, you can see evidence of early planning dedicated toward making the city of Portland a "living room" for all of its citizens. Earliest plot plans (circa 1845) called for 200-square-foot blocks (approximately 1 acre and half the size of the city's counterparts) downtown with a 60-foot public right-of-way in between so that there would be ample street room for the citizens to enjoy their city. Portland citizens today still enjoy their streets and sidewalks and think of them as an extension of their own homes.

In 1974 the Office of Neighborhood Associations began as a platform for discussion and decision-making between City Hall and the citizens of Portland. Hundreds of people are involved on a volunteer basis in more than 90 neighborhood associations. Portlanders care about their city, its environmental health, its appearance, and its future. To that end,

PORTLAND TIME LINE

1805 The Lewis and Clark Expedition reaches the Columbia River in August. In November they arrive at a village of 25 houses and 200 Flathead Indians. The village later became Portland.

1825 Fort Vancouver is built on the north side of the Columbia River.

1829 Etienne Lucier, a French Canadian, becomes the first white man to settle on land that would later become Portland.

1843 Provisional government formed.

1844 Lovejoy and Pettygrove build a cabin near what is now Front Street and Washington. These two men toss a coin to name the city.

1848 Oregon territorial government formed.

1849 A massive flood sweeps the Willamette Valley.

1850 Census reports indicate 805 white residents in Portland.

The brig *Emma Preston*, under the command of Captain John Couch, becomes the first vessel to sail between Portland and Hong Kong. She carried lumber and wheat.

1851 William S. Ladd, who later became one of Portland's leading merchants and bankers, arrives in town with a shipment of liquor.

1853 The Willamette Engine Company No. 1 is formed, offering the first fire service in Portland, complete with buckets and ladders.

1858 Congregation Beth Israel founded.

1859 Oregon becomes a state.

1863 City of Portland collects licenses for 38 dogs and 25 barrooms.

Henry Weinhard builds Portland's first brewery.

1864 First telegraph dispatch to Portland.

1870 Captain John Couch dies of typhoid pneumonia.

1872 New Market Theatre opens.

1872/1873 Two disastrous fires destroy much of Portland.

1876 Willamette River floods, reaching a high-water mark on June 24.

1880 Portland population has increased to 18,000.

1883 Stephen Skidmore bequeaths to the city a drinking fountain for "horses, men, and dogs."

1887 The Morrison Bridge becomes the first bridge across the Willamette in Portland.

1889 Portland holds its first rose show, which later develops into the Portland Rose festival, an annual citywide event in June.

1890 Portland Hotel opens at the terminus of the Northern Pacific Railroad, where Pioneer Square sits today.

1891 Port of Portland formed by Oregon state legislature.

1891 Ladd's Addition is platted as one of the country's first planned communities.

1895 Sign on Morrison Bridge reads, "Ordered that No Person Shall Ride or Drive Over This Bridge Faster than an Ordinary Walk."

Oregon Symphony founded.	**1896**
Meier and Frank Department Store constructed.	**1898**
The Lewis and Clark Centennial Exposition brings more than 1.5 million visitors to Portland.	**1905**
Officials make space in City Hall for a children's free dental clinic.	**1910**
Simon Benson donates 20 bubbling drinking fountains for the citizens of Portland.	**1912**
Women's suffrage passes in the Oregon legislature.	**1912**
Portland's population is 276,000.	**1913**
Portland is home to three working movie studios.	**1916**
International Rose Test Gardens established as country's first.	**1917**
Portland Knitting Company becomes Jantzen, the country's oldest swimwear manufacturer.	**1918**
Bonneville Power Administration established.	**1937**
Carhops begin service at 'Yaw's Top Notch" in the Hollywood District, where a milkshake was 55 cents.	**1944**
White Stag, a clothing company, is established by German-born Henry Wemme.	**1947**
Pietro Belluschi's Equitable Building is constructed as one of the world's first International Style office buildings.	**1948**
The disastrous Van Port flood causes $100 million in damage.	**1948**
First international flights depart from Portland Airport.	**1948**
Portland Development Commission formed to oversee urban development and renewal.	**1958**
The nation's largest shopping center, Lloyd Center, opens.	**1960**
Portland-born Linus Pauling wins his second Nobel Prize.	**1962**
Governor Tom McCall's Willamette Greenway Project begins to create "an accessible and inviting front porch for the city." Part of that project is Tom McCall Waterfront Park.	**1970s**
Kobos opens as Portland's first specialty coffee company.	**1973**
Portland Mounted Patrol formed.	**1979**
Mt. St. Helen's erupts and spews ash all over Portland.	**1980**
Bridgeport, Oregon's first microbrewery, is opened.	**1984**
Portlandia, 6.5 tons of hammered bronze, arrives in pieces on a barge for dedication at the Portland Building.	**1984**
The Columbia River National Scenic Area is established.	**1986**
MAX, Portland's benchmark light rail system, officially opens.	**1986**
Portland wins US Conference of Mayors' most livable city award.	**1988**
Barbara Roberts becomes Oregon's first woman governor.	**1991**
The "spring break quake" awakens Portlanders at 5:34 a.m. with a 5.6 on the Richter scale.	**1993**
Mr. Holland's Opus is filmed at Portland's Grant High School.	**1996**
Portland's Central Library, built in the early 1900s, reopens after extensive renovation.	**1997**

the city and the citizens work together through the neighborhood associations to monitor land-use decisions, improve traffic patterns, preserve historical landmarks, and promote local businesses. Also under the auspices of the Office of Neighborhood Associations, the Neighborhood Watch program was initiated to combat crime and has had tremendous success. The association's members also help to organize social activities like block parties, neighborhood fairs, and community fundraisers. In Portland, it's important and fun to get to know your neighbors, and the Office of Neighborhood Associations is a good place to begin.

For more information or to learn more about a specific neighborhood by talking to one of its representatives, you can call the Office of Neighborhood Associations at 823-4519 or 823-4000. The association has an office in City Hall where you will find neighborhood maps, meeting information, and referral programs for a wide variety of needs, including refugee assistance, media relations, fiscal policies, elderly or disabled services, and more.

Portland's neighborhoods vary not only in location, but also in personality and architecture. Many of those neighborhoods established in the early days still manage to maintain their historic charm and charisma. The newer neighborhoods around Portland are full of personality, too, but of a different kind. Descriptions of some of Portland's most interesting and well-known neighborhoods follow.

Westside Neighborhoods

Council Crest

On the city's Westside, up in the hills, Council Crest began as a home site for one John Talbot, a New Englander who settled in Portland in 1849. His original land claim of 640 acres appealed to him because he sought seclusion and a good place to raise a family. Malaria was a problem in Portland at that time, and Talbot sought a place "high enough to be healthy." In 1851, the same year that Portland officially became a city, Talbot built a log cabin for his family, just to the south of his original claim, where he and his family lived a fairly solitary life until the city began expanding its boundaries and other families moved in.

There are several stories about how the area got its name. One version claims that Chief Multnomah of the Willamette Indian Tribe held "council" meetings in the area with other tribal leaders. One other legend says that, since Council Crest was so high in the hills, it was a prime spot for sending smoke signals. According to yet another account, a group of ministers named it during a hike in 1888. Nobody knows for sure, but one thing is certain: Council Crest still offers panoramic vistas and a rather "woodsy" feeling.

When the Vista Avenue Bridge was constructed in 1908, a streetcar line came shortly thereafter, making transportation to Council Crest much easier. When Talbot settled here, there was little more than a rutted wagon trail up a muddy hillside. At one time, an amusement park at the top of the hill attracted thousands of people to ride the Ferris wheel and the roller coaster or sneak a risqué kiss in the Tunnel of Love. The amusement park is no longer there, but one of the early homes in the area (built in 1912) still stands. Originally this home was built for the amusement park's doctor. One can't help but wonder if accidents happened so frequently that the park required a physician to live nearby.

Today, the homes scattered in the area are an eclectic mix. Some of the homes built in the early 1900s still remain, but most were built in the 1930s. Council Crest is an interesting neighborhood, to say the least, and families still find it a somewhat secluded, yet popular, spot to settle.

Portland Heights

In the same general area, you will find Portland Heights, one of Portland's most exclusive and well-preserved areas. Bordered by the west hills, the heart of the city to the east, Canyon Road on the north, and Council Crest on the south, this neighborhood exudes European charm. Many of the homes were built in the 1920s. Again, varied architecture is the norm. You'll see everything from English Tudor to California Mission right beside Arts and Crafts–style homes.

Portland Heights is known for its sharp winding roadways and curved terraces. Intricate stone walls grace many of the streets, along with wrought-iron fences and walking paths. The quiet, elegant area is filled with 100-year-old azalea trees, dogwoods, and magnolias, and it's just a ten-minute drive from the heart of downtown.

The views from Portland Heights are second to none. On a sunny day, you can see the river and Mt. Hood. Portland's twinkling nighttime skyline provides a favorite backdrop to cocktail parties and patio dinners hosted by Heights residents, many of whom have lived here a long time. Portland Heights is a very "settled" area, and its denizens remain dedicated to preserving their own piece of Portland history.

TRIVIA

There is no sales tax in Portland—nor, for that matter, in all of Oregon.

Corbett/Terwilliger

The Corbett/Terwilliger neighborhood lies closer to the Willamette River and not so high up in the hills. This area found its beginnings in 1842, when William Johnson, a sailor and fur trader, settled his homestead. At that time, Portland was not even an official city, and was really little more than a convenient resting place for the trappers of the Hudson Bay Company. Johnson's cabin was the first structure built in Portland.

The name Terwilliger is derived from another of the early settlers. A blacksmith named James Terwilliger also took up residence in the area and bought three parcels of land here. It is said that in 1860, Terwilliger sold part of his original land holdings for $500 and a bottle of whiskey. The new owners built the Jones Lumber Company Steam Sawmill in what was then called South Portland. This resulted in a spurt of growth and an influx of industry. A railroad line was built in 1868, followed by another in 1887 and horse-drawn streetcars in 1886. Because of the ease of transportation and close proximity to the river, manufacturing and sawmills flourished here during the late 1800s. This area became a favorite landing spot for the growing immigrant population, who brought their own special influence to the district.

The early homes here reflected the immigrants' individual tastes, resulting in an array of styles, from small bungalows with simple porches to brightly colored Victorian mansions adorned with intricate details. Sadly, although you will find some of the original dwellings preserved, most of these homes no longer exist.

This colorful area of Portland was subject to body blows by industry, which resulted in a mass exodus from the neighborhood lasting more than 30 years. From the 1930s until the 1960s, disillusionment and safety issues caused people to find other places to call home. In the 1960s the construction of the Ross Island Bridge and Interstate 405 nearly killed the spirit of this lively area.

However, in true Portland fashion, the neighborhood rallied by forming the Community Planning Committee, which adopted an alternative development plan designed to maintain the integrity of the area and save what was left of it. Thus began an era of revitalization and restoration.

Today's Corbett/Terwilliger is another testament to Portland's commitment to its neighborhoods. No longer a decaying urban wound, the area is a fascinating and popular place to live. The erstwhile factories and sawmills are now sleek office buildings. Many homes have been restored, and even the newer condominium projects reflect a stylistic range similar to that found in the old days. The neighborhood is made up of young professionals living alongside many retired couples. Diversity has returned to the area and, with it, a wide range of things to do.

Multnomah

A ten-minute drive from downtown will take you to one of Portland's most affordable and quaint neighborhoods. Multnomah is an Indian name that

Lewis and Clark spelled "Mulknomah." It is said to be a name for a certain section of the Willamette River, a tribe, and an Indian chief, Chief Multnomah, from the Willamette Tribe.

In February 1850, President Ulysses S. Grant donated a 640-acre land claim to Mr. and Mrs. Thomas Tice. Their tract is now the heart of Multnomah Village.

The homes here are full of character and vary in style from Victorian to Arts and Crafts to modern duplexes and apartment buildings. The streets are punctuated by fir trees and azalea bushes, parks, gardens, and winding sidewalks. Houses seem to be "tucked in" in the village, safe and sound. Some of the streets aren't even paved, so the pace is a bit slower and it seems that people even breathe a bit more deeply and smile more often here. The relaxing pace of Multnomah is spiked with busy restaurants, art galleries, and coffee shops. The Multnomah Community Center provides a gathering place and learning facility for children and adults, and also serves a town hall kind of function. College students, retirees, and families all find Multnomah an enticing place to live.

Westover

Westover is one of Portland's smallest neighborhoods. Less than a square mile (bounded on the east and north by Cornell Road, and on the west by Macleay Park) of prime real estate provides some of the most panoramic views in the city. Cul-de-sacs, terraces, and short winding streets are lined predominantly with English manor houses, but there are a few other styles mixed in. Residing in Westover is as near to living in the country as you can get without leaving the city. The city center lies just 2 miles away, so many of Westover's residents think they have the best of both worlds.

Part of the country charm of the area is a result of the neighborhood's parks. Macleay Park is bounded by two other parks, one of them the 5,000-acre Forest Park, the nation's largest park within city boundaries. The other is the Audubon Society's bird sanctuary, also adjacent to the Westover neighborhood.

Just a short walk down the hill, you'll find yourself at one of Portland's favorite shopping areas. Northwest 23rd is a tree-lined avenue brimming with eclectic shops, fine restaurants, and coffee shops. The presence of quiet, peaceful parks so near to the heartbeat of the city center makes this a popular and exclusive area.

Nob Hill

Elegance. That about says it in a word. From the neighborhood's beginnings, in the mid-1800s, Nob Hill has enjoyed a reputation that rivals its San Francisco namesake's. It seems that construction of homes turned into something of a contest in the 1800s, as business tycoons, lumber barons, and shipping magnates designed homes bigger and grander than their neighbors'. Styles varied according to individual taste. Although many of the

TRIVIA

The area code for all of Portland is 503. South of the state capitol of Salem, the area code changes to 541.

original ornate mansions fell victim to the Depression and to row-house development, you can still see French-style chateaux, Georgian architecture, and even a turreted Germanic castle in the area.

Interspersed with Victorian homes, many of which have been converted to apartments and condominiums, are unique shops, fine restaurants, and bookstores that almost seem indigenous to the area. The commercial development here has not been without controversy, but through it all, the integrity of the area and the charming Victorian atmosphere have been fairly well preserved. Nob Hill is a reincarnated area, its ambiance full of subtle reminders of the past.

The Pearl District

The Pearl District, an old warehouse zone that sits just a little north of Burnside and east of Nob Hill, is a haven for artists and young professionals. Some of the streets are cobblestone. Warehouses have been turned into lofts for both business and living spaces. You'll find working artists, photographers, and writers living in the area.

The streets are lined with an assortment of coffee shops, art galleries, and retail shops. The vibrant Pearl District has a unique flavor all its own.

Eastside Neighborhoods

Sellwood

Sellwood is one of Portland's most distinctive neighborhoods. Located on the south end of the Eastside, this area began in the late 1800s as the brainchild of two preachers, the Reverends John and James Sellwood, who hailed from South Carolina. The Episcopal diocese of the new Oregon Territory and its bishop, Thomas Scott, needed help in church development; enter the brothers Sellwood.

Not entirely consumed by their religious affairs, the brothers knew that the fertile tract along the Willamette River just south of the burgeoning city of Portland would prove to be prime real estate for future settlers and their businesses. Shortly after the Sellwood brothers bought their first 320 acres, home sites were beginning to sell for $125. Soon other real estate investors saw the possibilities, and their prediction that the area would be a lucrative investment paid off. Within a few short years, schools, churches, and businesses sprouted up all over the area, and the City of Sellwood was officially incorporated.

Saloons, blacksmith shops, hotels, and a hospital evolved. The City of

Sellwood was officially annexed by Portland in 1893. Though the annexation changed the politics of the city, it did not change its original small-town atmosphere.

In 1905 John Caples began his cable ferry service at the foot of Spokane Street across the Willamette River. The advent of the ferry brought even more business and trade to Sellwood. Today, the ferry is gone, but it's not hard to imagine how busy it was and how varied the cargo and people it carried.

Today's Sellwood is alive and thriving while maintaining its vintage village charm. The old county road is now known as SE 17th and still provides a roadway to downtown Portland. Sellwood's SE 13th Street is fondly referred to as Antique Row. Old homes now house antiques from all over the world. You can still visit the little church, built in 1851, where Reverend John Sellwood preached his sermons to the pioneers. It doesn't sit at its original site, but it has been restored and is maintained as the Sellwood Historical Museum.

Historic pride resounds on every corner. Throughout Sellwood you will see brass identification plaques on buildings. The plaques tell the building's original construction date and use, along with the name of the owner.

Homes in Sellwood tend toward Victorian and Arts and Crafts styles. Their owners are a mix of urban professionals, families, artists, musicians, and shopkeepers. Visiting Sellwood is comfortable, rather like sitting on your grandmother's velvet sofa in the summertime while you sip a tall, cool lemonade. Satisfying, to say the least.

Mt. Tabor

It is said that Mt. Tabor was named after Mt. Tabor in then-Palestine by a group of Methodist families in the early 1850s. The neighborhood clusters around a 200-acre park with an extinct volcano at its core. It's thought that this volcano was active even before Mt. Hood spewed fiery ash into the skies.

The Mt. Tabor area grew from a wooded wilderness into a rural community dotted with farms and orchards and is today a sophisticated neighborhood in Southeast Portland. Near the historic Hawthorne District, Mt. Tabor families enjoy sweeping vistas, quiet streets, and elegant homes. According to old records, a home in the area in the early 1900s cost

TRIVIA One of Portland's most unique shopping malls, Johns Landing, is located in the old B.P. Johns Furniture manufacturing plant along Macadam Avenue. Inside, you'll find an eclectic array of shops, restaurants, and businesses. Microbreweries and lower shops, delicatessens and art shops add to the "neighborhood" feel of the area.

Mt. Tabor, in Southeast Portland, is the only extinct volcano within city limits in the country.

anywhere from $5,000 to $20,000, depending on lot location, views, and proximity to the verdant hills of the dormant volcano.

Through the years, the scenery has changed from horse-drawn wagons and ferries to streets filled with commuters on their way downtown to work. The orchards are gone, but gardening is still a favorite hobby of many of the residents. Walking through the area, you will see examples of creative gardening design along with stands of 100-year-old trees. The homes in the area range from Arts and Crafts to English Tudor mixed in with some newer modern homes.

Mt. Tabor is known for its block parties and neighborhood gatherings. It's a close-knit community with the family as its cornerstone. Mt. Tabor Park is a favorite gathering place for families but can also serve as a quiet spot for secluded reflection. The view toward the city is breathtaking and one not to be missed.

Ladd's Addition

William S. Ladd, a local banker and Portland's fifth mayor, acquired his 367-acre parcel in the 1880s. Originally, he intended the land to be used for agricultural and industrial investment purposes only. But, as Portland's boundaries crept closer and closer to what was at that time Ladd's raw land, he saw that his land values had increased markedly.

Influenced by a trip to Washington, D.C., where he was awed by the beauty of the city's parkways, traffic circles, and flower-filled boulevards, Ladd began dreaming of a new neighborhood in Portland. This neighborhood, however, had a very specific design. It was Ladd who envisioned a central park, filled with roses and other flowers, as the heart of the area. Ladd saw tree-lined streets emerging in a spokelike pattern from the central park, with four other diamond-shaped parks as beauty marks. Slow traffic, safe streets, and visible beauty were paramount in Ladd's design of a neighborhood built with people in mind.

Today, the area is still much the same as it was in the early 1900s. There is a central park in the heart of the area, and four diamond-shaped secondary parks are equidistant from the center of the neighborhood. These gardens are maintained through a cooperative community effort and with the help of the city's parks department.

Most of the homes in Ladd's Addition, constructed between 1910 and 1925, were located in the northern section of the neighborhood. Their grand-scale size and design favored large families and sometimes featured separate servants' quarters. Homes were often three stories of brick and stone, or "Decorator Box" style, while some were Craftsman style. You will also find an Asian influence in some of the homes, as well as a Swiss Chalet look and even some neo-Gothic architecture.

Construction halted during World War I and, when it resumed after the war, the appearance of the dwellings changed to reflect the times. The postwar homes were smaller, because families were smaller. Most homes typical of that later period were one- or two-story bungalows, and were located in the southern section of the neighborhood.

Ladd's unique street pattern, which prevented much development, was largely responsible for the area's immunity to urban decay in later years. In addition, residents have fiercely defended their lifestyle and their neighborhood. Today, the neighborhood organizations tackle everything from new construction approval to block parties. Ladd's Addition residents are stalwart in their loyalty to Ladd's original plans, and although you can see modern-day influences scattered throughout the area, much of the historic appeal is clearly intact. Construction is limited to single family homes.

The central park is still the dominant influence in the area, and the streets are still quiet. The new owners of the old homes are dedicated to restoration and civic pride. It may be difficult to find a home for sale in this much-sought-after neighborhood because the people who buy here tend to stay put. Today, Ladd's Addition is known as one of the most vital and community-oriented neighborhoods in Portland.

Eastmoreland

Eastmoreland is one of Portland's proudest possessions. It's a pricey neighborhood filled with elegant homes in a range from Tudors to colonials to stone and stucco mansions. Eastmoreland boasts one of the best-known and most beautiful municipal golf courses in the United States. Opened in 1918 by the City of Portland, Eastmoreland ranks as one of the top 25 courses in the country. The city's oldest golf course, it is open to the public.

Along with the golf course, Eastmoreland prides itself on Reed College. Founded in 1909, Reed actually held its first classes in 1911 in a downtown office building. The present campus was established in 1912, and since then has offered a highly respected program of liberal arts and sciences to students from all over the world. The college blends in well with the surrounding area, and its historic significance and beauty are among Eastmoreland's prime attractions. Citizens of Eastmoreland often partake

TRIVIA

According to Eugene Snyder in his book *Portland Names and Neighborhoods*, most people think that "moreland" was derived from "moorland" because of the area's marshy lowlands. But, he says, the name actually comes from a real estate developer named J. C. Moreland, whose full name was Julius Caesar Moreland.

of the college's cultural activities and community events, for some residents just a quiet stroll away from home.

William S. Ladd's influence can be felt here, too. In the late 1800s he owned Crystal Springs Farm, nestled in the hills and woods of Eastmoreland. Ladd's beliefs in farmers as the foundation of a thriving society and in real estate, rather than gold, as a lasting investment led him to acquire significant holdings all around Portland. Eventually, his farm was sold, and today, Crystal Springs Rhododendron Gardens provides a quiet memorial to Ladd's original philosophy. Reed College and the Eastmoreland Golf Course were also part of Ladd's farm.

Alameda

Alameda is one of the few neighborhoods in Portland where most of the houses were built during one time period—the 1920s—and they reflect much the same architectural style. Translated from Spanish, *alameda* means "a tree-shaded promenade," which aptly describes this neighborhood. Picturesque cottages and handsome mansions sit side by side on the hillsides. Winding little streets lead past houses built of brick and stone. Wrought-iron fences, leaded-glass windows, and shake roofs are just some of the common denominators that testify to the classic architecture and refined workmanship found in Alameda.

Alameda is close to several parks. Grant Park, for instance, is a popular spot for swimming, a game of tennis, or a boisterous family reunion. Two bus lines and the light rail are near the district, so commuting to downtown is easy. The major cross streets in Alameda are Fremont Street and Alameda Drive. Shopping at Lloyd Center is within a few minutes' drive, as is the more eclectic Hollywood district near 42nd and Sandy.

Even though the neighborhood is close to urban activity, it is quiet and secluded. First-time visitors to Alameda have commented on the charming "English village feel" of the area.

Portland's Weather

It's been said that the Devil himself won't take Oregonians because they are too wet to burn. Yes, it rains in Portland, but, surprisingly, it rains more in Houston and Atlanta than it does in this green city.

Oregonians love the rain. (Those west of the Cascades do, at least.) When they go for too long without seeing any, they start to complain about

TRIVIA

In Oregon it's illegal to pump your own gas. You'll pay more for gas, too, in Portland than in most cities across the country.

Portland's Weather

	Average Daily High / Low Temperatures (degrees Fahrenheit)	Average Monthly Precipitation (inches)
January	45 / 34	5.50
April	60 / 41	2.30
July	79 / 57	.63
October	64 / 45	2.60

Source: U.S. Department of Commerce, National Oceanic and Atmospheric Administration.

their joints drying up, their skin flaking off, and the streets looking dusty. In fact, they call the rain "liquid sunshine" and will tell visitors that, if they make up their minds, they really don't get wet on most rainy days in Oregon anyway, because Oregon rain is so soft and gentle most of the time.

Since it's rather cumbersome to carry an umbrella everywhere, lots of Portlanders boast that they never do—even in December, Portland's wettest month, when average rainfall is more than 6 inches. A pair of "duck boots" is a necessity, though, especially in the winter, at least until visitors stay long enough to grow their own webbed feet.

There's plenty to do in the rain in Oregon. Espresso shops, bookstores, restaurants, and art galleries are open for business and friendly conversation. The proprietors think nothing of visitors' wet shoes, either, and many post umbrella stands at the door.

November through April tend to be the rainiest months in Portland. Temperatures remain fairly moderate, though, with averages in the mid-30s to the 50s. An occasional freeze in December, January, or February brings the mercury down lower, but it usually lasts only a day or two. Springtime brings cherry blossoms and coaxes dogwood to bloom all over the city. Parks come alive with color and ornate flowering gardens.

Summertime temperatures commonly hover in the 80s, sometimes reaching as high as the upper 90s. The summer sun evokes a characteristic laid-back feeling in the city. Picnics and box lunches in the parks are popular this time of year, and many of Portland's downtown businesspeople can be seen enjoying a lunchtime respite from the work world. Evening strolls along the waterfront are a favorite pastime, too, as are river cruises and outdoor concerts.

Portland Style

Dressing in layers here is a good idea in any season. In fact, Oregonians dressed in layers long before it became a fashion statement. Even during

Never a Dull Climatic Moment . . .

Oregon enjoys seven of the world's ten climate zones, so weather can be unpredictable. If Portland's winter rains are bogging you down, you can drive east to the other side of Mt. Hood, where you'll be treated to sunshine in the high desert. Or, if you want a really dramatic experience, head to the Oregon Coast (only a 90-minute drive), where Pacific fronts, wild ocean currents, and fog banks create a commotion so volatile that storm-watching has become a favorite pastime and tourist attraction. Observing hearty winter weather can be a heady experience; you're missing something if you've never stood on a cliff and watched a storm approach from the depths of the Pacific Ocean.

the heat of high summer, a sweater or light jacket is often necessary after the sun goes down. Summer sun brings need for sunblock, polarized sunglasses, and a wide-brimmed hat. In the winter you'll probably want a jacket with a hood, some waterproof shoes, and an umbrella.

Portland is a casual city. Though you'll want to "upgrade" your style a bit for a five-star dinner, only rarely will an occasion require a coat and tie. Most restaurants encourage patrons to be comfortable but presentable. When attending the theater or opera, you'll see everything from jeans and tweed jackets to tuxedos and evening gowns. Portlanders pride themselves on lack of pretense when it comes to enjoying the city's offerings.

When to Visit Portland

Given that the weather can change any minute, there is no "best" time to visit Portland. Many of the locals favor the weather in early fall. From August through mid-October, you are likely to be blessed with long sunny days, coral sunsets, and velvety black nights. These are the least rainy months of the year.

High summer (which typically doesn't start until July) brings a plethora of festivals, so there's always something to do. On any given weekend, the waterfront is alive with crowds enjoying events such as the Oregon Brewers Festival, The Bite, the Blues Festival, and many others.

Winter, of course, is ski season. And with Mt. Hood just a 90-minute drive away, the downhill slopes and cross-country terrain offer popular recreation to visitors and locals alike. Some of the slopes are open at night, too, allowing many nine-to-fivers to ski in the evening after a day at the office.

Calendar of Events

JANUARY

Reel Music
Northwest Film Center
221-1156

This is the Northwest Film Center's annual celebration of music on film. It takes place annually at the film center, adjacent to the Portland Art Museum. Shows vary from year to year, but you can depend on good quality entertainment and learning experiences.

Wrangler Jeans Pro-Rodeo Classic
Memorial Coliseum
235-8771

This annual indoor event offers country music, wild broncs, and cowboys galore. Call for dates.

FEBRUARY

Greater Portland International Auto Show
Oregon Convention Center
235-7575 or 800/732-2914

Design concepts from the future as well as a preview of what's coming in the next year are two popular features at the show.

International Film Festival
Northwest Film Center
1219 SW Park Ave.
221-1156

The film festival features both first-run foreign films, classics, award winners, and little known works. It's one of Portland's most popular events.

Pacific Northwest Sportsmen's Show
Portland Expo Center
246-8291

This is the largest sports event on the West Coast. Some 450 exhibitors show you what's new in fishing, boating, hunting, golfing, skiing, and just about anything else you can imagine in the sporting world.

MARCH

America's Largest Antique & Collectible Show
Portland Expo Center
282-0877 or 285-7756

Portlandese: How to Talk like a Local

This guide to local slang and pronounciation will help even first-time visitors sound like they've been living in Portland all their lives.

Portland Term	Definition or Pronunciation
The Banfield	Interstate 84 (runs east from Portland)
The Sunset	Highway 26 (Portland to Oregon Coast)
Big Pink	US Bancorp Tower—the 43-story, rose-colored building at 111 SW 5th
The Ban Roll-on Building	Highrise at 1000 Broadway (a glance at the top of the building explains why)
Pill Hill	Oregon Health Sciences University, which sits on top of Marquam Hill in SW Portland
Fareless Square	The 300-block downtown square where public transit is free
MAX	Metropolitan Area Express, Portland's light-rail line
PDX	Portland International Airport
The Schnitz	Arlene Schnitzer Concert Hall
The Big O	The Oregonian, Portland's daily newspaper
WW	Willamette Week, Portland's weekly newspaper
Nordie's	Nordstrom department store
Freddy's	Any of the Fred Meyer stores
Mega-Fred's	The Fred Meyer at NE 33rd and Broadway
Trendy Third	Portland's NW 23rd area, known for unique shopping and dining
Reedies	Students at Reed College in Southeast Portland; connotes smart, hip, and more-than-a-little offbeat individuals
OMSI	Oregon Museum of Science and Industry
PICA	Portland Institute of Contemporary Art
Twin Peaks	The Oregon Convention Center, with its twin glass spires
The Mountain	Mt. Hood
Oregon	Pronounced "OR-uh-gun," not "OR-uh-gonn"
Willamette	Pronounced "Wil-LAM-et"
Couch Street	Pronounced "Kooch"
Glisan	Pronounced "GLIH-son"

Almost 1,500 booths cover 7 acres, so if antiques are your passion, this is the place to be.

Annual Winter Games of Oregon
Mt. Hood
520-1319
Alpine and Nordic competitions take place on Timberline, Mt. Hood Meadows, Ski Bowl, and Teacup ski areas on Mt. Hood.

Northwest Quilters Show
Portland State University
222-1991
The university provides space for quilters to show their work. More than 200 quilts are exhibited, and quilters are on hand to answer questions.

APRIL

Annual Rhododendron Show
8005 SW Grabhorn Rd., Aloha
642-3855
Enjoy the vibrant hues of Oregon's famous "rhodies" on 68 wooded acres of the historic Jenkins estate. Great place for a picnic. Held the third week in April.

MAY

Annual Ceramic Showcase
Oregon Convention Center
238-0973
A dazzling display of the finest in ceramic art brought to you by the Oregon Potter's Association.

Cinco de Mayo Festival
Waterfront Park
823-4572
The flavor of Mexico abounds in Waterfront Park during this well-attended festival.

Designer Showhouse
228-4294
A historically significant home is completely renovated and decorated. Fee. Sponsored by the Oregon Symphony.

JUNE

Annual Chamber MusicNorthwest Summer FestivalReed College and

Catlin Gabel School
223-3202 or 294-6400
Musical excellence in a casual setting. Some outdoor concerts, some indoors.

Gallery in the Woods
The Grotto
254-7371
Fine arts and specialty crafts exhibits, strolling minstrels, classical and jazz musicians, and a culinary feast highlight this annual festival.

Native American Pow Wow
Delta Park
630-5195
Ceremonial dancing, crafts, and indigenous foods are featured at this Native American festival.

Portland Rose Festival/Grand Floral Parade
227-2681
Portland's premier event actually lasts all month long. Starting with the Queen's coronation on the first Thursday in June and ending with the Budweiser/G.I. Joe's 200 IndyCar World series the last weekend, the month is dedicated to roses in Portland. Of special note is the KUPL Rose Festival Fireworks Display in Waterfront Park on the first Friday in June. Literally thousands gather for this amazing display of pyrotechnics. Other favorites are the Starlight Parade and the Grand Floral Parade, which attract thousands.

Your Zoo and All That Jazz
Washington Park Zoo
226-1561
Regional and national artists perform some of the best jazz around each Wednesday evening. Outdoors in the amphitheater at the zoo, the event features food, wine, and beer. But you can bring your own picnic, too, and enjoy a spectacular setting for kids and adults alike.

JULY

G.I. Joe's Camel Grand Prix by Nissan
Portland International Raceway
236-8006
The world's fastest sports cars return annually for this event.

Oregon Brewer's Festival
Waterfront Park
241-7179 or 281-2437

This is America's largest outdoor gathering of independent brewers. More than 80 different brews can be tasted along with some of Portland's finest food.

Portland Croquet Tournament
Reed College

A fundraiser for the Northwest Film Center, this is the largest nine-wicket croquet tournament in the country.

Portland Scottish Highland Games
Mt. Hood Community College
293-8501

It's about a 30-minute drive to Gresham, east of Portland, and well worth the effort. At the games, you will find traditional food, pipes, and beer. This annual celebration of the Scottish heritage is attended by people from all over the world.

Waterfront Blues Festival
282-0555

International celebrities and Oregon's finest blues artists gather in the park on three different stages to present some of America's greatest blues. Food booths and some craft booths accompany the music.

AUGUST

Bank of America Slam 'n' Jam
Civic Auditorium
234-9291

Starring those famous Blazers and other NBA players, this is a basketball and musical blowout to benefit high school athletics.

Dragon Boats, Portland Rose Festival

Portland Oregon Visitors Association

The Bite: A Taste of Portland
Waterfront Park
249-0600

Northwest bands, food, and camaraderie accentuate one of Portland's most popular events. It's all about eating, and there's no limit to the amount of food you can consume in the city's most delicious festival.

Homowa Festival for African Arts
Washington Park

288-3025

Music, dance, crafts, and food from several African nations. The family-oriented festival takes place in the amphitheater at the park.

Mt. Hood Festival of Jazz
Mt. Hood Community College
666-3810

This is Oregon's largest jazz festival. Featuring world-renowned artists, the festival is an outdoor event complete with food and lots of people. Plan to go early. Traffic can be a nightmare, but the music is sublime.

SEPTEMBER

Oktoberfest Celebrations

Fall German folk festivals featuring German music, brats, and beer are celebrated at Oaks Amusement Park (232-3000), Mount Angel (845-9440), and Waterfront Park (230-1056).

Pacific Northwest Dahlia Conference Show
Clackamas County Fairgrounds, Canby
665-2870

Thirty minutes from Portland (to the south and west), you'll find some of the most beautiful dahlia fields in the country. The conference brings experts and growers together to answer questions and help in planning gardens.

Table Lamp and Chair
226-3556

An art show honoring outstanding achievement in innovative furniture and lighting fixture design. Call for location.

OCTOBER

Greek Festival
Holy Trinity Greek Orthodox Church
234-0468

Authentic Greek dinners, imported gifts, and entertainment.

Portland Marathon
226-1111

TRIVIA

Portland has more than 1,100 high-tech companies, employing more than 50,000 people.

More than 11,000 people participate in the 26.2-mile marathon, a 5-mile run, the mayor's walk, a kid's run, and a sports medicine and fitness fair. It's fun to watch as well as participate.

NOVEMBER

Christmas at Pittock Mansion
Pittock Mansion
823-3624
Overlooking the city, this three-story Victorian mansion is extravagantly decorated for the holidays.

Meier & Frank Holiday Parade
Downtown Portland
203-9166
This festive event will get you in the mood for the holidays. Floats, bands, horse-drawn carriages, celebrities, and Santa all join together to bring on the Christmas madness.

Washington County Wine Tour & Open House
Washington County
357-5005
A drive through the picturesque wine country features specialty foods, wines, and gifts. When you visit at least four wineries, you receive a free Christmas ornament.

Wooden Toy Show
World Forestry Center at Washington Park
228-1367
Wooden-toy makers from throughout the Pacific Northwest converge for a three-day showing and sale of some very unique toys. Good for Christmas shopping.

Young People's Film & Video Festival
Northwest Film Center
221-1156
Young film- and video-makers from the Northwest screen their best new works.

DECEMBER

Annual Festival of Lights at the Grotto
National Sanctuary of Our Sorrowful Mother
254-7371
Celebrate a message of hope, peace, and love at the largest choral festival in the Northwest.

Holiday Lights Displays
Portland is known for its lighting displays at Christmas. There are several locations throughout the city that are worth noting: Peacock Lane, between SE Belmont and Stark, 222-2223; Ridgewood Drive, off of SE Webster Road, Milwaukie, 222-2223; Shilo Inns Executive Offices, 11600 SW Barnes Road, 641-6565.

Portland Parade of Christmas Ships
Willamette and Columbia Rivers
222-2223
Decorated and lighted boats navigate the Willamette and Columbia Rivers nightly. Varying schedule.

Zoolights Festival
Washington Park Zoo
226-1561
The zoo dazzles after dark in a carnival of sparkling lights. A Christmas fairyland for the whole family.

Business and Economy

Portland's diverse economy revolves around manufacturing, trade, and business services. Sixteen percent of the work force is employed in manufacturing industries that include machinery, electronics, metals, lumber, transportation equipment, and wood products.

Portland's access to West Coast and Asian markets make this area ripe for industry expansion and relocation. Known as the Northwest Gateway to the Pacific Rim, the city can easily compete in the international marketplace. Many international companies relocate to Portland because of its prime location, its low cost of electricity, and its transportation infrastructure. Portland is served by three railway lines, excellent highway connections, and one of the West Coast's busiest seaports.

For detailed information about property taxes, contact the following offices:

Clackamas County Tax Department
168 Warner Milne Rd., Oregon City, OR 97045
655-8411

Multnomah County Assessment & Taxation
610 SW Alder St., Portland, OR 97204
248-3326

Washington County Assessment & Taxation
150 N. 1st Ave., Hillsboro, OR 97123
648-8741

Cost of Living

According to the ACCRA, a national association of community and economic development research professionals, in the third quarter of 1995, Portland ranked 9.1% above the nationwide average cost of living.

Typical costs of everyday items and services include the following:

A 5-mile taxi ride	$10
Hotel, double room	$90
Average dinner	$12
Movie admission	$7 ($3.75 matinee)
Daily newspaper	$.35 ($1.50 Sunday)
Double tall latte	$2.50
Pint of microbrew	$2.75
Gallon of gasoline	$1.27
Monthly bus pass	$35
Club cover charge	$5

Median Real Estate Prices by Region

The following information is from an area report provided by Windemere Cronin-Caplan, one of Portland's most reliable and helpful realty groups. Its relocation department specializes in tours of the city's neighborhoods, shopping districts, and businesses. Although there are many offices throughout the city, the relocation department is located at 636 NW 21st Avenue in Portland. You can reach it at 800/654-5457 or, locally, at 220-4500.

The prices below reflect a range from data compiled in January 1998. Prices fluctuate, just as interest rates do, but this list should give you a pretty good idea of average sale prices of two-bedroom houses.

The City:

Northeast Portland	$139,000
Southeast Portland	$125,000
West Portland	$207,000
(includes both NW & SW)	

Suburban Areas:

Gresham/Troutdale	$150,000
Milwaukie	$154,000
Oregon City	$163,000
Beaverton	$150,000
Lake Oswego/ West Linn	$267,500

Other Areas:

Yamhill County	$131,000
North Washington County	$250,000

Rental Prices

The following average monthly rents are based on two-bedroom/two-bath units.

Northwest Portland	$875
Southwest Portland	$700
Northeast Portland	$550
Southeast Portland	$600

Taxes

There is no sales tax in Oregon. There is a 5¢ bottle deposit required on all recyclable bottles sold in Oregon. Personal income tax is based on federal taxable income. Employers withhold taxes from wages. For more detailed information, contact the Oregon Department of Revenue, 955 Center Street NE, Salem, OR 97310; 378-4988. Property taxes have, in the past, varied according to location. In November 1990, Oregonians passed a ballot measure that phased in property tax reductions so that as of 1996, property taxes could not exceed $15 per $1,000 of assessed value. Local governments levy taxes on real property. Properties are appraised every six years.

Tri-Met

2

Getting around Portland is easy. Whether you choose to walk, ride, drive, or bike your way around the city, you'll find easy-to-follow directions and quick access to a variety of transportation modes.

The Lay of the Land

The Willamette River, the longest north-flowing river in the United States, divides the city in half, east from west. In fact, at one time Portland was really two cities—East Portland and Portland. Today, it's one city with east and west linked together by eight bridges covering a 2.3-mile span in the downtown area. Easy access to all parts of Portland is provided by these arteries, as they carry the pulse of the city back and forth across the river.

The city is basically divided into four sections, grid-style. Locals refer easily to these sectors as Northwest, Southwest, Northeast, and Southeast. North Portland is a smaller section that is adjacent to the Northeast section; for ease, in this book we will include North Portland in the Northwest section. You'll hear locals refer to "the little cafe in Southeast" or "shopping in Northwest." After you get the lay of the land, talking like this will become second nature to you, too.

The north and south sections of town are divided by Burnside Street, which runs east-west across the Willamette. Anything north of Burnside is known as Northeast or Northwest, depending on which side of the river you are on. Anything south of Burnside is called Southeast or Southwest.

> **Portland is bordered on the north by the mighty Columbia River. When you cross the Columbia River, you end up in Vancouver, Washington.**

Westside

Front Avenue, recently renamed Naito Parkway in honor of one of Portland's favorite citizens, runs north-south parallel to the Willamette. It meanders along the river adjacent to Tom McCall Waterfront Park and continues north to the industrial district. This is the major street for access to downtown.

After turning off Front, as you head away from the river toward the West Hills, the numbered avenues run north and south. The further west from the river, the higher the number. The named streets (such as Yamhill, Taylor, and Washington) run east and west. As in most cities, there are exceptions. Broadway, a major street, is one of them. It runs north and south (one-way south in the heart of downtown), leading to some of the city's major attractions, such as the Portland Center for the Performing Arts and Nordstrom.

North of Burnside, the streets run in alphabetical order, starting with Couch Street and moving on to Davis, Everett, Flanders, and so on. The numbered avenues still run north and south.

Eastside

On the Eastside, Interstate 5 (I-5) runs parallel to the Willamette River, north to the Columbia River.

Again, the numbered avenues run east and west; the named streets run north and south. Martin Luther King Jr. Boulevard is a major street that offers easy access to interesting points on the Eastside, such as the Oregon Convention Center and the Lloyd Center shopping mall. The twin spires of the Convention Center are visible all over town and are a useful landmark if you lose your bearings. If you're lucky and the sky is clear, you'll be able to see Mt. Hood looming in the distance to the east.

Tri Met: Public Transportation

Tri-Met, Portland's award-winning mass transit system, is held in high regard throughout the country. All Tri-Met routes are wheelchair accessible except for a small number of rush-hour trips. Look for the wheelchair access symbol on buses, schedules, and bus stop signs. Call 238-4952 or (TTY) 238-5811 for information.

Fares are standard throughout Tri-Met's system, whether you're riding a bus or Metropolitan Area Express (MAX), the city's light rail system. Any Tri-Met ticket is good on any Tri-Met route. Keep your ticket with you, as you may be asked to show it. Kids under six can travel free if accompanied by an adult.

Tri-Met has an excellent safety record, but it's always a good idea to be aware of your surroundings and use good common sense when riding public transportation. At night, always stand in a well-lit area. If you are traveling alone after 8 p.m., you can ask your driver to let you off anywhere a safe stop can be made, whether it's a bus stop or not. Tri-Met drivers tend to be friendly and helpful, so don't hesitate to ask questions or let them know if you need something.

Metropolitan Area Express (MAX)

MAX

The city's light rail system, Metropolitan Area Express, or MAX, which officially opened in September 1986, is free in the 300-block area of downtown Portland.

Originally known as the Banfield Transitway Project, the multi-milliondollar venture was begun during Oregon's economic recession and helped to create more than 12,000 jobs over its four-year construction period.

MAX is so efficient and innovative that transportation representatives from around the world come to study it.

The Portland Guides

If you have a question like, "Where's Pioneer Square?" or "Where can I buy a good tie?" or even "Where's an authentic Greek restaurant?" there's help at virtually every street corner. The Portland Guides are dressed in kelly green jackets, and you'll see them all over the downtown area traveling in teams of two. The Portland Guides are a walking concierge service. Trained by the Association of Portland Progress, they are on the streets to serve you. It's their job to know the secrets to downtown as well as to offer helpful information about "how to get there from here," even if you're not sure where "here" is.

The new Westside light rail system not only transports, it entertains. Art can be found all along the way. Especially interesting is the Washington Park Station. The station's underground platform has a 260-foot timeline made of Earth's core samples. Its accompanying sketches highlight the geological events that occurred in the tunnel's 17-million-year history.

The trains, powered by overhead electrical wires, run on standard railway gauge tracks at speeds from 35 to 55 mph. MAX enjoys a right of way over bus and automobile traffic, so the trains can bypass all the stop-and-go traffic of rush hour. A rush-hour MAX ride between Portland and the suburb of Gresham takes about 45 minutes, a considerably shorter time than driving or taking the bus.

MAX operates nearly 200 trains per day. With the recent multimillion dollar expansion of the MAX line to Hillsboro, commuters can now ride the rails for a total of 33 miles, with stops at 50 different stations. Trains run every 15 minutes on weekdays, twice as often during the rush hours. After 10 p.m. on weekdays, the trains run every 30 minutes. On weekends, MAX runs every 23 minutes from 6:30 a.m. to 10:30 p.m.

Customers can purchase MAX tickets at any station (you must buy before boarding the train).

Bus Service

Blue and white bus stop signs, which give routes and bus numbers, are posted every two or three blocks throughout Tri-Met bus routes. It's fairly safe to say that you can catch a bus going anywhere (with some connections) from the SW 5th Avenue transit mall downtown. Buses tend to run every 15 to 30 minutes, so if you miss the first one, another will be along shortly.

Pay your bus fare when you board, using exact change. You can easily determine your fare by using the convenient charts found at all stops. The Tri-Met service area is divided into just three zones. Simply count the number of zones you'll travel through and add up the numbers. If you get confused, ask the driver. They know their way around and are happy to answer questions about routes, bus numbers, and schedules.

Driving in Portland

Driving in Portland is fairly easy. Rush hours can be brutal, though, so it's not a good idea to try to learn your way around between 7 and 8:30 a.m. or 4 and 6 p.m. Front Avenue, on the Willamette River, is especially congested because it is the main thoroughfare to southbound I-5 and to Highway 43, the route to Lake Oswego. The Sunset Highway (#26) is at a dead stop

FARELESS SQUARE

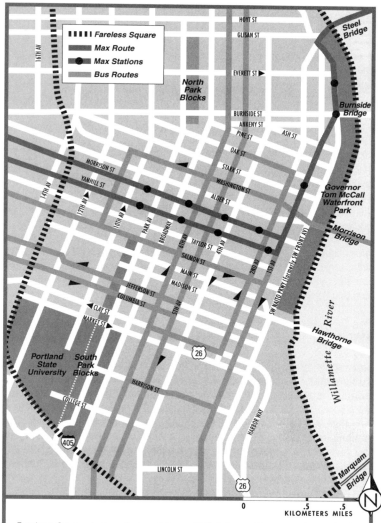

Fareless Square is bounded as follows: NW Johnson Street on the north, the Williamette River on the east, and I-405 on the south and west. If you will be travelling by bus or MAX entirely within Fareless Square, there is no fare. If you board inside but travel outside Fareless Square, you will have to pay a standard fare.

Tri-Met serves over 600 square miles of the Portland metropolitan area. Some visitor stops include the Memorial Coliseum and the Rose Garden, the Oregon Convention Center, Pioneer Courthouse Square, the Portland Art Museum, Lloyd Center, and the Washington Park Zoo.

Tri-Met schedule and route information is subject to change without notice; you can obtain the most current route and scheduling information by calling 503/238-RIDE for an information packet.

ART on Wheels

ART, the Cultural Bus, is a three-dimensional interactive piece of art on wheels. You can't miss its wildly decorated body on the street. ART travels on line 63 throughout Portland's inner core and is part of the Tri-Met system. ART will connect you to Portland's many cultural centers. Stops include Washington Park, the Rose Quarter (Coliseum), Lloyd Center/Oregon Square Pacific Northwest College of Art, Portland Center for the Performing Arts, and OMSI.

much of the time during rush hour, so just have a cup of coffee or a nap in your hotel and forget trying to get anywhere.

Other than during rush hours, the city streets are pretty friendly. Nobody seems to be in much of a hurry in Portland. In fact, a few years ago, a national magazine did a study on how long it takes people to "go on the green light" around the country, and Portland came in last! There isn't any wild careening around corners like you find in Los Angeles or New York, but slow drivers can be hazardous, too. Just watch the car in front of you and you'll do fine.

Parking

Downtown street parking can be difficult during business hours. Plan on circling the block a few times if you want to park in front of a business or across the street from a hotel. In Portland, the meter patrol takes its job very seriously. It's illegal to replug the same meter if you run over time—and they *will* catch you doing it. Parking tickets can run from $12 to $50, depending on your infraction. You don't have to plug the meters on Sunday, but you do on Saturday. After 6 p.m. every day, parking at downtown meters is free. Beware: Some meter patrols have been known to ticket cars parked at 5:55 because it was not yet exactly 6 p.m.

The SmartPark garages are a better alternative. Look for the SmartPark symbol on the red and white signs. Evening parking is $1.50, and on weekends you can park all day for $3. During business hours, it's only 95¢ per hour for the first four hours. There are six different SmartPark locations throughout the city. Other parking garages (privately owned) can run $1.50 per hour and up—sometimes as high as $4 per hour.

Many downtown merchants will validate your parking for two hours if you spend $25 or more on merchandise. If you park longer than two hours, you can use a validation from an additional store where you purchased $15 worth of goods.

Bicycling in Portland

Bicycling magazine recently named Portland as the most bicycle-friendly city in the country. The City of Portland Bicycle Program is in constant motion, always striving to improve its high-quality network of bicycle pathways.

There is ample parking within the city for your bike, too. More than 700 racks are scattered throughout the city, on both sides of the river, and you can even rent a bike locker from the city if you want to store your bike overnight.

Bicycle Safety

Though bicycle helmets are not mandatory for adults, cyclists under 16 years old must wear a helmet. It's the law. Bikes are considered part of the traffic system in Portland and therefore must follow general traffic rules. Bicyclists should obey all regulatory signs and traffic lights, never ride against the traffic, and ride in a straight line. Also, you are not allowed to ride bikes on any sidewalk in Portland. When riding at night, you must be equipped with a white light visible for at least 500 feet in the front and a red light or reflector visible for at least 600 feet to the rear. Remember always to lock your bike, no matter where you are.

You can bicycle safely across six of Portland's downtown bridges. Bicyclists most frequently choose either the Broadway, the Burnside, or the Morrison Bridge to cross the Willamette River. No bikes are allowed on the Fremont Bridge or the Marquam Bridge, because they are both part of the freeway system.

There are quite a few good publications to assist you in routing your way around Portland by bicycle. For a free Multnomah County bike map and brochure, call 248-5050. The book *Best Bike Rides Around Portland* is available at many bike shops in Portland for $9.95.

Take your bike on MAX

Portland Bureau of Traffic Management

Bikes on Buses

Portland is the first city in the United States to outfit all of its buses with bicycle transport. Each Tri-Met bus (except the mini-shuttle buses) is equipped with a bike rack. You can also take your bike on MAX, but you'll need to contact the office for rules and regulations.

To take your bike on the bus, you'll need to obtain a $5 permit from

For more information on biking in Portland, contact the City of Portland Bicycle Program, 1120 SW 5th Ave., Room 730, Portland, OR 97204; 823-7082.

the Tri-Met office (Pioneer Square or at 4012 SE 17th Avenue). You will be asked to watch a short safety and instructional video, and then you're on your way. It's an easy, safe, and convenient way to enjoy bike travel at the speed of bus!

Taxi Service

Don't forget (although you're not likely to), you're not in New York City—Portland cabbies can be hard, if not impossible, to flag down from a corner. It's best to stop at your hotel lobby and call ahead for a pick-up. Occasionally you can hail a cab (after all, nothing's impossible), but most often, passing cabs are en route and can't stop for impromptu passengers. Portland taxi companies include Portland Taxi, 256-5400; Broadway Cab, Inc., 227-1234; and Radio Cab, 227-1212.

Other Transportation Services

Coachman Express Towncar Service
Not just a cab ride! You'll want to dig deep in your pockets for a ride in a Bentley, a stretch limo, or a Lincoln Town Car. But if you don't mind spending from $40 to $125 per hour, you can enjoy some true VIP service. Coachman specializes in wine country tours, tours of downtown Portland, and scenic drives up the Columbia Gorge. And you definitely get what you pay for. The drivers are friendly, informed, and flexible. And the cars are beautiful. For more information, call 761-1986.

Carriage Rides
Vintage carriage rides can be a romantic way to see the city sights. Horse-drawn carriages are popular in Portland, especially on hot summer nights. They'll drop you off at a restaurant, pick you up after dinner, and then take you around the city for a historical tour, if that's what you desire. Or you can spend an hour on a Sunday afternoon touring specific sights. All four companies offer basically the same service, but their rates vary, so call ahead for custom itineraries and rates: Palmer House, 284-7789; Classic Carriages, 631-8777; Golden Times, 256-5609; and Rose City, 823-3378.

Portland: Cycling City USA
by Jo Ostgarden

Jo Ostgarden, a Portland bicycle enthusiast, fitness buff, and freelance writer, offers the following bicycling ideas. Jo's work has appeared in *Bicycling* magazine and other national fitness publications. She knows what she's talking about!

Named number one in the country and runner-up in North America by Bicycling *magazine, Portland reigns at the top with a plethora of bicycling opportunities. Premier bikeways exist within minutes of the town square, allowing you to travel north or south along the Willamette corridor and connect with bike-friendly neighborhoods along the way. The Hawthorne and Burnside Bridges offer easy access to the Eastside.*

A 20-minute trek south along Waterfront Park takes you over the Sellwood Bridge into Southeast Portland and to Tacoma Street, the start of the superb multiuse Springwater Corridor trail, a hard sand–seal surface that travels east along an old railroad bed for 17 miles. You'll get knockout views of Mt. Hood while traveling through an industrial area, farmland, and an urban wetland teeming with birds and wildlife. A turnoff about halfway east leads to Powell Butte, a mountain bike–friendly park that overlooks Portland suburbs.

Forest Park, in Northwest Portland, is the brightest jewel in the city's crown. Mountain bikers will love the 10 miles of upward-wending dirt road that offer incredible views of Portland's port and freighter terminals, as well as awesome glimpses of Mt. St. Helen's, across the Columbia River in Washington State. Several offshoots lead to a maze of more technical riding.

RAZ Transportation
246-3301

RAZ offers basic no-frills airport shuttle service to downtown hotels and to some on the Eastside, near Lloyd Center mall. RAZ also stops at Union Station and the bus station downtown. It leaves from the airport every half-hour from 5 a.m. to 11:30 p.m. Catch it at the airport on the downstairs baggage claim level, just across the street near the parking garage. The fare is $8.50 one way and $15.50 round trip, but you must purchase the round-trip ticket on the first leg of the journey to get the discount.

Water Taxi, Willamette River Services
244-2534
Owners Jack and Suzie Stiles run the only water taxi in town. They'll happily make arrangements to pick you up dockside from several points downtown, deliver you to dinner, and retrieve you when you're finished. If you don't know quite what you want, Suzie and Jack will help you to custom design a cruise around the area. Their routes include both north and south on the Willamette, on the Columbia River, and just about anywhere the river leads. This is a unique way to see the city lights at night or to enjoy one of Waterfront Park's many festivals. Fees start at $10 per person for a simple shuttle from point to point. Scenic cruises begin at $25.

Willamette Shore Trolley
222-2226
The tracks along the Willamette were built in the 1880s, and the restored trolley is vintage, too. Riding the rails parallel to the Willamette River gives you a peek at parts of Portland that are hidden from the road. The ride takes you through a 1,400-foot tunnel, in front of some of Portland's most prestigious homes in the Dunthrope area, and winds up in Lake Oswego, an upscale bedroom community south of Portland. There's not much to do once you get off in Lake Oswego, but there are a couple of restaurants, a beer garden down the street, and the Tillamook Creamery, an old-fashioned ice cream parlor. Round-trip schedules change with the seasons, so call ahead for reservations and ticket information.

Portland International Airport

7000 NE Airport Way
800/547-8411 or 231-5000
Portland International Airport (PDX) is about 20 minutes from downtown, just off Interstate 205. Once at the airport, you can choose from two parking options: short-term ($2 per hour) and economy ($6 per day or $36 per week). Free shuttle buses run between long-term and economy lots every five minutes. The lots are open 24 hours per day.

The Port of Portland, which owns and manages Portland International Airport, is one of the most significant enterprises in the Pacific Northwest. Created more than a century ago, the port's scope includes three general aviation airports, five deep-water marine terminals, the Portland Ship Yards, and six industrial parks. Together, these different facilities provide about 25 percent of the jobs in the Portland metropolitan area.

Portland International Airport

Portland International Airport has recently expanded its parking facilities and remodeled the inside of the airport. Though the look is different, the inside layout is much the same. Airport parking, however, is much more convenient and accessible.

Getting around PDX is fairly simple. It's a brightly lit, colorful airport with ample lobby areas and relatively uncrowded concourses. If you have to wait or are stuck on a layover, there's a lot to do right at the airport. The new Oregon Market retail area features upscale shops specializing in Oregonia that aren't any more expensive than they would be downtown. Retailers are required to keep the same prices as their nonairport locations'.

The airport is "kid-friendly," too. The Kids Flight Deck area allows children to play in a scale-model aircraft fuselage and a control tower, and to listen to aircraft-to-tower communications and weather reports. Scattered throughout PDX are "Lego Tables" offering a bit of relief, too.

The food court in the main area of the airport has something for everyone. From espresso and croissants to full meals, there's plenty to choose from. Concourses have special stops, too. There's a microbrewery pub on Concourse D and a bar and grill on Concourse E.

Information kiosks are scattered throughout the terminal. Some offer interactive videos in Japanese, Chinese, German, Korean, Spanish, and English. During peak periods, Volunteer Information Persons (VIPS) provide travel assistance, information, directions, and escort. You can't miss them—they're dressed in teal shirts and purple cardigan sweaters sporting the "Ask Me!" logo.

The PDX Conference Center is located at the top of the stairs near the clock tower in the main area. To reserve a conference room, call 335-1050. You'll find a notary public there, a photocopy machine, a fax, and computer

TRIVIA

Portland International Airport (PDX) serves almost 12 million passengers and transports some 180,000 tons of cargo each year.

ports. Concourse D Service Center is located near Gate D7 and is equipped with a copy machine, a fax, change machines, stamp machine, and a mail drop, as well as telephone workstations.

Foreign language assistance is available through AT&T at the information booths in the ticket lobby and baggage claim area. Airport information brochures are also available in six languages at the booths.

Disabled services: Restrooms are located at the South Service Center near Concourses B/C security checkpoint and near Gate D2. Text Telephones (TTY) are located throughout the terminal; visual paging telephones exist in the main terminal. For wheelchair or porter service, contact your airline.

Major Airlines Serving Portland International Airport

AirBC (Air Canada), 800/776-3000
Alaska, 800/426-0333
American Airlines, 800/433-7300
America West, 800/235-9292
Delta, 800/221-1212
Hawaiian Airlines, 800/367-5320
Horizon Air, 800/547-9308
Northwest, 800/225-2525
Reno Air, 800/736-6247
Southwest, 800/435-9792
Trans World Airlines (TWA), 282-1111
United, 800/241-6522
United Express, 800/241-6522

Useful Numbers

Airport Limousine Service, 800/697-5466 or 283-5182
Broadway Cab, 227-1234
Metropolitan Airport Shuttle, 331-2335
RAZ Transportation Airporter, 246-4676

PORTLAND INTERNATIONAL AIRPORT

Concourse C

Concourse D

Shops and Restaurants

Concourse B

Ticket Lobby

Concourse A

Concourse E

← Departures/Upper Roadway

Baggage Claim

← Arrivals/Lower Roadway

Due to ongoing construction, the information on this map is subject to change.

Ground Transportation

The RAZ Downtowner Shuttle picks up passengers every 15 minutes and is located on the lower roadway between baggage claim and the short-term parking garage.

Rental cars are located on the ground level of the short-term parking structure.

Other Area Airports

Troutdale Aviation
920 NW Perimeter Way, Troutdale
661-4940

This airport is 15 miles east of downtown Portland at the west end of the Columbia Gorge near Interstate 84. It offers a range of services, including scenic flights, helicopter and fixed-wing flight training, and aircraft maintenance services.

Hillsboro Airport
1040 NE 25th
648-2831

Fifteen miles west of downtown Portland, just south of Highway 26, the Hillsboro Airport is Oregon's second-busiest airport and considered one of the top general aviation facilities in the United States. Hillsboro Airport is the site of the Portland Rose Festival Association Air Show and home to a variety of corporate aircraft, including Louisiana Pacific's and Nike's.

Mulino Airport
26926 S. Airport Rd.
231-5000
Ten miles south of downtown Portland along Highway 213, Mulino Airport plays an important role as a reliever airport for small propeller-driven aircraft and serves the aviation growth of Clackamas County.

Train and Bus Travel

Union Station
800 NW 6th Ave. (just north of West Burnside)
800/872-7245 (Amtrak)
273-4866 (local information)
273-4871 (baggage information)
Union Station, which got its name from the three major railroad lines that converged here, is a Portland Historic Landmark and is also on the National Register of Historic Places. In 1996 Union Station celebrated its 100th anniversary, and much repair and renovation were done to retain the building's Old World feel, with its massive entrance, highly detailed ceiling, and marble interior. The ticket counter, wooden benches, and signage inside help recall the station's heyday, when about 150 trains per day arrived and departed. The pace is slower today. Only nine trains arrive and depart and, in typical Amtrak fashion, they're often late. But if you're a railroad fan, there's still no more romantic way to travel. Even if you don't intend to ride the train, the station itself is worth a look. And, if you're on a layover, Wilf's piano bar and restaurant, next door, has a fun Fifties feel.

Greyhound-Trailways Bus Lines
550 NW 6th Ave.
800/231-2222
243-2357
Next door to Union Station, you'll find one of the cleanest and brightest Greyhound-Trailways bus stations in the country. It's within walking distance of the downtown and Old Town sectors. Though the station is quite safe, it is sometimes a gathering place for transients—caution is advised.

The Lion and the Rose Victorian Bed & Breakfast

3

WHERE TO STAY

Long known for its love affair with renovation, Portland offers a textured variety of lodging options. Once you start exploring, you'll recognize and appreciate the subtle romance of the city's hotels, some of which are noted for their exquisite dining rooms, while others are praised for their luxurious suites. Though there are new gleaming towers cropping up all the time, some of the most unusual rooms can be found in restored vintage buildings. You can stay in a property listed on the National Historic Register in the heart of the city, or, a little further afield, you'll find eclectic rooms with adjacent theaters and brewpubs. Spas are becoming de rigueur for many travelers, and finding one near your hotel is easy.

Whether your tastes run toward cozy B&Bs, upscale chain properties, or historical interest hotels, you're sure to a place that pleases. No matter where you end up, you'll discover that, for the most part, hoteliers in Portland are proud of their establishments and will welcome you like an old friend. Don't hesitate to ask for a preview of your room and spend a few moments relaxing in the lobby before signing on the dotted line. Feel free to ask for a room with a view or a feather pillow to soothe your weary soul. Most importantly, be willing to immerse yourself in the experience—once you check in, you may not want to check out.

Price rating symbols:
$	$65 and under
$$	$66 to $80
$$$	$81 to $150
$$$$	$151 and up

Note: Prices reflect a general range and may fluctuate depending on season and availability.

DOWNTOWN PORTLAND

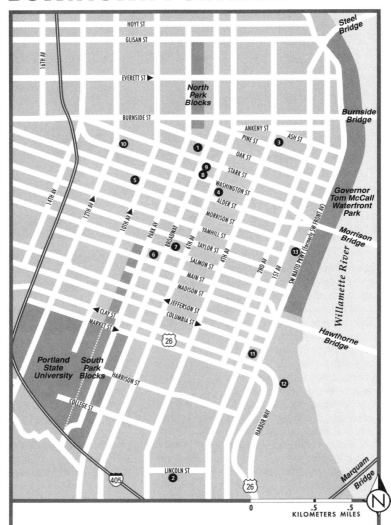

Where to Stay in Downtown Portland

1 Benson Hotel
2 Doubletree Downtown
3 Embassy Suites Hotel
4 Fifth Avenue Suites Hotel
5 Governor Hotel
6 Heathman Hotel
7 Hilton Hotel Portland

8 Hotel Vintage Plaza
9 Imperial Hotel
10 Mark Spencer Hotel
11 Marriott Hotel Downtown Portland
12 RiverPlace Hotel
13 Riverside Inn

DOWNTOWN

Hotels

BENSON HOTEL
309 SW Broadway
Portland, OR 97205
228-2000
$$$$ DT

A $17-million restoration a few years ago has brought the Benson back. It was built in 1912 by Simon Benson (one of Portland's wealthiest lumber barons) during the city's early heyday. The first thing you'll notice about the Benson is the cloaked doormen who greet you. They are noted for their excellent service and friendly ways, but don't expect first-name basis here. Inside the hotel, you'll see imported Russian walnut panels, a huge fireplace, chandeliers, and marble. The lobby exudes warmth and European charm. The guest rooms are elegant. Ask for a top floor room with a view. They're a bit more pricey, but the view is worth it. The Benson is a favorite haunt for film stars and the corporate set, and, even if you don't stay here, have a drink in the lounge, a cozy place to unwind and people-watch.

DOUBLETREE DOWNTOWN
310 SW Lincoln St.
Portland, OR 97201
221-0450
$$$$ DT

Formerly a Red Lion, this hotel has some remodeled rooms. Ask for one. This particular hotel has a reputation for dark rooms without adequate reading light, sometimes even in the remodeled rooms. Nice amenities, though, including coffee pots and hairdryers. An outdoor pool sits in the middle of a landscaped courtyard, and that's about it for

"special" at this standard hotel. The front desk staff does not seem particularly knowledgeable about the area, so you're better off taking your questions elsewhere.

EMBASSY SUITES HOTEL
319 SW Pine St.
Portland, OR 97204
279-9000
$$$$ DT

Opened in October 1997, the former Multnomah Hotel (built in 1912) was once Portland's grandest hotel and is now on the National Historic Register. Queen Marie of Romania was a guest in 1924. Restored to near its original splendor by the great-grandson of the original builder, the hotel also boasts furniture designed to replicate the old days. Each of the 276 rooms is a suite complete with a microwave and refrigerator. The hotel features an indoor swimming pool and a fitness room, 24-hour room service, complimentary breakfast, and parking just across the street.

FIFTH AVENUE SUITES HOTEL
506 SW Washington St.
Portland, OR 97204
222-0001
$$$$ DT

This is a stellar Kimpton property, opened in May of 1996. The historic and elegant ten-story building was erected in 1912 and was once a distinguished department store. It has been refurbished in a charming American country home style with all the savvy of a luxury hotel. The adjacent restaurant, the Red Star Tavern and Roast House, which features brick wood-burning ovens and French-style grills, artwork, and cozy seating, offers classic American cuisine. More than half of the

221 guest rooms are spacious suites. All rooms have writing tables, dataports, plug-ins for PCs, and plush terry robes.

GOVERNOR HOTEL
611 SW 10th Ave.
Portland, OR 97205
224-3400
$$$$ **DT**

The Governor is resplendent with Northwest ambiance. Built in 1909, the hotel was originally known as the Seward Hotel, and the rooms rented for $1.50 to $2 per night, breakfast included. Listed on the National Register of Historic Places, the Governor, known in the old days as "the hotel of quiet elegance," is an architectural treat. The architect, William C. Knighton, was known for incorporating bells in his designs. Look for them throughout the building, especially on the outside wall facing SW 10th and in the stained-glass dome in the restaurant. The dome was part of the original hotel and has been painstakingly restored. Although much of the interior today is reproduction, restorers studied historic photographs to accurately duplicate the hotel's original splendor. Even the carpet is patterned after the original design. The mahogany and sweeping murals in the hotel lobby, the leather chairs, and a crackling fireplace make the Governor a comfortable treasure. All 100 rooms are historically appointed. If you feel like luxury, ask for a suite with a fireplace and/or balcony.

HEATHMAN HOTEL
1001 SW Broadway
Portland, OR 97205
241-4100
$$$$ **DT**

Just across the street from the Performing Arts Center, the Heathman is one of Portland's treasures. The doormen are renowned for their courtesy and willingness to help, and the personal service is second to none. It's likely that the staff will know you by name before you leave, even if you stay only a day or two. The guest rooms are small but elegantly appointed and comfortable. One of the hallmarks of the Heathman is its library. Located on the mezzanine level above the bar, the shelves are filled with books signed by the authors, most of whom have stayed here. Artwork also abounds. Note especially the Andy Warhol works in the restaurant. Afternoon tea is a sumptuous affair, served near the fireplace off the lobby.

HILTON HOTEL PORTLAND
921 SW 6th Ave.
Portland, OR 97204
226-1611
$$$$ **DT**

A major facelift at the Hilton made big news in Portland's hotel world. The lobby now looks like something out of Hollywood. Every guest room has been remodeled to exude modern richness. The Hilton is a hub for conventioneers and well-heeled business travelers. Of special note is the state-of-the-art fitness club. The views (from rooms on the upper floors of the hotel) are all magnificent, whether from the city side or east, toward the mountains. Room service can be a little slow, but the food is good.

HOTEL VINTAGE PLAZA
422 SW Broadway
Portland, OR 97205
228-1212
$$$$ **DT**

The Hotel Vintage Plaza (a Kimpton

Hilton Hotel Portland

property), where most rooms are named after Oregon wines, has been compared to some of Europe's fine small hotels. The lobby, furnished in dark wood and elegant but comfortable pieces, is much like a large living room. You'll often see guests just relaxing and reading by the fire or watching passersby from an old easy chair. Afternoons bring complimentary wine tasting and conversation in the lobby. Of particular interest are the bilevel suites with 1½ baths. The guest rooms are decorated in various styles. Some are done in rich cherry-wood and wine colors, others are light and airy, with wicker furniture and neutral tones. Be sure to check out Pazzo, the hotel's restaurant, which features some of the best Italian food in town.

IMPERIAL HOTEL
400 SW Broadway
Portland, OR 97205
228-7221
$$$ **DT**

If you tell locals that you're staying at the Imperial, they'll likely raise their eyebrows and wonder why. The Imperial is not known as one of the ritzy places downtown, but it is more than adequate if it's just a comfy spot you're looking for. It's clean (recently remodeled), charming, and much less expensive than its pricey neighbors. The staff is very friendly and eager to please, which counts for a lot when you're a weary traveler. The Imperial is a good value in a safe downtown area. The rooms are equipped with two-port telephones, remote control TVs, free HBO, and a state-of-the-art security system. Another plus: Check-out time is 2 p.m.

MARK SPENCER HOTEL
409 SW 11th Ave.
Portland, OR 97205
224-3293
$$ **DT**

The Mark Spencer is especially nice for longer stays because many of the rooms have kitchen facilities. The building itself is rather bland—no charming landmarks here—but the inside of the hotel is clean and hospitable. Lighting can be a problem in some of the rooms, but if you ask the front desk to recommend a bright room, they'll be happy to accommodate you. Laundry facilities and free parking are not often found in downtown hotels, but they actually exist at the Mark Spencer. It's a good bargain for a no-frills stay. Within walking distance of Powell's Books.

MARRIOTT HOTEL DOWNTOWN PORTLAND
1401 SW Front Ave.
Portland, OR 97201
226-7600
$$$$ **DT**

This is a typical ritzy downtown highrise hotel that caters to the business and conventions crowd. The busy hotel has more than 500 guest rooms, a 24-hour health club, two restaurants, and two bars. Ask for a room with a river view. Service is Marriott-standard, and the rooms are spacious. It's located across the street from Tom McCall Waterfront Park and Riverplace Marina, a bonus for runners and walker. The hotel sits at the edge of the financial district, close to downtown business and the arts and culture scenes.

RIVERPLACE HOTEL
1510 SW Harbor Way
Portland, OR 97201
228-3233
$$$$ **DT**

Plush and cushy, the RiverPlace is the only Portland hotel on the marina. Be sure to ask for a room with a river view, because the life on the waterfront is fascinating 24 hours a day. Service is excellent, and the staff is very prompt and courteous. This is an elegant hotel with a subdued ambiance and gorgeous decor. Huge bouquets of fresh flowers in the

RiverPlace Hotel

lobby are just one of the added touches it's known for. The rooms are deliciously decorated, and the bathrooms are big, a pleasant plus. If you like, you can have a complimentary continental breakfast, accompanied by the *New York Times*, in your room. Upscale shops abound on the riverwalk, and it's just a short walk to one of Portland's favorite brewpubs, the Pilsner Room. In the summertime, patio seating is available outside the hotel, a splendid way to enjoy a meal and watch the happenings along the Willamette River. The RiverPlace is especially popular during the Rose Festival. The view of the opening night fireworks over the river is stunning.

RIVERSIDE INN
50 SW Morrison St.
Portland, OR 97204
221-0711
$$ **DT**

The inn sits a half-block off the waterfront, within easy walking distance of major downtown attractions. All 139 rooms, the lobby, and

New Hotels in Portland

Several new hotels in Portland are slated to open in late 1998 through 1999. As of this printing, not all phone numbers were available. The hotels and approximate opening dates are as follows:

The Westin Portland
SW Alder and Park Avenue
Autumn 1998

Marriott City Center
SW Broadway and Washington Street
January 1999

The Paramount Hotel (a West Coast property)
SW Park Street and Taylor Avenue
441-9856
Spring 1999

Sheraton Hotel Downtown
SW 6th Avenue and Oak Street
Autumn 1999

the restaurant have been recently remodeled. Guests can use the fitness center in the Bank of America building across the street. Free covered parking.

SOUTHWEST

Hotels

MALLORY HOTEL
729 SW 15th Ave.
Portland, OR 97205
223-6311
$$$ **SW**
Oh, the Mallory. Many repeat travelers won't stay anywhere else. Even the bellmen have been here forever, and they enjoy telling you stories about guests, happenings, and history. Built in 1912, the Mallory is one of the last establishments to retain a quaint Fifties sort of charm. The guest rooms are a bargain (ask for a corner suite with a view of the city) and very clean. It's a quirky place, so be prepared. You'll see old folks who used to live here (when it was a residence hotel) dining in the restaurant or sitting in the expansive bright green lobby. The hotel is often full, so you may want to reserve a room early. The lounge just off the lobby is truly memorable, one of the last of

GREATER PORTLAND

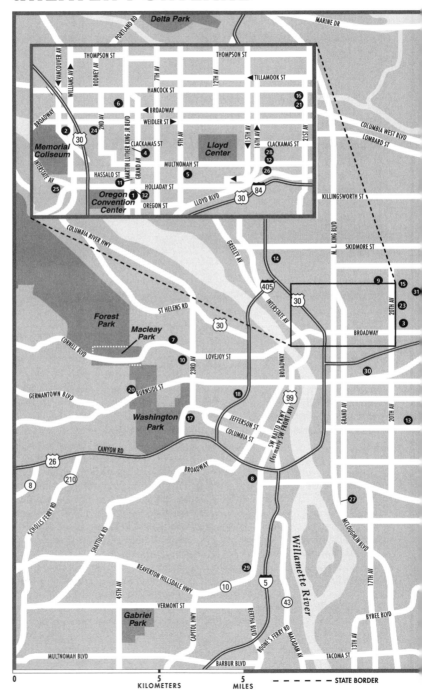

0 ___ 5 ___ 5 ___ — — — — — STATE BORDER
    KILOMETERS   MILES

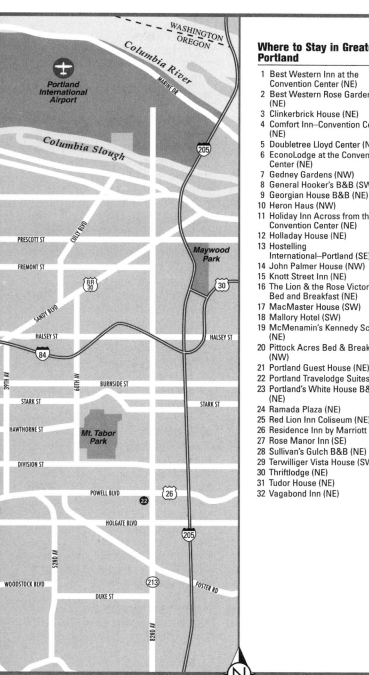

Where to Stay in Greater Portland

1 Best Western Inn at the Convention Center (NE)
2 Best Western Rose Garden (NE)
3 Clinkerbrick House (NE)
4 Comfort Inn–Convention Center (NE)
5 Doubletree Lloyd Center (NE)
6 EconoLodge at the Convention Center (NE)
7 Gedney Gardens (NW)
8 General Hooker's B&B (SW)
9 Georgian House B&B (NE)
10 Heron Haus (NW)
11 Holiday Inn Across from the Convention Center (NE)
12 Holladay House (NE)
13 Hostelling International–Portland (SE)
14 John Palmer House (NW)
15 Knott Street Inn (NE)
16 The Lion & the Rose Victorian Bed and Breakfast (NE)
17 MacMaster House (SW)
18 Mallory Hotel (SW)
19 McMenamin's Kennedy School (NE)
20 Pittock Acres Bed & Breakfast (NW)
21 Portland Guest House (NE)
22 Portland Travelodge Suites (SE)
23 Portland's White House B&B (NE)
24 Ramada Plaza (NE)
25 Red Lion Inn Coliseum (NE)
26 Residence Inn by Marriott (NE)
27 Rose Manor Inn (SE)
28 Sullivan's Gulch B&B (NE)
29 Terwilliger Vista House (SW)
30 Thriftlodge (NE)
31 Tudor House (NE)
32 Vagabond Inn (NE)

its kind around—it looks like it stepped directly out of a Bogey movie. It can get pretty smoky in here because the ventilation isn't top-notch, but if you want to sip a Manhattan or a martini in Fifties style, this is just the place to do it.

Bed and Breakfasts

GENERAL HOOKER'S B&B
125 SW Hooker St.
Portland, OR 97201
222-4435
$$$ **SW**
All rooms feature desks, cable TV, VCR, phones, and an honor bar. You can enjoy an extensive library here, too. Lori is a fourth-generation Portlander who knows the city inside and out, so she is an excellent resource for tourists. No smoking or children under 10 allowed.

MACMASTER HOUSE
1041 SW Vista Ave.
Portland, OR 97205
223-7362
$$$ **SW**
This 17-room mansion sits near Washington Park in a lovely neighborhood made for walking and jogging. Each room has its own library, desk, and dressing table. European antiques and seven fireplaces add to the ambiance.

TERWILLIGER VISTA HOUSE
515 SW Westwood Dr.
Portland, OR 97201
244-0602
$$$ **SW**
Set in the wooded Terwilliger Corridor in Portland's exclusive West Hills, this Georgian Colonial is close to downtown but is surrounded by serene walking paths and views of Portland's rolling hills. Children are welcome here. The Terwilliger Vista House has five rooms, all with private baths.

NORTHWEST

Hotels tend to be fairly sparse in Northwest Portland. There are, however, several nice bed and breakfasts to choose from. If you will be doing business in the area, keep in mind that it's an easy commute from downtown's many choices—usually a simple 15-minute bus trip or an affordable cab ride.

Bed and Breakfasts

GEDNEY GARDENS
2651 NW Cornell Rd.
Portland, OR 97210
226-6514
$$ **NW**
Built in 1907, Gedney Gardens was once owned by Portland's first pediatrician. There are three rooms with a shared bath. Two of these have fireplaces, and all three have views of the city, rivers, and mountains. Gedney Gardens features full breakfasts.

HERON HAUS
2545 NW Westover Rd.
Portland, OR 97210
274-1846
$$ **NW**
You can walk to the Nob Hill shopping district from this elegant old mansion that sits high in the hills of Northwest Portland. All rooms have a sitting/work area and a private bath, TV, phones, and queen- or king-size beds.

JOHN PALMER HOUSE
4314 N. Mississippi Ave.

Portland, OR 97217
284-5893
$$$ NW
This family-run historic Victorian inn
has 11 rooms, four with private baths.
Hosts Mary and David Sauter pride
themselves on their great breakfasts
and their humorous approach to life.
You'll feel like one of the family in this
restored home. They have a beautiful
bridal suite.

PITTOCK ACRES
BED & BREAKFAST
102 NW Pittock Ave.
Portland, OR 97210
226-1163
$$$ NW
This warm, contemporary home
boasts three guest rooms and is located in a scenic urban area. It's a
little more than a mile to downtown
and convenient to the historic Pittock Mansion. Full breakfast.

NORTHEAST

Hotels

BEST WESTERN INN AT THE
CONVENTION CENTER
420 NE Holladay St.
Portland, OR 97232
233-6331
$$ NE
Located across the street from the
Convention Center, this is a prime lo-
cation for conventioneers. There is a
restaurant but no pool. Laundry facil-
ities on premises.

BEST WESTERN ROSE GARDEN
10 N. Weidler St.
Portland, OR 97227
287-9900
$$$ NE
Formerly known as the Best Western

at the Coliseum, the hotel has 178
rooms, an indoor swimming pool, and
a 24-hour restaurant.

COMFORT INN-CONVENTION
CENTER
431 NE Multnomah St.
Portland, OR 97232
233-7933
$$ NE
All rooms include an upgraded conti-
nental breakfast and cable TV. Some
of the king rooms have a spa in them.
The pool is open 24 hours. There is no
restaurant here, but the motel is
within easy walking distance of more
than 40 eateries.

DOUBLETREE LLOYD CENTER
1000 NE Multnomah St.
Portland, OR 97232
281-6111
$$$$ NE
Another former Red Lion, little has
changed since it was purchased by
the DoubleTree Corporation. Some-
times getting through on the phone is
a trial, and the front desk personnel is
not particularly helpful. DoubleTree
has added a concierge to this 476-
room hotel. Adjacent to Lloyd Center
Mall, the hotel is convenient to the
light rail and shopping.

ECONOLODGE AT THE
CONVENTION CENTER
305 N. Broadway
Portland, OR 97227
284-5181
$$ NE
This is a very small motel, with only
20 rooms, some with king-size beds.
No restaurant.

HOLIDAY INN ACROSS FROM THE
CONVENTION CENTER
1021 NE Grand Ave.
Portland, OR 97232

235-2100
$$ NE
Suites with king-size beds and sitting rooms, some with wet bars, are available here. The Master Suites all feature a Jacuzzi and wet bar. A restaurant, room service, lounge, and cable TV with HBO are some of the amenities at this establishment.

MCMENAMIN'S KENNEDY SCHOOL
5736 NE 33rd Ave.
Portland, OR 97211
249-3983
$$$ NE
It's hard to know if this property should be classified as a brewpub with rooms or an inn with a brewpub. Either way, it's a treat not to be missed. Formerly a schoolhouse built in 1915, the McMenamin brothers have restored and rejuvenated this lovely building in one of Portland's oldest neighborhoods. Sleeping rooms are former classrooms, so they all come with a chalkboard! Each room has a private bath and a queen-size bed. There's an on-site movie theater, a Japanese soaking tub, a community garden, and, of course, the brewpub.

RAMADA PLAZA
1441 NE 2nd Ave.
Portland, OR 97232
233-2401
$$$ NE
Located close to the Convention Center and the Rose Garden, this ten-story hotel has 236 guest rooms, an outdoor pool, an indoor exercise room, restaurant, and laundry facilities.

RED LION INN COLISEUM
1225 N. Thunderbird Way

Georgian House B&B

Portland, OR 97227
235-8311
$$ NE
One of the older Red Lion Inns. It's dark here, but the lounge offers a great river view. Although the service is good, don't expect much from the staff with regard to answering questions.

RESIDENCE INN BY MARRIOTT
1710 NE Multnomah St.
Portland, OR 97232
288-1400
$$$$ NE
This is a five-year-old property that boasts 168 suites ranging from studio-size to one- and two-bedroom units. It's clean, comfortable, and well furnished. All suites are fully equipped with a kitchenette and a living area. Many units have king-size beds, and all rooms (except studio with king bed) have fireplaces. Residence Inn is close to restaurants and the Lloyd Center mall. Although there is no food service at the Residence

Inn, Stanford's, a good restaurant nearby, will bill to your room if you like.

THRIFTLODGE
949 E. Burnside St.
Portland, OR 97214
234-8411
$ **NE**
This is a no-frills place: no restaurant, no room service, no suites. Located on a main route to downtown with bus service every ten minutes.

VAGABOND INN
518 NE Holladay St.
Portland, OR 97232
234-4391
$$ **NE**
This used to be the EconoLodge, and all that has changed is the name. This small motel has 35 rooms. There is no restaurant, but a nice continental breakfast is offered in the lobby. Cable TV in all rooms.

Bed and Breakfasts

CLINKERBRICK HOUSE
2311 NE Schuyler
Portland, OR 97212
281-2533
$$ **NE**
Clinkerbrick House is a 1908 Dutch Colonial with comfortable oversized rooms decorated with antiques and quilts. Ten minutes from downtown and close to Lloyd Center and the Convention Center. A full gourmet breakfast is served.

GEORGIAN HOUSE B&B
1828 NE Siskiyou
Portland, OR 97212
281-2250
$$ **NE**
This handsome brick Georgian Colonial resides in a quiet, established neighborhood. Antiques, stained glass, and a winding stairway provide that Old World feel in a homey atmosphere. The rose garden blooms all summer. A gazebo and a sun deck offer a relaxing place to read or enjoy a cup of tea.

HOLLADAY HOUSE
1735 NE Wasco
Portland, OR 97232
282-3172
$ **NE**
Named after Ben Holladay, one of Portland's early leading citizens, the Holladay House is close to shopping and parks. There are only two guest rooms here, with a shared bath, so it's quiet. Service is personal without being intrusive.

KNOTT STREET INN
2331 NE Knott
Portland, OR 97212
249-1855
$$ **NE**
This Portland Craftsman house was built in 1910 and sits in the heart of the historic Irvington District, where you can enjoy a safe stroll through the neighborhood. Filled with antiques and Laura Ashley charm, the inn features three rooms, but only two have private baths.

THE LION & THE ROSE VICTORIAN BED AND BREAKFAST
1810 NE 15th Ave.
Portland, OR 97212
287-9245
$$$$ **NE**
You'll feel like you've been transported back in time when you step into the Lion & the Rose. The house, built in 1906, is a Victorian mansion in the Irvington District

and is listed on the National Register of Historic Places. It's elegant and, at the same time, very comfortable.

PORTLAND GUEST HOUSE
1720 NE 15th Ave.
Portland, OR 97212
282-1402
$$ NE
Vintage linens and luscious breakfasts are two of the charms here. The herb, vegetable, and flower gardens are open for strolling. Close to public transit and shopping, the exquisite accommodations feature air conditioning and wonderful, fluffy beds.

PORTLAND'S WHITE HOUSE B&B
1914 NE 22nd Ave.
Portland, OR 97212
287-7131
$$$ NE
Greek columns and a circular drive greet you at this stately historic landmark, the epitome of romantic elegance. Fountains, a carriage house, and an impressive ballroom add to the period furnishings and decor. All six rooms have private baths. The White House has been the setting for many weddings and private parties.

SULLIVAN'S GULCH B&B
1744 NE Clackamas St.
Portland, OR 97232
331-1104
$$ NE
This B&B is definitely not Laura Ashley. Western art and Indian artifacts grace this 1907 4x4 Portland Craftsman home. Sullivan's Gulch celebrates diversity, and all are welcome here. It's in a quiet Northeast Portland neighborhood within walking distance of an eclectic mix of coffeehouses, boutiques, and micro-breweries. There are three rooms, two with private baths. The Northwest Room features Northwest Coast art and handpainted furniture. Skip Rognlien, one of the owners, describes his B&B as "Frank Lloyd Wright meets Buffalo Bill." Animals abound, so if you are allergic or averse to dog smells, you may want to think twice about staying here.

TUDOR HOUSE
2321 NE 28th Ave.
Portland, OR 97212
287-9476
$$$ NE
This Tudor-style house is only 62 years old, but it looks like a piece of Elizabethan England. Hedged in rhododendrons and azaleas, the yard is one of Portland's largest. Furnished in French and English antiques, the home is interesting and eclectic. The Getaway Suite is especially unique. It has a queen-size bed, a fireplace, and a lavender bathtub. The tub and tiling are original to the house. All the rooms have TV and phone. Full breakfast is served.

SOUTHEAST

Hotels

PORTLAND TRAVELODGE SUITES
7740 SE Powell Blvd.
Portland, OR 97206
788-9394
$$ SE
All rooms include a microwave, coffeemaker, refrigerator, and hairdryer. Free carport parking.

ROSE MANOR INN
4546 SE McLoughlin Blvd.

Portland, OR 97202
236-4175
$$$ **SE**

The inn offers kitchenette rooms and regular rooms. The former have stoves and refrigerators but no dishes or cooking utensils. The outdoor pool is open only during the summer.

Hostels

HOSTELLING INTERNATIONAL-
PORTLAND
3031 SE Hawthorne Blvd.
Portland, OR 97214
236-3380
$ **SE**

Open in the morning and evenings after 6 p.m. Reservations must be made 24 hours in advance with a major credit card. This is a typical hostel, with bunk beds, shared bath, and "no frills." The front desk is extremely helpful and knowledgeable about the area. It's virtually guaranteed that you will meet interesting folks here, too.

4

WHERE TO EAT

Portland has lively restaurants that are over a century old and others that have existed for only a few weeks. Though the city supports hundreds of eating establishments, the dining scene is still plagued by contradictions. Adventurous diners can enjoy excellent Ethiopian, Salvadoran, or Gulf Coast fare, but good Chinese food is almost impossible to find. There are dozens of Thai and Japanese restaurants, but most people still have to stand in line for a simple Sunday breakfast.

Portland's restaurant scene seems conflicted because the city is still in the heady experimental process of figuring out fine dining. During the past decade or two, the culinary arts have exploded in the Rose City, resulting in some of the finest restaurants in country, as well as a delicious type of Northwest cuisine unique to Portland. Fine chefs from around the world are flocking here, eager to take part in a culinary renaissance that is capturing international attention.

But in spite of a new cosmopolitan influence, Portland remains a city of neighborhoods. Each pocket of community loyally supports a variety of restaurants. Neighborhood bistros are abundant, with intimate cafes that specialize in international concepts executed with local ingredients. The dining dress code is occasion-driven rather than venue-driven. Blue jeans, Chanel suits, and leather shorts often coexist comfortably in the same dining room. Dress for comfort—it's Portland.

The following list of restaurants is a selection of the some of best dining establishments in Portland. But since the scene is rapidly changing, visitors shouldn't hesitate to try a place not listed if it looks interesting.

The price rating indicates how much you can expect to spend for a typical appetizer, entree, and dessert.

Price rating symbols:
  $ **$10 and under**
  $$ **$11 to $20**
  $$$ **$21 and up**

African
Abyssinia (NE), p. 76
Jarra's Ethiopian Restaurant (SE),
  p. 81

American Comfort Food
Besaw's Cafe (NW), p. 72
Huber's Cafe (DT), p. 64
Jo Bar & Restaurant (NW), p. 74
RingSide (NW), p. 75
Three Square Grill (SW), p. 72

Best Breakfast
Bijou Cafe (DT), p. 62
Fat City Cafe (SW), p. 70
La Cruda (SE), p. 81
The Original Pancake
  House (SW), p. 72
Shakers Cafe (NW), p. 67
Zell's: An American Cafe (SE), p. 83

Caribbean
Sweetwater's Jam House (SE), p. 81

Chinese
Hunan (DT), p. 65

Continental
Cafe des Amis (NW), p. 73
Couvron (SW), p. 71
Three Doors Down Cafe (SE), p. 83
Toulouse (DT), p. 70
Vignale (NW), p. 76
Zefiro (NW), p. 76

Greek
Alexis (DT), p. 62
Berbati (DT), p. 62
Greek Cusina (DT), p. 64

Hawaiian
Noho's Hawaiian Cafe (SE), p. 81

Indian
India Grill (SE), p. 80
India House (DT), p. 65
Indigine (SE), p. 80

Italian
Caffe Mingo (NW), p. 73
Genoa (SE), p. 80
Il Fornaio (NW), p. 74
Mama Gianetta's (NE), p. 74
Pazzo Ristorante (DT), p. 66

Japanese
Koji Osakaya (DT), p. 66
Restaurant Murata (DT), p. 67
Saburo's Sushi House (SE), p. 81

Late Night Spots
Bistro Montage (SE), p. 78
Brasserie Montmarte (DT), p. 63
Fellini (DT), p. 63
Jake's Grill (DT), p. 65

Middle Eastern
Abou Karim (DT), p. 60
Al-Amir (DT), p. 60
Casablanca (SE), p. 79

Native American
Fiddleheads (SE), p. 79

Neighborhood Sandwich Spots
Dot's Cafe (SE), p. 79
Good Dog/Bad Dog (DT), p. 64
Kornblatt's Delicatessen (NW), p. 74
Leaf and Bean (NE), p. 77
Marco's Cafe and Espresso Bar
  (SW), p. 71

Northwest Fine Cuisine
Atwater's Restaurant & Bar (DT),
  p. 62
Avalon Grill (SW), p. 70
Bread and Ink Cafe (SE), p. 78
Caprial's Bistro and Wines (SE), p. 78
Higgins (DT), p. 64
Jake's Famous Crawfish (DT), p. 65

Paley's Place (NW), p. 75
Papa Haydn Westside (NW), p. 75
Ron Paul Charcuterie (NE), p. 77
Wild Abandon (SE), p. 83
Wildwood (NW), p. 76
Winterborne (NE), p. 78

Pan-Asian
Saucebox Cafe Bar (DT), p. 67
Tiger Bar (DT), p. 67

Pizza
Paparazzi (NE), p. 77
Pizzicato (DT), p. 66

Southern
Bima (NW), p. 62
Doris' Cafe (NE), p. 73
Esparza's Tex-Mex (SE), p. 79
O'Connor's (SW), p. 71

South-of-the-Border
Chez Grill (SE), p. 79
La Sirenita (NE), p. 76
Mañana (SW), p. 71
Oba! (DT), p. 66
Salvador Molly's (SW), p. 72

Spanish
Fernando's Hideaway (DT), p. 64
Tapeo (NW), p. 75

Steak, Seafood, and Pasta
Esplanade at Riverplace (DT), p. 63
Heathman Restaurant and Bar (DT),
    p. 64
Henry Ford's (SW), p. 71
Red Star Tavern and Roast House
    (DT), p. 66
Ruth's Chris Steakhouse (DT), p. 67

Thai
Beau Thai (NW), p. 72
Bird of Paradise (DT), p. 62
Lemongrass Thai Restaurant (NE),
    p. 77
Typhoon! (NW), p. 75

Atwater's, p. 62

Vietnamese
Misohapi (NW), p. 74
Saigon Kitchen (NE), p. 77
Yen Ha (NE), p. 78

DOWNTOWN

ABOU KARIM
221 SW Pine St.
223-5058
$$ **DT**
The fragrance of garlic fills this
busy, well-established Lebanese
cafe that offers standard Middle
Eastern fare, including lamb ke-
babs, cabbage rolls, and hummus.
The *mezza*, a family-style feast
combining a scrumptious bit of
everything, is an excellent selec-
tion. Lunch and dinner. No Discover
Card.

AL-AMIR
223 SW Stark St.
274-0010
$$ **DT**

DOWNTOWN PORTLAND

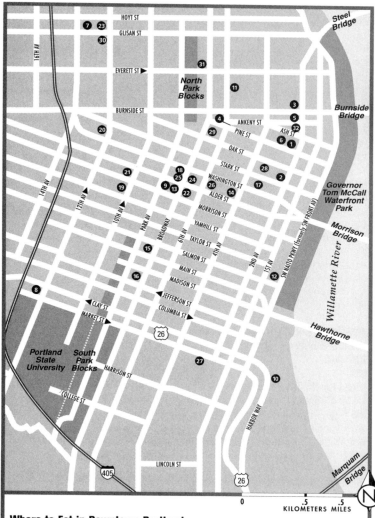

Where to Eat in Downtown Portland

1 Abou Karim
2 Al-Amir
3 Alexis
4 Atwater's Restaurant & Bar
5 Berbati's Pan
6 Bijou Cafe
7 Bima
8 Bird of Paradise
9 Brasserie Montmarte
10 Esplanade at Riverplace
11 Fellini
12 Fernando's Hideaway
13 Good Dog/Bad Dog
14 Greek Cusina
15 Heathman Restaurant & Bar
16 Higgins
17 Huber's Cafe
18 Hunan
19 India House
20 Jake's Famous Crawfish
21 Jake's Grill
22 Koji Osakaya
23 Oba!
24 Pazzo Ristorante
25 Pizzacato
26 Red Star Tavern & Roast House
27 Restaurant Murata
28 Ruths' Chris Steakhouse
29 Saucebox Cafe and Bar
30 Shakers Cafe
31 Tiger Bar
32 Toulouse

Located in the historic and architec-turally interesting Bishop House, this exotic Middle Eastern restaurant provides elegant meals and a full bar. Try the Al-Amir special, a tasty con-coction of chicken filet and lamb shank. Just remember to save room for a sweet piece of baklava. Lunch and dinner served all day.

ALEXIS
215 W. Burnside St.
224-8577
$$ DT
The family-run Alexis enjoys a repu-tation for friendliness and fun that few restaurants achieve. This lively establishment serves excellent Greek food with gusto and flair. Don't be surprised to see people flinging plates or dancing with chairs in their mouths in the old-style Greek tradi-tion. Lunch and dinner. Reservations recommended for groups of ten or more.

ATWATER'S RESTAURANT & BAR
111 SW 5th Ave., 30th Floor
275-3600
$$$ DT
High atop the US Bancorp Tower, At-water's offers a hypnotizing view of the city. The superb Pacific North-west cuisine is French influenced. But if the venerable dining room seems too pricey, consider appetiz-ers in the lounge, which commands the same view and features excellent jazz on weekend nights. Lunch and dinner. Reservations recommended.

BERBATI'S PAN
19 SW 2nd Ave.
226-2122
$$ DT
This Old Town mainstay recently opened a rocking music club next door, but it still offers the most im-pressive and interesting Greek food in town. The *Pikilia* combination plate combines seven of the best dishes Berbati has to offer and is huge enough for two. Lunch and dinner. Closed Mondays. Reservations rec-ommended for large parties.

BIJOU CAFE
132 SW 3rd Ave.
222-3187
$–$$ DT
Expect a wait on weekend mornings at this funky cafe well known for pro-viding the best breakfast in the downtown area. The portions are huge and prepared with a healthy twist. Favorites include hearty snap-per hash, heavenly pancakes, and eggs cooked to perfection. Breakfast and lunch. Closed Mondays. No reservations.

BIMA
1338 NW Hoyt St.
241-3465
$$ DT
The cocktails are tropical, and the food is exotic. This spacious Pearl District restaurant brings a bright taste of the Gulf of Mexico coast to Portland. Jambalaya, baby back ribs, and crab cakes shine on the dinner menu. The bar can provide a decent meal as well. Lunch and dinner. No lunch on weekends.

BIRD OF PARADISE
1533 SW 12th Ave.
796-9131
$ DT
This immaculate cafe offers fantastic Thai food prepared without oil, sugar, or salt. The friendly owners will help novices through the ordering pro-cess and prepare each meal to order. Every artistically arranged dish ex-plodes with fresh flavors and pure

ingredients. Lunch and dinner. No lunch on Sunday. No credit cards.

BRASSERIE MONTMARTE
626 SW Park Ave.
224-5552
$$ **DT**
This bistro-style downtown eatery has gained a reputation for great jazz and disdainful service. Although popular for lunch, the restaurant really shines in the evening, when people of all ages, classes, and political beliefs gather to enjoy music and food into the wee hours. Lunch, dinner, and late night. Reservations recommended.

ESPLANADE AT RIVERPLACE
1510 SW Harbor Way
295-6166
$$$ **DT**
This hotel dining room on the shores of the Willamette River provides an appropriate forum for business lunches and dinners. The food, decor, and service are tasteful and upscale but unobtrusive. Perfect for expense account power dining. Breakfast, lunch, and dinner.

FELLINI
125 NW 6th Ave.
243-2120
$ **DT**
Located adjacent to Portland's grungiest nightclub, this clean and casual hole-in-the-wall offers simple fare a step beyond regular pub grub. Burgers, souvlaki and interesting specials are available until 4 a.m. on weekends. Lunch, dinner, and late night. No credit cards.

Portland's Homegrown Cuisine

The Pacific Northwest is host to a bounty of homegrown gastronomical wonders. From hazelnuts to Willapa Bay oysters to marionberries, some of the most unique food items in the world are grown in Oregon and southwest Washington. Portland chefs are realizing the potential of local ingredients. In ever-increasing numbers, restaurant owners are modifying their menus to take advantage of the glorious abundance that grows in Portland's backyard. One chef, Greg Higgins, plans to eventually use only locally grown food in his restaurant, Higgins. He believes that using products from a local, sustainable agriculture saves energy, boosts the local economy, and results in tastier, more creative dishes. Portland's better restaurants already use locally grown ingredients, many bought from small, organic farms. And as more and more chefs arrive to execute international ideas with local ingredients, a new style of uniquely Portland cuisine blossoms.

FERNANDO'S HIDEAWAY
824 SW 1st Ave.
248-4709
$$$ **DT**

Eat, drink, and be private at this romantic spot where the Spanish food is almost as heady as the at-mosphere. The lamb dishes are particularly good, but everything is prepared with a wonderful flair. The elegant bar serves a delicious sangria that is the perfect lubricant for any social event. Lunch and dinner. Dinner only on Saturdays. Closed Sundays.

GOOD DOG/BAD DOG
708 SW Alder St.
222-3410
$ **DT**

Sausage lovers will be in dog heaven at this cafe that serves handmade wieners from around the world. The spicy Oregon Smokey is a good choice for out-of-towners. And the canine-inspired decor will charm even cat people. Lunch and dinner. Closed Sundays. No credit cards.

GREEK CUSINA
404 SW Washington St.
224-2288
$–$$ **DT**

Plate-throwing is required on weekend evenings at this popular, noisy, family-run restaurant in the heart of downtown. Good Greek food, friendly service, and a full bar keep the place packed the rest of the time. Lunch and dinner.

HEATHMAN RESTAURANT AND BAR
1001 SW Broadway
241-4100
$$$ **DT**

Hotel restaurants are hit-and-miss when it comes to food quality, but the Heathman is always a big, big hit. Chef Philippe Boulot makes excellent use of fresh Northwest ingredients to create outstanding, memorable meals. The Fireplace Room is a comfortable spot for solo diners to indulge in excellent dining without feeling conspicuously alone. And don't dare leave the premises without sampling one the divine desserts. Breakfast, lunch, and dinner.

HIGGINS
1239 SW Broadway
222-9070
$$$ **DT**

Chef Greg Higgins serves up a delicious slice of Portland night after night. Using the freshest regional ingredients to their fullest, Higgins' ever-changing menu offers some of the best Northwest Cuisine available anywhere. The atmosphere is comfortable, just the right ambiance to enjoy a meal to remember. Lunch and dinner.

HUBER'S CAFE
411 SW 3rd Ave.
228-5686
$$ **DT**

Portland's oldest restaurant, bustling

TRIVIA

In 1904 Henry Weinhard built his brewery just a block from Jake's Famous Crawfish Restaurant, either to aid beer delivery or because Weinhard wanted to be within crawling distance of his favorite restaurant. Both establishments are still operating.

Collections in Good Taste

Most Portland restaurants attract customers by providing good food and friendly service. But some establishments boast an added attraction that draws patrons just as strongly as a delicious meal: collectibles. Shakers Cafe (1212 NW Glisan St.) is famous for its huge collection of salt- and pepper shakers from around the world. Gina of Gina's Place (901 NW 21st Ave.) displays her charming collection of ceramic cookie jars. And kids of all ages are delighted by the quirky assemblage of canine art objects at Good Dog/Bad Dog (708 SW Alder St.) that ranges from stuffed toy poodles to German shepherd figurines. Each of these restaurants has an added dimension that makes eating out more fun. Go for the good food and friendly service, but stay for the kitsch.

since 1879, is most famous for its turkey dinner with all the fixings. The gorgeous wood-paneled dining room, with its stained-glass ceiling, is made homey by such details as fresh roses and perfectly mashed potatoes. Lunch and dinner. Closed Sundays.

HUNAN
515 SW Broadway
224-8063
$ DT
Some like it hot, and Hunan delivers. This pleasantly decorated Chinese restaurant provides Portland's best General Tso's chicken, as well as consistently fine versions of other favorites. Hunan is an oasis in a town with a surprising lack of good Chinese food. Lunch and dinner.

INDIA HOUSE
1038 SW Morrison St.
274-1017
$$ DT

The spicy dishes at this popular Indian restaurant cut the gloom of even the grayest Portland day. The lunch buffet is an excellent deal, allowing unlimited amounts of authentic Indian fare. This is a good spot for vegetarians. Lunch and dinner. No lunch on Sundays.

JAKE'S FAMOUS CRAWFISH
401 SW 12th Ave.
226-1419
$$$ DT
Jake's is Portland's true landmark restaurant. The century-old seafood house is always packed, and not just with tourists. Locals enjoy the scrumptious food, impeccable service, and rollicking bar time after time. Perusing the huge menu is just the beginning of a truly memorable meal. Lunch and dinner. Reservations recommended.

JAKE'S GRILL
611 SW 10th Ave.

220-1850

$$ DT

This relatively young cousin of Jake's Famous Crawfish is located in the newly renovated Governor Hotel. Businessmen rule here, conducting important power lunches in a manly environment. Grilled meat, fish, and poultry dominate the menu, with special late-night fare from 11 p.m. to 1 a.m. Breakfast, lunch, and dinner.

KOJI OSAKAYA
606 SW Broadway
294-1169

$$–$$$ DT

Koji's cramped quarters are usually packed with an interesting cross-section of hungry Portlanders. The sushi bar is an excellent spot to grab a quick bite while the chefs perform a working dance. Cooked food at individual tables is available as well. Lunch and dinner. Closed Sundays.

OBA!
555 NW 12th Ave.
228-6161

$$ DT

If style matters more than substance in your world, then Oba! is the place to dine. This super-slick warehouse turned stunning corporate eatery boasts new-wave Mexican food that is almost as spicy as the atmosphere. Those who wish to be seen may strut their stuff here. The cocktails are the most refreshing aspect of this heavily designed spot. Dinner only.

PAZZO RISTORANTE
627 SW Washington St.
228-1515

$$ DT

Pazzo is a comfortable fit for serious and casual diners alike; it's a favorite among business people, singles, and families. Italian dishes prepared with some interesting twists help this bustling restaurant maintain its status as one of Portland's finest. Breakfast, lunch, and dinner.

PIZZACATO
705 SW Alder St.
226-1007

$$ DT

The owners of this gourmet pizza outfit are slowly building an empire across the city. The cutting-edge pies are topped with such offbeat ingredients as roasted potatoes, barbecued chicken, and even peanut butter. They are delicious and different. Lunch and dinner.

RED STAR TAVERN AND ROAST HOUSE
503 SW Alder
222-0005

$$–$$$ DT

This relatively new spot boasts a metropolitan ambiance that is often lacking in other Portland restaurants, even though the large win-

---

TRIVIA

McCormick & Schmick's seafood restaurants are now spread in a chain across the country, but Portland is home to the charming original that started it all. Partake in M&S's specialty, alder-smoked salmon, at 235 SW 1st Ave., 224-7522.

---

dows look out over the mundane bus mall. Since this is a roast house, expect wonderful eats to emerge from the wood-burning oven. Pork is definitely spoken here, served alongside such delicious Southern treats as cornbread, sweet potato hash, and corn salad. Breakfast, lunch, and dinner.

RESTAURANT MURATA
200 SW Market St.
227-0080
$$ **DT**
This small dining room in an unlikely location provides the best Japanese food in Portland. Dishes range from intricate sushi to delicate tempura to adventurous specials. One of the many authentic treats includes an ice cream dessert powdered with tea leaves. Lunch and dinner. No lunch on Saturdays. Closed Sundays.

RUTH'S CHRIS STEAKHOUSE
309 SW 3rd Ave.
221-4518
$$$ **DT**
Portland's installation of this national restaurant chain was popular as soon as its doors opened early in 1997. The upscalecomfort/Flintstone fare boasts spectacular meat and potatoes—and vegetables if you insist. This beefy, old-fashioned spot is not the place to eat before your annual cholesterol test. Dinner only.

SAUCEBOX CAFE AND BAR
214 SW Broadway
241-3393
$$ **DT**
The owners of Zefiro had a stroke of genius when they envisioned this Asian-style restaurant that features exotic Eastern food from Japan to Java. The adventuresome diner will

TRIVIA

Fat City Cafe has a plaque on the wall commemorating the "Fat City Massacre." In 1987 then-Mayor J.E. "Bud" Clark fired the police chief in one of the turquoise vinyl booths, popularizing the phrase "read my lips" long before George Bush uttered it.

be in ecstasy here, and the excellent staff will hold the hands of those who aren't quite as daring. The bar is one of the hotter spots in town. Lunch and dinner. Dinner only on Saturdays. Closed Sundays and Mondays.

SHAKERS CAFE
1212 NW Glisan St.
221-0011
$ **DT**
Breakfast tastes even better when eaten at one of the happiest places in town. Invigorating music, peppy servers, kitschy decor, and first-rate food support this diner's claim as one of the best breakfast spots around. Expect a wait on weekends. Breakfast and lunch. No credit cards.

TIGER BAR
317 NW Broadway
222-7297
$ **DT**
This elegant dive of a cocktail lounge has quickly become a mainstay for the young and broke, mostly because the Thai food is plentiful and affordable. The choice of *satays*—skewers of various meats, seafood, or vegetables—is mindboggling. The wild greens with eggplant dressing or vegetable *yakisoba* will fuel a hungry hipster for the rest of the evening. Dinner only.

GREATER PORTLAND

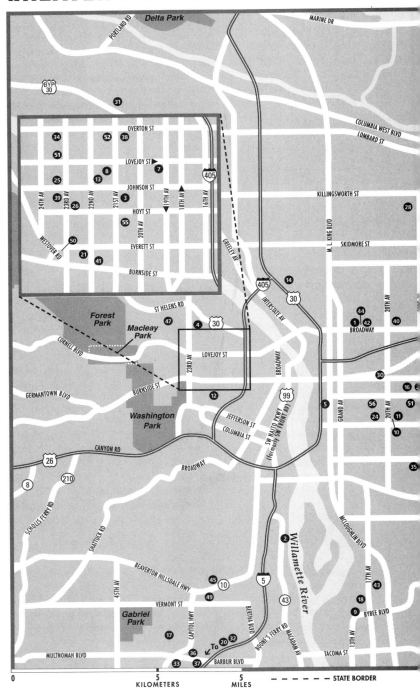

Delta Park

MARINE DR

PORTLAND RD

BYP 30

COLUMBIA WEST BLVD

LOMBARD ST

31

Overton St

34   52   38
51
25   13   8
24TH AV 39 23RD AV 26 22ND AV 21ST AV
55
WESTOVER RD 50
21 41

Lovejoy St   7
405
Johnson St   3
19TH AV 18TH AV 16TH AV
Hoyt St   20TH AV
Everett St
Burnside St

KILLINGSWORTH ST
28

M. L KING BLVD
SKIDMORE ST

Forest Park
ST HELENS RD
47
Macleay Park
CORNELL BLVD

GREELEY AV
405 14
30 INTERSTATE AV

44
1 42
BROADWAY
40

20TH AV

4   30
23RD AV LOVEJOY ST BROADWAY
12
30
16

Washington Park
GERMANTOWN BLVD
BURNSIDE ST

JEFFERSON ST
COLUMBIA ST
99
5
56
24 20TH AV 51
11
10

GRAND AV

CANYON RD
26
8 210

SW MAITO PKWY (formerly SW FRONT AV)
BROADWAY

MCLOUGHLIN BLVD

35

Willamette River

SCHOLLS FERRY RD
SHATTUCK RD
45TH AV

BEAVERTON HILLSDALE HWY
45
49
10
VERMONT ST

Gabriel Park
17 CAPITOL HWY

BERTHA BLVD
5
43

BOONE'S FERRY RD MACDAM AV
43
18
9 BYBEE BLVD
17TH AV

13TH AV

MULTNOMAH BLVD
36
33 37 BARBUR BLVD
To 20 32
TACOMA ST

0   5
KILOMETERS   MILES   – – – – – STATE BORDER

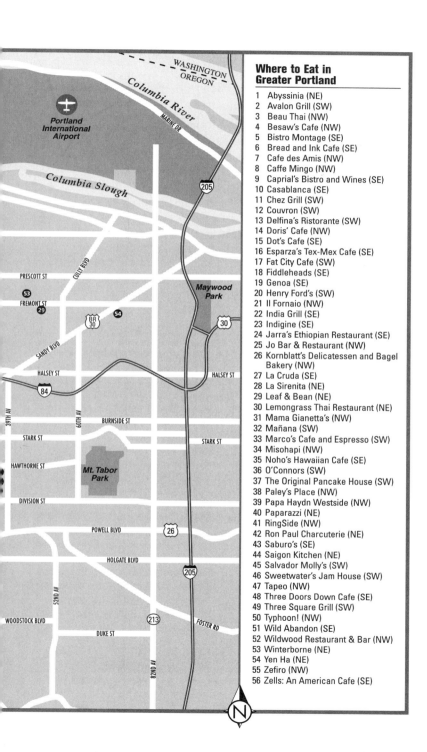

Where to Eat in Greater Portland

1. Abyssinia (NE)
2. Avalon Grill (SW)
3. Beau Thai (NW)
4. Besaw's Cafe (NW)
5. Bistro Montage (SE)
6. Bread and Ink Cafe (SE)
7. Cafe des Amis (NW)
8. Caffe Mingo (NW)
9. Caprial's Bistro and Wines (SE)
10. Casablanca (SE)
11. Chez Grill (SW)
12. Couvron (SW)
13. Delfina's Ristorante (SW)
14. Doris' Cafe (NW)
15. Dot's Cafe (SE)
16. Esparza's Tex-Mex Cafe (SE)
17. Fat City Cafe (SW)
18. Fiddleheads (SE)
19. Genoa (SE)
20. Henry Ford's (SW)
21. Il Fornaio (NW)
22. India Grill (SE)
23. Indigine (SE)
24. Jarra's Ethiopian Restaurant (SE)
25. Jo Bar & Restaurant (NW)
26. Kornblatt's Delicatessen and Bagel Bakery (NW)
27. La Cruda (SE)
28. La Sirenita (NE)
29. Leaf & Bean (NE)
30. Lemongrass Thai Restaurant (NE)
31. Mama Gianetta's (NW)
32. Mañana (SW)
33. Marco's Cafe and Espresso (SW)
34. Misohapi (NW)
35. Noho's Hawaiian Cafe (SE)
36. O'Connors (SW)
37. The Original Pancake House (SW)
38. Paley's Place (NW)
39. Papa Haydn Westside (NW)
40. Paparazzi (NE)
41. RingSide (NW)
42. Ron Paul Charcuterie (NE)
43. Saburo's (SE)
44. Saigon Kitchen (NE)
45. Salvador Molly's (SW)
46. Sweetwater's Jam House (SW)
47. Tapeo (NW)
48. Three Doors Down Cafe (SE)
49. Three Square Grill (SW)
50. Typhoon! (NW)
51. Wild Abandon (SE)
52. Wildwood Restaurant & Bar (NW)
53. Winterborne (NE)
54. Yen Ha (NE)
55. Zefiro (NW)
56. Zells: An American Cafe (SE)

Ten Best Places to Eat with Kids in Portland

by Rocky Raccoon (Bob Hill), mascot, Portland Rockies baseball team

1. **Civic Stadium** 1844 SW Morrison St., 223-2837, during a Portland Rockies baseball game.
2. **RingSide**, 2165 W. Burnside St., 223-1513.
3. **Esparza's Tex-Mex**, 2725 SW Ankeny St., 234-7909.
4. **Good Dog/Bad Dog**, 708 Adler St., 222-3410.
5. **The Old Spaghetti Factory**, 0715 SW Bancroft St., 222-5375.
6. **Jamie's Great Hamburgers**, 838 NW 23rd Ave., 248-6784.
7. **The Original Pancake House**, 8601 SW 24th Ave., 246-9007.
8. **Mañana**, 8981 SW Barbur Blvd., 245-6501.
9. **Ivy House**, 1605 NE Bybee Blvd., 231-9528.
10. **Der Rheinlander**, 5035 NE Sandy Blvd., 288-5503.

TOULOUSE
71 SW 2nd Ave.
241-4343
$$ **DT**

At first glance, this French restaurant seems as if it could be an uptight, overpriced nightmare. But don't be fooled by stereotypes: Toulouse is as comfortable as any American neighborhood bistro. The food is artfully prepared and presented, and the wine selection is superb. Finish off a delightful meal with a nightcap at the adjoining nightclub, Bar 71. Lunch and dinner. No lunch on weekends. Closed Mondays.

SOUTHWEST

AVALON
4630 SW Macadam Ave.
227-4630
$$$ **SW**

This elegant restaurant boasts one of the best views of the Willamette River. Internationally renowned Chef Roy Brieman offers an extensive and interesting menu that will satisfy appetites of all sizes. The service is excellent. Dinner, weekday lunch, Sunday brunch.

COUVRON
1126 SW 18th Ave.
225-1844
$$$ **SW**

The food is the thing at this cozy, special-occasion restaurant. Complicated dishes feature excellent ingredients presented in delightful combinations. Prepare for the unexpected, but expect a hefty bill at the end of the meal. Dinner only. Closed Sundays and Mondays.

FAT CITY CAFE
7820 SW Capitol Hwy.

245-5457
$ SW

Long before Multnomah Village became a haven for antique hunters, Fat City Cafe was serving up good, cheap food to long lines of patrons. Homemade cinnamon rolls, gooey sandwiches, and thick milkshakes are just a few reasons folks return to this neighborhood mainstay. Breakfast and lunch. No credit cards.

HENRY FORD'S
9589 SW Barbur Blvd.
245-2434
$$$ SW

This richly elegant restaurant has barely changed since Mr. Ford built it in 1955. The menu changes seasonally, offering such selections as hand-cut steaks, rack of lamb, salmon, and razor clams. Discriminating diners, or those celebrating a special occasion, won't mind the equally impressive bill.

MAÑANA
8981 SW Barbur Blvd.
245-6501

$ SW

This family-run cafe is a neighborhood favorite. Choose from consistently prepared and affordable Mexican food that ranges from combination plates to daily specials to a lunch buffet. Kids may join some of the servers' children playing in the corner. Lunch and dinner.

MARCO'S CAFE AND ESPRESSO BAR
7910 SW 35th Ave.
245-0199
$–$$ SW

Newly remodeled, clean, and bright, Marco's is a Multnomah Village institution that offers something delicious for every member of the family. The classic American fare, prepared with a healthy twist, is best topped off with one of Marco's awesome desserts. Breakfast, lunch, and dinner. No reservations.

O'CONNORS
7850 SW Capitol Hwy.
244-1690

One of the many fine dishes at Genoa, p. 80

© John Rizzo

The Western Culinary Institute (1316 SW 13th Ave., 223-2245), one of the finest cooking schools in the country, lures people into its dining room to act as guinea pigs for experimenting students. The reward is usually an excellent meal for a low price.

$ **SW**

O'Connors' motto is "Where Montana people meet the rest of the world," but the transplanted Big Sky cafe has been in Portland since 1934. This casual diner is known for hefty portions of good food leaning toward the spicy. Breakfast, lunch, and dinner.

**THE ORIGINAL
PANCAKE HOUSE
8601 SW 24th Ave.
246-9007**

$ **SW**

Expect the ultimate in pancakes, pancakes galore, flapjacks, hotcakes, and crêpes. Not to be confused with the dingier Original Hotcake House across the river, this cheery breakfast spot is heaven for pancake lovers, although the wait for a table is excruciating on the weekends. Breakfast and lunch. Closed Mondays and Tuesdays. No credit cards.

**SALVADOR MOLLY'S
1523 SW Sunset Blvd.
293-1790**

$$ **SW**

The little strip mall maze known as the Hillsdale neighborhood hosts one of Portland's most unique restaurants. Bask in the warmth of such Gulf Coast–inspired treats as jerk chicken, black-eyed pea fritters, and Cuban stuffed sandwiches. The exotic drink selection is surpassed only by the variety of hot sauces. The rickety deck is an excellent destination on hot summer evenings, though the interior's island trinket–inspired decor is delicious as well. Closed Sundays and Mondays.

**THREE SQUARE GRILL
6320 SW Capitol Hwy.
244-4467**

$$ **SW**

Restaurants in strip malls don't have to be fast food. This cheery shopping center cafe offers an eclectic selection of international comfort food: latkes, chili, meatloaf and crushed potatoes, or sausage with kraut. Lunch, dinner, and weekend brunch. Closed Mondays.

NORTHWEST

**BEAU THAI
730 NW 21st Ave.
223-2182**

$ **NW**

This relatively new Thai restaurant expanded just a few months after it opened, but it's still tough to find an open table. The wait is worth just one mouthful of the delicious food, served in plentiful portions. Lunch and dinner. No lunch Mondays or Saturdays. Closed Sundays. No reservations.

**BESAW'S CAFE
2301 NW Savier St.**

228-2619

$$ **NW**

This venerable eatery has learned something since it opened in 1902; the service is impeccable. The ever-changing dinner menu usually offers pasta, seafood, and meat dishes, all carefully prepared. Do not leave this restaurant without sampling a fabulous des-sert. Breakfast, lunch, and dinner. Closed Mondays.

CAFE DES AMIS
1987 NW Kearney St.
295-6487

$$$ **NW**

This wonderfully romantic bistro offers delightful French fare influenced by the great Northwest. Owner/chef Dennis Baker has carved a strong niche with his intimate menu of classic continental cuisine prepared with local ingredients. A perfect place for lovers. Dinner only. Closed Sundays.

CAFFE MINGO
807 NW 21st Ave.
226-4646

$$ **NW**

Many Portlanders consider this the friendliest of all Rose City Italian restaurants. The robust peasant-style food is enhanced by the happy ambiance of pleased patrons. The pastas are especially delicious, all cooked with loving care and interesting ingredients. The line stretching out the door of this excellent spot is there for a very good reason. Dinner only. Closed Sundays.

DORIS' CAFE
325 N. Russell St.
287-9249

$$ **NW**

Doris' just keeps getting bigger and bigger. Stop in for the ribs and catfish but stay for any one of such delicious side dishes as black-eyed peas, hush puppies, or greens cooked in pot

Ten Hippest Places to Eat in Portland
by Richard Martin, Music Columnist,
Willamette Week

1. **Zefiro**, 500 NW 21st Ave., 226-3394.
2. **Wildwood**, 1221 NW 21st Ave., 248-9663.
3. **Esparza's Tex-Mex**, 2725 SE Ankeny St., 234-7909.
4. **Pazzo Ristorante**, 627 SW Washington St., 228-1515.
5. **Bima**, 1338 NW Hoyt St., 241-3465.
6. **Fellini**, 125 NW 6th Ave., 243-2120.
7. **Il Piatto**, 2348 SE Ankeny St., 236-4997.
8. **Bistro Montage**, 301 SE Morrison St., 234-1324.
9. **India House**, 1038 SW Morrison St., 274-1017.
10. **Typhoon**, 2310 NW Everett Ave., 243-7557.

likker. Enjoy live music on weekend
evenings. Lunch and dinner.

IL FORNAIO
115 NW 22nd Ave.
248-9400
$$–$$$ **NW**
This restaurant chain is gradually
spreading forth from its Italy-to-
California roots, and its first Oregon
store is a hit. The beautiful people
have flocked to this sophisticated
and trendy site like pigs to a trough.
But the delicious bread alone is
reason enough to pig out here. Atten-
tive servers make it easy to navigate
the massive menu of Italian fare. An
additional monthly list of items from a
particular region of Italy is a special
treat. But start with the bread, end
with the bread, and then take some
with you when you leave. Lunch and
dinner.

JO BAR & RESTAURANT
701 NW 23rd Ave.
222-0048
$$ **NW**
San Fransisco seems right outside
the door at this tony spot where calo-
ries are king, and martinis are manda-
tory. The restaurant's best dishes
come from the rotisserie that encom-
passes an entire wall. The wonderful
roast chicken has crispy skin cover-
ing the tenderest of meat. The Thai

chicken ravioli is becoming a local
legend, along with the fabulous drink
specials and excellent service. Lunch
and dinner.

KORNBLATT'S DELICATESSEN
AND BAGEL BAKERY
628 NW 23rd Ave.
242-0055
$ **NW**
New Yorkers can get a taste of
home without the surly attitude at
this cramped and bustling deli/
diner. The food is traditional deli fare
such as knishes, lox and bagels,
chopped liver, and gargantuan
three-decker sandwiches. The
Reubens are outstanding. Breakfast,
lunch, and dinner. No American
Express.

MAMA GIANETTA'S
5264 N. Lombard St.
285-8863
$$ **NW**
Sometimes heavy Italian fare is the
most appropriate selection for dinner on a rainy night. Mama's motto,
Mangiere o Morire, means "Eat or
Die." The warmth of the luscious
five-cheese lasagna is exceeded
only by the graciousness of the wonderful staff. Takeout is available. Dinner only.

MISOHAPI
1123 NW 23rd Ave.
796-2012
$$ **NW**
There aren't many things as satisfy-
ing as a huge bowl of hot noodles on
a cold, rainy night. This echo-cham-
ber of a noodle house has a variety
of good pan-Asian dishes, but the
noodle or ramen bowls will make
you-so-happy. Watch out for single
doctors on break from Good Samarit-
an Hospital, located right across the

street. Lunch and dinner. Closed Sundays.

PALEY'S PLACE
1204 NW 21st Ave.
243-2403
$$$ **NW**
Vitaly and Kimberly Paley moved from New York City to open this intimate bistro that quickly captured the hearts, and stomachs, of Portland. The Paleys serve meticulously prepared French cuisine that takes advantage of Oregon's bountiful food supply. Dinner only. Closed Sundays and Mondays.

PAPA HAYDN WESTSIDE
701 NW 23rd Ave.
228-7317
$$ **NW**
Although best known for sinfully decadent desserts, Papa Haydn also has a reputation for good grilled meat dishes, interesting specials, and thoughtful service. Outdoor seating is available during warm weather. The original Eastside location (5829 SE Milwaukie Ave.) is more quiet and laid-back. Lunch, dinner, and Sunday brunch. Closed Mondays.

RINGSIDE
2165 W. Burnside St.
223-1513
$$ **NW**
A restaurant with a boxing theme is unique in itself, but the rustic Ring-Side is the place to go for an excellent steak and outrageous Walla Walla sweet onion rings. For over 50 years this cozy spot has been a local favorite. Lunch and dinner. Reservations recommended.

TAPEO
2764 NW Thurman St.
226-0409
$–$$ **NW**
Spanish food is definitely making a splash in Portland, due in part to this brilliant spot that offers the best of Madrid with a decidedly Northwest spin. The menu consists of only tapas, small appetizer plates of magnificently diverse dishes. Order as many or as few as your interest or hunger dictate. The chefs crank out beautiful plates, from scallops in saffron sauce to gazpacho. The dining room is anything you want it to be: friendly and boisterous or quietly romantic. Tapeo is leading local dining into a wonderful era of distinctive taste. Dinner only. Closed Mondays.

TYPHOON!
2310 NW Everett Ave.
243-7557
$$ **NW**
Imagine nearly 60 varieties of tea under one roof. This Thai restaurant, along with a new store near PSU, offers unusual, intricate dishes served with grace and flair. The food is excellent, but the extensive tea list is

RingSide

Brewster Associates Ltd.

worth a stop in itself. Lunch and dinner. No lunch on Sundays.

WILDWOOD RESTAURANT & BAR
1221 NW 21st Ave.
248-9663
$$$ **NW**

Chef Cory Schreiber deserves the credit for making this wildly popular and energetic restaurant one of Portland's best. The wood-burning oven turns out excellent pizza, roast duck, and bread. The margaritas are legendary, and the desserts are awesome. Lunch, dinner, and Sunday brunch. Reservations recommended.

ZEFIRO
500 NW 21st Ave.
226-3394
$$$ **NW**

The owners of this exceptional restaurant have heightened Portlanders' dining expectations. The constantly changing menu challenges diners to experiment with cuisines from all over. Although the fare frequently changes, the friendly, hip ambiance remains delightfully the same. Lunch and dinner. No lunch on Saturdays. Closed Sundays.

NORTHEAST

ABYSSINIA
801 NE Broadway
281-1975
$ **NE**

The decor may seem all-American, but the food is deliciously, authentically Ethiopian. Sop up spicy lamb, lentil, or chicken stew with soft *enjera* bread. The portions are huge, but the price is small. Hungry diners will be pleasantly stuffed with interesting, affordable food. No lunch on Saturdays or Sundays.

LA SIRENITA
2817 NE Alberta St.
335-8283
$ **NE**

Cheap, authentic Mexican fare is the selling point at this casual, indoor/outdoor *taqueria*. The food is great—sample the awesome chile relleno burrito—and the prices are reasonable—a winning combination. Adventurous diners can try tacos stuffed with tripe or tongue. *Horachata*, a cinnamon flavored milk, is a perfect beverage to compliment a spicy meal. A hungry family can stuff themselves for mere pesos. Lunch and dinner. Cash only.

LEAF AND BEAN
4936 NE Fremont St.
281-1090
$–$$ **NE**

Though this austere cafe serves marvelous lunches and dinners (specializing in super-huge sandwiches), it truly shines in the morning, with a spectacular array of interesting breakfast dishes. Try a "stacked" omelette: a baked casserole of egg, bacon, mushrooms, onions, and ricotta. Solo diners will find company in the

TRIVIA

Fans of Portland movie director Gus Van Sant may recognize the Pharmacy Fountain (2334 W. Burnside St.), where he filmed scenes for his 1989 movie *Drugstore Cowboy*.

The Skyline Tavern (8031 NW Skyline Blvd.) hosts "The Montana Party" for anyone who hails from Montana. The bash always happens in July, after the NBA playoffs are over.

mountain of current publications. Breakfast, lunch, and dinner daily.

LEMONGRASS THAI RESTAURANT
1705 NE Couch St.
231-5780
$$ **NE**

One of the most heated arguments in town rages over who makes the best Thai food. Lemongrass has a strong faction of defenders, who cite tasty dishes prepared with fresh ingredients, served in a delightful dining room. Worth the wait for a table. Dinner only. Closed Wednesdays. No credit cards.

PAPARAZZI
2015 NE Broadway
281-7701
$$ **NE**

Pizza is the specialty here, cooked in the Neapolitan style, with thin crispy crusts and light toppings. Antipasto, salads, soup, and pasta are available as well, along with a merciless *tiramisu* for dessert. This family-run storefront operation is a refreshing change from most pizza parlors. Dinner only. Closed Mondays.

RON PAUL CHARCUTERIE
1441 NE Broadway
284-5347
$$ **NE**

Ron Paul is one of Portland's premier catering companies, but his restaurant offers the same great food regardless of the occasion. The salads are fabulous, and so are the internationally influenced casseroles. The casual dining room is often packed. The other location in John's Landing (6141 SW Macadam) may be quieter. Lunch and dinner. No dinner on Sundays.

SAIGON KITCHEN
835 NE Broadway
281-3669
$$ **NE**

This brightly decorated Thai and Vietnamese restaurant remains a favorite among locals. The enormous menu can be intimidating, but nearly everyone can find a personal favorite. Spring rolls, Thai noodles, and curry chicken are popular choices. Eat in or take out. Lunch and dinner.

WINTERBORNE
3520 NE 42nd Ave.
249-8486
$$ **NE**

Recently redecorated, this tiny unpretentious neighborhood bistro provides excellent French-influenced meals in an intimate setting. Owner/ chef Gilbert Henry uses unlikely spices and fresh seafood to create some very memorable dishes. Try anything chocolate for dessert. Dinner only. Closed Sundays, Mondays, and Tuesdays. Reservations recommended.

YEN HA
6820 NE Sandy Blvd.
287-3698
$–$$ **NE**

Don't be confused by the 160 different dishes on the menu. The helpful servers know what is good and what is great at this Asian cafe with mostly Vietnamese influences. Trust them. The outstanding specials are also a good bet. The accommodating cooks will pump up the heat on any dish, or turn down the volume for the spice-challenged. Lunch and dinner.

SOUTHEAST

BISTRO MONTAGE
301 SE Morrison St.
234-1324
$$ **SE**
Not for the uptight, anything goes at this hippest of all Portland restaurants. If the cartoon mural of the Last Supper isn't offensive or the Green Eggs and Spam on the menu sounds interesting, then enjoy some great Southern cooking and fun people. Dinner and late night. No credit cards.

The entrance to Cafe des Amis, p. 73

BREAD AND INK CAFE
3610 SE Hawthorne Blvd.
239-4756
$$ **SE**
Eclectic dishes and a refined air preside at this casual and bright neighborhood cafe. The menu changes often, offering fare that ranges from cheese blintzes to roasted lamb chops. An excellent place to stop while shopping on Hawthorne Boulevard. Lunch and dinner.

CAPRIAL'S BISTRO AND WINES
7015 SE Milwaukie Ave.
236-6457
$$$ **SE**
Caprial and John Pence cook up some of Portland's best food using regional ingredients in wonderfully creative ways. The cafe is also a wine shop, so diners may purchase a bottle, then drink it with dinner for a mere extra $3 corkage fee. Everything is delicious, but try to save room for dessert. The Pences plan to expand the dining room and add a bar in mid-1998. Lunch and dinner. Closed Sundays and Mondays.

CASABLANCA
2221 SE Hawthorne Blvd.
233-4400
$$$ **SE**
The beautifully ornate front door alerts hungry diners to the delicious Moroccan mysteries that await inside. The decor is straight out of a Middle Eastern fantasy, and the food fits the finery. Arrive with a healthy appetite, then order the sumptuous Royal Feast Dinner that includes an entree of Moroccan stew or shish kebab, salads, lentil soup, a delightful blend of rice and egg encased in phyllo, and a decadent piece of baklava for dessert. It will definitely be the

beginning of a beautiful friendship. Dinner only.

CHEZ GRILL
2229 SE Hawthorne Blvd.
239-4002
$$ **SE**

The owners of Portland's two immensely popular Chez Jose restaurants certainly knew what they were doing when they created this cool character. The cuisine is an eclectic, multicultural blend of Tex-Mex, California, and Southwestern heat prepared with a very cool twist. The result is a delightful array of unexpected gastronomical treasures. Add one of the marvelous margaritas, and this cafe becomes one of the most comfortable *casas* in town. Lunch and dinner.

DOT'S CAFE
2521 SE Clinton St.
235-0203
$ **SE**

Visitors who want to view real live Portland slackers in their natural habitat need look no further than Dot's Cafe. The patrons of this popular diner are so relaxed, they're almost asleep. Best known as a subcultural watering hole, the Mexican-influenced food is filling and cheap. Lunch, dinner, and late night. No credit cards.

ESPARZA'S TEX-MEX CAFE
2725 SE Ankeny St.
234-7909
$$ **SE**

Joe Esparza, Portland's undisputed king of Tex-Mex food, often sits at the counter and gazes over his realm. The place is usually packed with happy diners chowing down on cactus, buffalo, and house-smoked meats. The decor is *muy divertido.*

TRIVIA

The Goose Hollow Tavern (1927 SW Jefferson St.) is best known as the home of the beer that made its owner, J. E. "Bud" Clark, mayor. But it's also Portland's first tavern to install condom machines in the women's restroom.

Lunch and dinner. Closed Sundays and Mondays.

FIDDLEHEADS
6716 SE Milwaukee Ave.
233-1547
$$–$$$ **SE**

This immensely popular restaurant draws it name from succulent, immature ferns found deep within the forest. The foraging theme permeates the Native American cuisine from all the Americas, prepared with a pre-Columbian sensibility. Chef Fernando Divina takes advantage of the Pacific Northwest bounty to create aboriginal foods for contemporary tastes. A favorite dish is grilled venison with Zuni-style succotash. The soups, such as a steelhead and Dungeness chowder, are sublime. The Native American art is nearly as interesting as the cuisine. Lunch, dinner, and weekend brunch.

GENOA
2832 SE Belmont St.
238-1464
$$$ **SE**

For 25 years, Genoa has represented the finest that Portland has to offer, both in service and food. The menu

Chef Caprial Pence of Caprial's Bistro and Wines, p. 78

changes every two weeks, providing perfect seven- or four-course Northern Italian meals that last for hours. A truly refined experience. Dinner only. Closed Sundays. Reservations required.

INDIA GRILL
2924 E. Burnside St.
236-1790
$$ **SE**

A converted two-story house offers a homey feel to this quiet restaurant. The food is consistently delicious. Start with the India Grill Combo Platter, meat or vegetarian, for a taste of everything. The tandoori entrees are especially tasty. Lunch and dinner.

INDIGINE
3723 SE Division St.
238-1470
$$ **SE**

The tables fill quickly at this charming Indian-influenced restaurant. Expect the unexpected, whether dining casually on a weeknight, enjoying

the multicourse Saturday night feasts, or partaking in the popular Sunday brunch. The outdoor tables are wonderful. Dinner and Sunday brunch. No dinner on Sundays. Closed Mondays.

JARRA'S ETHIOPIAN RESTAURANT
1435 SE Hawthorne Blvd.
230-8990
$$ **SE**

The hottest food in town is Ethiopian. Jarra's friendly owners offer menu guidance and cultural direction, as well as plenty of cold water. Combination platters are a good way to experience the wonders of Africa in the midst of the Rose City. Lunch and dinner. Closed Sundays and Mondays.

LA CRUDA
2500 SE Clinton St.
233-0745
$ **SE**

La Cruda means "hangover" in Spanish, and this funky find specializes in healing that certain affliction.

The Bite: A Taste of Portland

Every August Portland restaurants and regional wineries strut their best stuff at The Bite: A Taste of Portland (248-0600). Food lovers roam amid food and wine booths that fill the expanse of lawn at Tom McCall Waterfront Park, next to the Willamette River. Hungry crowds sample the best that local chefs and vintners have to offer while enjoying a variety of live music from a number of venues. This family-oriented event is one of the more popular festivals that happen each summer at Waterfront Park. Outlying suburbs are now following Portland's lead by organizing food and wine fetes of their own. Proceeds from The Bite benefit Oregon Special Olympics.

Spicy Mexican breakfast is served all day long here. The tacos are excellent, certain to cure whatever ails you. A handful of tasty dishes, soups, and appetizers rounds out the menu. Add a searing dose of hot sauce from the amazing salsa bar. Brunch and dinner.

NOHO'S HAWAIIAN CAFE
2525 SE Clinton St.
233-5301
$ SE
Those who can't slip off to Hawaii for dinner can get halfway there at this charming island-style cafe. Patrons pack the intimate space for chicken, ribs, beef, and fish prepared with a variety of delicious sauces. Huge portions of tasty *yakisoba* noodles are an excellent value. Lunch and dinner. Closed Mondays.

SABURO'S
1667 SE Bybee Blvd.
236-4237
$$ SE
When it comes to sushi, there's no room for error. Saburo's sushi is the best in town: exceedingly fresh, imaginatively prepared, and very reasonably priced. Ignore the menu and stick with the sushi. Since seating is limited, expect a wait. Dinner only. Closed Mondays.

SWEETWATER'S JAM HOUSE
3350 SE Morrison St.
233-0333
$$ SE
This bright and lively cafe—recently relocated in bigger digs—provides a refreshing breeze from the Caribbean Islands. Listen to reggae music and sip a tropical drink while eating conch fritters, pork spare ribs, and other delicacies from paradise. The servers are often on island time, so relax, take a gulp from a Winston's Rum Punch, and bask in the warm ambiance. Don't worry, be happy. The food is fabulous; sunscreen is not included. Lunch, dinner, and Sunday brunch.

THREE DOORS DOWN CAFE
1429 SE 37th Ave.
236-6886

Portland's Exciting New Chefs

Chefs from New York, Los Angeles, even Paris, are stampeding to Portland in droves, and with good reason. The Rose City is garnering international attention as the biggest new thing in the culinary world. The mix is magic: excellent local ingredients, a population of eager restaurant patrons, a booming business climate, dramatic landscapes, and still-affordable living. From European Ricardo Segura (Tapeo) and New Yorkers Vitaly and Kimberly Paley (Paley's Place) to local boy via San Francisco Cory Schreiber (Wildwood), some of the finest chefs in the world have opened shop in Portland and are creating a restaurant scene that is diverse, exciting, and expanding.

But one culinary master has probably done more to heighten Portland's profile than any other. Caprial and John Pence were popular at Fuller's in Seattle when they sought a more relaxed place to raise their kids while still riding the cutting edge of food preparation. They bought Southeast Portland's Westmoreland Bistro in 1992. Since then, Caprial has gained national attention with her cooking show that first aired on the Learning Channel, then quickly moved to public television. But though Caprial may be an international star, she is still one of Portland's most accessible chefs. Whether she's hanging out at the restaurant—now named Caprial's Bistro and Wine—sharing her recipes through her popular cookbooks, or teaching intimate weekly cooking classes with her extremely charming husband, Caprial is quickly becoming Portland's most beloved chef.

The Pences are thriving in the Rose City culinary renaissance. In 1998 they will expand their restaurant to triple the seating, add a larger bar, and include a fancy classroom. The Pences are an excellent example of why Portland has attracted the world's best chefs. And Portland is grateful to have them. Even though they are famous, they still run a friendly neighborhood bistro.

$$ **SE**

The Hawthorne District was in need
of a casual but elegant neighbor-
hood bistro, and Three Doors Down
easily filled the gap. The lovingly
prepared, Italian-influenced fare,
mostly seafood, chicken, and pasta,
is worth the certain wait. Dinner
only. Closed Sundays and Mondays.
No reservations.

WILD ABANDON
2411 SE Belmont St.
232-4458
$$ **SE**

Not one single customer is tearing
his clothes off and running gleefully
through the room, though the food
is inspiring enough for that to happen. The specials change every
day, and the food is impossible to
classify. Suffice it to say that the
finest Northwest ingredients are
prepared in adventurous meals
influenced by cuisines from around
the world. Let yourself go and
expect the unexpected. Lunch, dinner, and Sunday breakfast.

ZELLS: AN AMERICAN CAFE
1300 SE Morrison St.
239-0196
$ **SE**

Though under new ownership, Portland's premier morning place still
provides the heartiest breakfast in
town, usually laced with local fruit.
Try the huckleberry pancakes or the
famous German pancake with ap-
ples. There will be a waiting line for
breakfast on weekends; lunches are
great, too. Breakfast and lunch.

5

MICROBREWERIES

So what gives? Why is it that Portland is home to more microbreweries per capita than any other city in the United States? Well, the brewers all say pretty much the same thing. It's that famous Oregonian creativity and dogged determination. Oregonians are known for their pioneering spirit, and the art of brewing beer has offered a whole new realm for innovation.

Seems it's no longer a simple matter of walking into a bar and ordering a beer—just as the espresso craze in neighborhood coffee shops drove the simple cup of joe to extinction. Now you order "an Americano" or a "double skinny latte" or "mocha grande, no foam." In bars and taverns people now ask, "Which porter do you have on tap?" and "Is there a fruit beer back there?"

Portland has become a mecca for beer lovers and, for neophytes, a great place to learn about the craft of brewing good beer. Bartenders and brewers alike are eager to share their "best of" secrets and are more than willing to offer advice to the novice.

What's the difference between a mass-produced beer and a micro-brew, you ask? Basically, it's the ingredients and the recipes. It's the craft, not the production schedule, that drives the final outcome. Portland's craft brewers take pride in their individual recipes and in their ability to improvise on Old World traditions.

Many Portland microbreweries offer tours and tastings. Most brew-pubs provide a "taster platter" filled with tiny glasses of the in-house brews. You can purchase a small taste of many beers and then decide for yourself which one to drink. Don't hesitate to ask questions of the wait-staff or the bartenders. They are all eager to share their stories and pref-erences, and they love to talk about their craft. Most brewpubs have some fine food, too.

BRIDGEPORT BREWING CO.
1313 NW Marshall
241-7179   **DT**
Founded in 1984, BridgePort is Oregon's oldest microbrewery. The "old warehouse" feel of the place is part of its charm. The outdoor patio is a popular spot in summer, where you can sit amid lush hop vines while savoring your favorite brew. A tour (Saturdays and Sundays at 2 p.m. and 3 p.m.) of the brewery is a voyage of discovery, and you'll learn much about the craft. Bridgeport specializes in true English-style ales, hand-pumped from beer engines. Ask the brewer about Portland's only Firkin beer.

FLANDERS ST. BREWPUB
1339 NW Flanders
222-5910   **DT**
Brewing since 1986, the pub is located in the historic Pearl District. Its woody atmosphere features a view of the brewing process that includes a custom-made copper kettle made in Portland. This pub also

A Matter of Taste

There are two basic types of beer: ale beer, which is fermented at a warmer temperature and for a shorter time, and lager beer, which is fermented cold for a longer time. Under each of these categories are many and varied subcategories.

Lagers lean toward a lighter, more bitter, crisper flavor. They are usually quite hoppy and fragrant, ranging in color from a light straw yellow all the way to shades of amber. Pilsener, bock, and dopplebock are all types of lager beer.

Ales are a more robust, full-flavored brew, ranging in color from a light burnished amber to a deep opaque brown, sometimes even black. Popular ales include malt, amber, brown, porter, and stout. Tastes range from a sweet chocolatey caramel to a dry-roasted barley and coffee essence.

Seasonals range from light fruit beers, perfect on a hot summer's afternoon, to hearty dark stouts. Traditionally, ales are strong winter brews and lagers, savored in summer—but, of course, some people like a raspberry beer at Christmas, and some insist on chocolate porter in the summer. It's all a matter of taste, but Portland's brewers seem to get quite a charge out of inventing new flavors for every season.

PORTLAND MICROBREWERIES

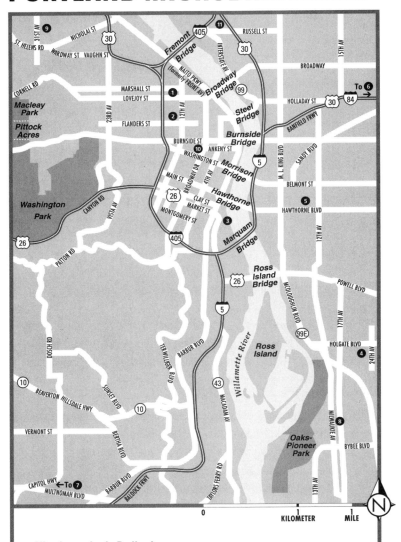

Microbreweries in Portland

1 BridgePort Brewing Co.
2 Flanders St. Brewpub
3 Full Sail Brewing Co. at RiverPlace
4 Hair of the Dog Brewing Company
5 Lucky Labrador Brewing
6 McMenamins Edgefield
7 Old Market Pub & Brewery
8 Philadelphia's
9 Portland Brewing Co.
10 Tugboat Brewing Co.
11 Widmer Brewing Co.

features an English-style beer engine and live music. Known for the MacTarnahan's Ale, the pub also offers carbonated cask-conditioned ales on tap.

FULL SAIL BREWING CO. AT RIVERPLACE
0307 SW Montgomery
222-5343 DT

Full Sail has been brewing one of Oregon's most popular brews since 1992. The small state-of-the-art facility in the Riverplace Marina just south of downtown brews about 5,000 barrels of beer every year, including seasonal offerings. Coppertopped tables in the Pilsner Room provide a comfortable place to watch, through a glass wall, the Full Sail brewers go about their business. Tours are available by appointment.

HAIR OF THE DOG BREWING COMPANY
4509 SE 23rd Ave.
232-6585 SE

Although it's not a brewpub, Hair of the Dog Brewing Company is worth mentioning because of its unique product. Hair of the Dog produces some of the best bottle-conditioned beer around. You can find it at grocery stores and in other brewpubs and restaurants. They brew only two beers. The stronger of the two, Adambier, is patterned after an ancient German recipe for Dortmund Adambier. This beer can be treated like a fine cognac, and, surprisingly, it's great for dessert with a bit of

BridgePort Brewing Company

BridgePort Brewing Company, p. 85

chocolate. You can even serve it in a wine glass. Owners Doug Henderson and Alan Sprints are happy to give you a tour of their small operation if you call ahead. Be sure to ask for directions—it's a hard-to-find spot in a warehouse district near Holgate Boulevard but well worth the hunt.

LUCKY LABRADOR BREWING
915 SE Hawthorne Blvd.
236-3555 SE

Housed in an old timbered warehouse, the "Lucky Lab," as it's affectionately called, has been around since 1994. Pub games like steel-tipped darts abound here. Known for its Black Lab Stout, the Lucky Lab also produces some other notable ales, such as its U.K. I.P.A., originally

> **TRIVIA**
>
> The Northwest corner of the United States produces 30 percent of the world's hops. Oregon's Willamette Valley alone boasts 12 different varieties.

What's in the Brew?

Brewers will tell you they use hints of this and bits of that in their brews, but there are only four basic ingredients necessary to make beer: water, grain (usually malted barley), hops, and yeast.

Hops: This bright green climbing vine grows rapidly, sometimes as much as eight inches on a warm spring day. At the end of the season, the vine makes a golden green flower, called the "cone" because of its structure. This flower is used in the brewing process to add characteristic bitterness and to give the beer aroma. Hops also enhances clarity and provides natural preservatives. Depending on the brewer's preference, hops can be added as whole flowers or in pellet or extract form.

Malt: Malt is basically two-row barley, the basis for most beer. The barley has been steeped in water and put into a germination bed, which brings it back to life, reawakening the enzymes. The barley is then dried and roasted. The roasting process gives the beer aroma and flavor.

Specialty malts such as chocolate, peated, and black are finished in much the same manner but in smaller quantities, and they are toasted or roasted differently to add color, flavor, aroma, and sweetness. Breweries usually use 80 percent pale barley and a small amount of specialty malts, depending on the recipe. Malts can add a range of flavors, from smoky to toasty, from sweet to espressolike.

made for travel from England to India in the 1800s.

MCMENAMINS EDGEFIELD BREWERY & POWER STATION
2126 SW Halsey St., Troutdale
800/669-8610 or 503/492-4648

Though technically McMenamins Edgefield is not in Portland, it's worth the 20-minute drive out Interstate 84 to see what the McMenamin brothers have done with the old Multnomah County Poor Farm. The Edgefield Brewery is not just a brewpub. You'll discover restaurants, a theater, a winery, and a distillery. History lives in the gardens at Edgefield, and you'll find it a relaxing place to spend an afternoon or even an entire night—Edgefield is also an inn. Some of the quaint rooms have private baths, but there are no telephones. If you want to tour the brewery, call ahead and they'll be happy to accommodate you.

For an informative booklet listing Oregon's breweries and brewpubs, call the Oregon Brewers Guild, 510 NW 3rd Ave., at 295-1862.

OLD MARKET PUB & BREWERY
6959 SW Multnomah Blvd.
244-0450 **SW**

This used to be an old produce market, and it still maintains that "old neighborhood" feel. Mr. Toad's Wild Red is the best-seller. With a name like that, who wouldn't try it? The folks at the Old Market pride themselves on their hand-built brewery. Bits and pieces of this and that come together here to create a truly one-of-a-kind establishment. Ask about the keg washer, known as the "looks-like-it-can't-work" end of the brewery.

PHILADELPHIA'S
6410 SE Milwaukie Ave.

239-8544 **SE**

Philadelphia's is one of the smallest licensed breweries around, but it has one of the most charming beer gardens. This pub offers a changing selection of ales brewed according to the brewer's whims and creative urges. The brewpub is located in the Westmoreland Business District in Southeast Portland, near antique shops, art galleries, and movie theaters. As you might guess, they also specialize in Philadelphia cheesesteak and hoagie sandwiches served on 11-inch torpedo rolls.

PORTLAND BREWING CO.
2730 NW 31st Ave.

The Manor at McMenamins Edgefield

Hugh Ackroyd

Handcrafted Brew in Revolutionary Style

Paula Fasano, marketing director at BridgePort Brewing Company, says that to know where the craft of beer is headed, you need only look at Oregon's microbrew history. BridgePort, founded in 1984, is Oregon's oldest microbrewery and was recently awarded a Gold Medal for their India Pale Ale at the Great American Beer Festival in Denver. Paula writes about the microbrewery revolution and how it all began:

"In 1984, when the trek westward for overworked yuppies was just beginning, busy executives traded in their golden handcuffs for an easier lifestyle in the Pacific Northwest. These modern-day pioneers shed their three-piece suits and Italian loafers in exchange for hiking boots and Gor-Tex™ jackets. It was a quest for a better quality of life in a region where the priorities were old-growth forests, clean streams, and family time. Many of these former executives set about a new business—that of brewing beer. They set up shop in old buildings, home garages, and communal kitchens. They stood united in their desire for independence and the pursuit of great beer. They began brewing beer with pride and passion, direct from the heart. Thus, the craft-beer revolution was born, and Portland, Oregon, became a pilgrimage destination for beer lovers.

Since those early days, the breweries have multiplied, but brewing integrity remains steadfast to tradition. Portland's brewers offer a wealth of styles, from traditional pale ales and porters to lemon lagers and berry beers. We all invite our customers for an afternoon or an evening of sampling our fares. You'll meet some interesting characters in Portland's brewpubs, learn a little something about their craft, and, who knows, you just may discover a new pilgrimage for yourself!"

Brewery kettle at Hair of the Dog Brewing Company, p. 87

228-5269   **NW**

This is the headquarters of the Portland Brewing Company, 27,000 square feet of brewpub in the heart of the Northwest Portland industrial district. The huge copper brewing vessels, originally from Sixenbrau Brewing (a Nordlingern, Bavaria, company dating from the sixteenth century), are a must-see if you want a thorough view of the Portland microbrew scene.

TUGBOAT BREWING CO.
711 SW Ankeny
226-2508   **DT**

Tugboat Brewing Company is one of Portland's most eclectic spots. You'll hear poets and musicians at adjacent picnic tables discussing the attributes of their favorite brew and sometimes, these characters will appear on stage. You never quite know what's going to be on tap, as this small brewery produces several delightful fresh brews, including fruit beers like Marion Berry or peach beer. If those don't suit your taste, try a Russian stout or a rye ale. The owners say they chose the name "Tugboat" because their brewery's character is stronger than its size suggests and, what's more, they're ready in any weather!

WIDMER BREWING CO.
929 N. Russell
281-3333   **NE**

Brothers Kurt and Rob Widmer started Oregon's first family-owned and -operated craft brewery. It's so German that they even use the traditional spelling—*Bier*. Widmer uses German *alt Bier* brewing techniques in combination with Northwest ingredients to produce some of Oregon's top-selling micros.

Children's Story Garden/Larry Kirkland

6

SIGHTS AND ATTRACTIONS

There is so much to see and do in Portland that it would be impossible to contain it all in one book. Upon arrival, stop by the Portland Oregon Visitors Association at Front Avenue and Salmon Street, near the waterfront. There you will find detailed brochures and friendly volunteers who will answer questions and provide you with ideas.

DOWNTOWN

BISHOP'S HOUSE
219 SW Stark   **DT**
Perhaps the most "Gothic" of Portland's old buildings, the Bishop's House was built in 1878 by the Roman Catholics. It has been many things since then—among them, a speakeasy, a Chinese club, and a musicians' gallery.

BLAGEN BLOCK
30–34 NW 1st Ave.   **DT**
Whimsical cast-iron motifs decorate this High Victorian Italiante building. You can see stars and stripes and arrows and leaves on the extravagant pastiches. The building design is one of the notable works by architect

Warren Williams, who was known for his creative designs.

CHILDREN'S STORY GARDEN
Tom McCall Waterfront Park
near the Burnside Bridge   **DT**
This is a children's park, but adults find it intriguing as well. Different from a traditional play park, it was designed by artist Larry Kirkland as a maze with a rather "fairy-tale" quality. Within cobblestone and grass areas are red granite squares with questions etched in them like, "What is your joy?" or "What do you remember?" It's a thoughtful journey through life for children and adults. There are "dangerous" stones, like the spider and the alligator. And there are safe-haven stones, like Venice

and a tropical paradise. The park is filled with visual puns, riddles, and carved animals. Free admission.

CHINATOWN
Entrance at NW 4th Ave. and
Burnside   DT
Portland's Chinese sister city of Kaohsiung and the People's Republic of China presented Portland with an elaborate ceremonial gate to mark the entrance to Chinatown. The gate is guarded by two larger-than-life lions and also includes 64 dragons and five roofs. Chinatown began in the 1850s, developed into the nation's second largest Chinese community in the 1890s, and remains a bastion of Chinese culture today. Stretching for several blocks, the district holds dozens of Chinese restaurants, markets, and traditional Asian architecture. Strolling down the streets is safe and can be quite a learning experience. You'll pass Chinese herb shops, grocery stores, and other kinds of markets. In the spring, blooming cherry trees fill the air with fragrance. A real treat is the dim sum served at Fong Chong's on Couch Street and 4th Avenue.

CHURCH OF ELVIS
720 SW Ankeny
226-3671   DT
It's been said that this tribute to The King is the world's first coin-operated art gallery. Filled with kitsch and charisma, this little novelty museum has been the scene for weddings, confessions, and sermons. You can even have your picture taken with "Elvis." Admission is free, but as the operators say, "We're a church and we operate on guilt, so if you make a donation or buy something, you'll feel a lot better." Open all year. Hours vary, but it's open most afternoons.

ERICKSON'S SALOON
9–15 NW 2nd Ave.   DT
August Erickson jumped ship in Astoria, came to Portland, and opened his saloon. Erickson's was popular with sailors, loggers, and working men in the 1800s. The saloon once boasted a 684-foot bar that was often lined two or three deep with thirsty men.

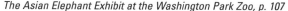

The Asian Elephant Exhibit at the Washington Park Zoo, p. 107

© Washington Park Zoo/Amy Ognall

DOWNTOWN PORTLAND

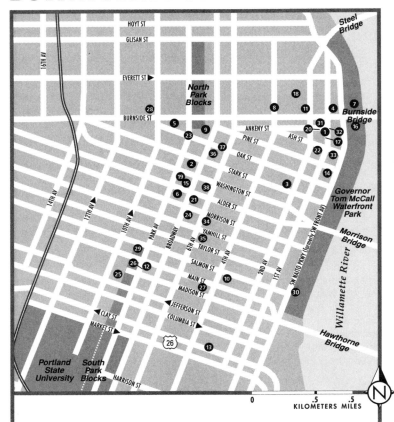

Sights in Downtown Portland

1 Ankeny's New Market Block
2 Bank of California
3 Bishop's House
4 Blagen Block
5 Campbell's Fountain
6 Charles F. Berg Building
7 Children's Story Garden
8 Chinatown
9 Church of Elvis
10 Elk Fountain
11 Erickson's Saloon
12 First Congregational Church
13 Forecourt Fountain
14 Hallock and McMillan Building

15 Hickox Salon and Spa
16 Japanese American Historical Plaza
17 Jeff Morris Fire Museum
18 Merchant's Hotel
19 Morgan Building
20 New Market Theater
21 Northwestern National Bank
22 Oregon Maritime Center and Museum
23 Pacific Telephone and Telegraph Company
24 Pioneer Courthouse Square
25 Portland Art Museum
26 Portland Town
27 *Portlandia*

28 Powell's City of Books
29 *Rebecca at the Well* Shemanski Fountain
30 Salmon Street Springs
31 Saturday Market
32 Skidmore Fountain
33 The Smith Block
34 Transit Mall Animal Fountain
35 Untitled Fountain
36 US National Bank
37 Wells Fargo Building
38 Wilcox Building

Pioneer Courthouse Square, p. 96

FIRST CONGREGATIONAL CHURCH
1126 SW Park Ave.   **DT**

This Venetian Gothic church was built in the 1890s and is one of Portland's favorite landmarks. Today it's the site of lectures and concerts as well as church services. The tower and the checkerboard stone gallery are especially interesting.

JAPANESE AMERICAN HISTORICAL PLAZA
North end of Tom McCall Waterfront Park along Front Ave. near the Burnside Bridge   **DT**

The plaza is a memorial to the 110,000 Japanese Americans placed in internment camps during World War II. Starting from the relief columns at the memorial's formal entrance, it's then best to walk the plaza's length from south to north, where you will see various stones engraved with haiku. The stones actually seem to stand up and speak to you. Some stones are fractured, others are cut, and some are broken to represent shattered hopes and dreams. The park is a moving experience, and while it symbolizes specifically the Japanese American experience, it tells a story for all of us. Free admission.

JEFF MORRIS FIRE MUSEUM
55 SW Ash   **DT**

Next door to Saturday Market, you'll see vintage horse-drawn, hand-pump fire wagons and other firefighting memorabilia. You can't actually enter the museum, but you can view the relics outside from behind huge glass walls. Some visitors have observed that the old fire engines look a lot like really expensive Italian espresso machines! It's worth looking for while you are at Saturday Market. Kids really love the old fire engines and photographs. Jeff Morris was one of Portland's best-known firemen, who became the Fire Bureau's unofficial good-will ambassador. He and his firehouse Dalmatian, Sparky, loved to visit with children and educate them on fire safety and prevention.

MERCHANT'S HOTEL
120–136 NW 3rd Ave.   DT
No longer a hotel, this building was built between 1880 and 1884. Of particular note are the female heads adorning the Italiante structure.

OREGON MARITIME CENTER AND MUSEUM
113 SW Front Ave.
224-7724   DT
The main attraction at the Oregon Maritime Museum is the steam-powered tugboat across the street. The tugboat houses a historic steamboat interpretive center and is located on the Portland seawall of the Willamette River. The museum building itself contains ship models, vintage photos, and antique navigational instruments. Hours and days vary according to season, so call ahead. Admission: $4 adults, $3 seniors and children, $10 families.

PIONEER COURTHOUSE SQUARE
701 SW 6th Ave.
Between 6th and Broadway on Yamhill and Morrison
223-1613   DT
In 1858 downtown's Pioneer Square was the site of Portland's first schoolhouse. Later, the Portland Hotel (no longer in existence) was erected and became the hub of the city's thriving social community. When the hotel was torn down in the Fifties, the city built a parking lot, but in the Seventies the land was donated to the city to be used as a public square. Nearly 70,000 citizens donated money for the construction of what is now fondly known as "Portland's living room." The square is paved with bricks bearing the names of those donors.

An amphitheater featuring day and evening concerts, a purple fountain, a Starbuck's coffee shop, and a Tri-Met ticket office are permanent residents here. Of special note is the 25-foot-tall weather machine, once featured on the *Today Show.* The animated machine spews mist, blasts trumpets, and raises whimsical creatures from within every day at noon. This attempt at predicting Portland's unpredictable weather is sometimes right, sometimes wrong, but always entertaining. There tend to be a lot of streetwise teens hanging around here; for the most part they're harmless and rather interesting to watch.

The square has recently undergone a $900,000 renovation that added fresh paint, wheelchair-accessible doors to the Tri-Met ticket lobby, and new pink granite walls to the fountain.

PORTLAND ART MUSEUM
1219 SW Park Ave.
226-2811   DT
The tree-filled Park Blocks surround this museum, known locally as PAM. Renovated in 1995, the museum is filled with light and displays abundant European and American art. Asian artwork and a stunning collection of Native American art are also featured in this airy museum. Open daily 9–7. Admission varies.

PORTLANDIA
Portland Building
SW 5th Ave. between Main and Madison Sts.   DT
She's 36 feet tall and weighs 6.5 tons. *Portlandia* has caused quite a fuss since she arrived on a barge in 1984. People seem either to like her or hate her. Either way, she is something to behold. *Portlandia* is a hammered copper statue (second in size only to the Statue of Liberty) that sits above the entrance to the Portland Building. Some find her a

Stumptown Architecture

From the postmodern design of Michael Graves' famous Portland Building, or the modernist sensibilities of a Pietro Belluschi church, to the earliest brick and cast-iron buildings, Portland's diverse designs take visitors down a verdant trail of discovery. Much like Oregon's weather, its architecture can be surprising. It, too, changes with the scenery and doesn't necessarily conform to any rules.

Oregon's original architects, the Chinook, Coast Salish, and Nootka Indians, used the Northwest's abundant timber supply to construct the first log homes in Oregon forests and along the riverbanks. Sheathed in cedar, these practical yet artistic plank buildings were constructed in permanent winter villages, a quiet and natural architectural beginning that set the tone for Oregon's inventiveness through the centuries. Early excavations along the Columbia River indicate that the area was inhabited by Indians of various cultures as far back as 6,000 years ago.

Since those crude beginnings, Portland's unique architectural interpretations have covered a broad spectrum of design, from ornate Victorian homes to modern steel and glass. European influence can be seen all over the city, reflecting the pioneers' need to recreate what was familiar to them, that which they left behind. The region's indigenous timber supply combined with Oregonians' proud work ethic to produce diverse buildings that have left an indelible mark on the pages of Portland's history.

Urban renewal projects continue to provide compelling proof that this is a city to be watched, a city whose citizens will not compromise beauty in the interest of growth. Romantic fountains and statues grace cobblestone streets and sidewalks. Gothic architecture, cast-iron buildings, and elaborate mansions help set the tone for a dignified burg whose other side is reflected in skyscrapers, modern art, and high bridges.

graceful representation of a city's modern mythology, others say she looks like she's shooting dice. She was intended to personify the spirit of Portland and is modeled after Lady Commerce, who appears on the city's seal. The Portland Building is a sight in itself. Designed by Michael Graves and built in 1982, this is the first major postmodern office building in the United States. Visit the second floor of the Portland Building to see the Metropolitan Center for Public Art and ask for the "Public Art Walking Tour Map" at the information desk.

PORTLAND TOWN MURAL
New Theatre Building at the Portland Center for the Performing Arts
SW Broadway and Main
248-4335   DT
Go through the Park Blocks entrance to PCPA, and you'll find a most interesting piece of work that will challenge your perception. Portland artist Hank Pender used "anamorphic perspective" in his mural, an illusory technique that gives viewers the impression that the further away the figures are, the more extended they become, vertically and laterally. Pander describes it as an "interactive work. When you walk through it, the thing changes, like theater." Many figures in the mural represent actors, dancers, and costume designers in Portland's theater community.

POWELL'S CITY OF BOOKS
1005 W. Burnside St.
228-4651   DT
The *Washington Post* calls it "one of the best bookstores in the English-speaking world." Roaming around Powell's can take all day. With more than a million new and used books in

stock, if you can't find it at Powell's, it probably doesn't exist. But then, the experts at the rare book division may be able to help. Powell's is definitely a big part of the Portland experience. You are invited to peruse your books or read a foreign magazine over a cup of cappuccino in the Anne Hughes Coffee Shop. Or you can just watch the hive of humanity at the bookstore. Stop at the information desk to get a map of the store and feel free to ask questions of the staff. They're all well-read, informed, and friendly. Hours: Mon–Sat 9–11, Sun 9–9.

SATURDAY MARKET
108 W. Burnside St.
222-6072   DT
Portland's festive Saturday Market, located in Old Town, is the largest continuously operating open-air crafts market in the United States. For a detailed description, turn to Chapter 10, "Shopping."

VINTAGE TROLLEY
323-7363   DT
Portland has always been big on mass transit, and the four reproductions of the city's original trolleys will give you a good idea of what commuting meant in the old days. The colorful trolleys operate on the MAX line every day from Memorial Day through December. You can catch the trolley at any light rail station between Lloyd Center and downtown Portland. If you plan to catch the arts scene of First Thursday, the trolley can help get you to the gallery tours, too. Call for schedules. Free.

Glazed Terra Cotta Historic District

The Terra Cotta District runs roughly from 10th Avenue on the west down

Glazed Terra Cotta

Most of Portland's many glazed terra cotta buildings were built between 1905 and 1930. During the Great Depression little construction occured in Portland, and when development began again after WWII, such handmade materials as terra cotta were deemed too expensive. Thus, the art of terra cotta was no longer used.

Architectural terra cotta is a hard-baked building material, usually constructed in hollow blocks about 12 inches deep. Portland's terra cotta is mostly off-white or cream-colored, although some have been fashioned to look like granite or copper. But it's not just blocks that are built from terra cotta. You'll also see lions' heads, griffins, and gargoyles on the buildings.

Most of Portland's terra cotta buildings were designed by A. E. Doyle, a prestigious architect whose studies at Columbia University led him to Europe and eventually to Portland. His Portland office opened in 1907. The first building Doyle designed was the Meier and Frank Company building at 6th and Morrison. Other significant architects of that era included William Shidden and Ion Lewis, who met at M.I.T. and later came to Portland to establish a partnership in 1889. Together they built the City Hall building in 1895.

to 5th on the east, and from Yamhill to Oak Street on the south and north, respectively. A few of the buildings fall outside these bounds, but you can see most of them within this area. This chapter details a few of the buildings. For a complete walking guide to the Terra Cotta District, pick up a brochure at the Portland Development Commission in the Portland Building at 1120 SW 5th, 10th floor.

BANK OF CALIFORNIA
6th and Stark DT
This is an unusual 1925 Italian Renaissance building, its terra cotta glazed to look like granite. The interior has been remodeled, but you can still see the original marble floor and plaster ceiling.

CHARLES F. BERG BUILDING
615 Broadway DT
This is Portland's only example of art deco terra cotta. Originally built in 1902, the building was remodeled in 1930 and features black terra cotta textured with "real gold of 18-karat fineness." It was one of only three buildings in the United States at that time that featured this finish. Don't miss the rain clouds, spirals, and peacocks on the building.

MORGAN BUILDING
720 SW Washington　　**DT**

Look for Neptune's trident in the frieze above the first floor. You'll also find dolphins and a variety of terra cotta details in this building, built in 1913. The columns on the storefront level are not original but have been finished with a ceramic veneer that looks much like the original terra cotta.

NORTHWESTERN NATIONAL BANK
Between Broadway and 6th, Alder and Morrison　　**DT**

This building was a combined effort, in 1913, of Henry Pittock and Frederick Leadbetter, two of Portland's leading timber and banking tycoons. On the upper floors are griffins and eagles in beautiful detail. The lobby was remodeled by A. E. Doyle from 1936 to '37.

PACIFIC TELEPHONE AND TELEGRAPH COMPANY
Corner of Park and Oak　　**DT**

This building was erected in two parts, the first in 1914, and the second in 1926. It is interesting to note that this is one of the few unaltered terra cotta buildings remaining in Portland.

US NATIONAL BANK
Between Broadway, 6th, Stark, and Oak　　**DT**

It's been called a "banking temple." Designed by A. E. Doyle in 1917, the building has 54-foot-high Corinthian columns intended to symbolize "the soaring power of finance in a wealthy civilization."

WELLS FARGO BUILDING
Corner of 6th and Oak　　**DT**

This was Portland's first skyscraper,

Portlandia, *p. 96*

built in 1907. Look for wreaths and "Wells Fargo" above the top story of this colorful building.

WILCOX BUILDING
6th and Washington　　**DT**

Look for lions' heads and urns loaded with fruit on the cornice here. The building was completed in 1911.

Skidmore/Old Town Historic District

Portland first developed along Front and 1st Avenues next to the Willamette River, which carried most of the traffic for Portland's thriving commercial core. The Skidmore/Old Town District is the very heart of Portland's historic beginnings. Although the district features many buildings of different styles and ages, this area is best known for its collection of cast-iron buildings. In fact, Portland has more cast-iron buildings than any city west of the Mississippi and, in the United States, is second only to New York's SoHo District. You might be fooled into thinking the cast iron is plaster. It's not. Look for occasional rust stains on some of the friezes, and you'll know you're looking at cast iron.

ANKENY'S NEW MARKET BLOCK
Bounded by Ankeny, Ash, 1st, and 2nd Aves. **DT**
The first commercial structure constructed by Ankeny in 1871 is an Italian-style building. Elaborate leaves and grape motifs decorate the building. Look for cast-iron thresholds and the letter "A" on the building.

HALLOCK AND McMILLAN BUILDING
237 SW Front Ave. **DT**
This is the city's oldest brick commercial structure. Though the cast-iron facade is no longer visible, you can see an 1858 drawing that shows the building's original appearance.

NEW MARKET THEATER
50 SW 2nd Ave. **DT**

This Italiante building features a 200-foot-long interior arcade and was once the cultural center for a thriving new city. In the old days, produce carts filled the first floor in stalls that are still easily visible. The second floor houses an elaborate 1,200-seat theater. Although the building was used as a warehouse for many years thereafter, and was once even a parking garage, today it is filled with retail shops, restaurants, and people. It's a beautiful building and definitely worth a visit. Notice all the old photographs throughout the building, and you'll get a good idea of what life was like in Portland's Old Town during the late 1800s.

THE SMITH BLOCK
North half of block bounded by Pine, Ash, 1st, and Front **DT**
Today the Oregon Maritime Center and Museum is housed here. The building was built in 1872 by Joseph Smith, a prominent Oregon attorney (and one of the state's first). This building gives a good idea of what

Historic District Renovation

Portland citizens place great importance on the significance of the city's older buildings and historic neighborhoods. In 1958 the City of Portland Development Commission was established and, since then, has played a major part in revitalizing Portland's downtown core. The street signs, brass plaques, and sidewalk stamps that identify boundaries within the historic district have been funded by the commission. You will also find historic markers identifying sites that were particularly important to the city's colorful heritage. Look for the markers and plaques on buildings and sidewalks during your exploration of Portland's Old Town and Skidmore Districts.

Benson Bubblers

In 1912 a local lumberman and civic leader offered the city $10,000 to place drinking fountains throughout downtown. His interest was as much in keeping his loggers sober as it was in art. He noted that if the men had fresh water available, perhaps they wouldn't spend so much time in the saloons drinking beer. In those days, taverns wouldn't give patrons a glass of water unless they ordered a beer first. Thus, the birth of the Benson Bubblers. By 1917 the City had installed 40 graceful bronze four-bowl fountains, which continue to operate today, along with 10 others. Though originally intended to run freely 24 hours a day, the fountains are now operated by push buttons in the interest of conserving water. Benson, by the way, noted that after the initial installation of his fountains, saloon sales had decreased by 40 percent. You will also find 75 other single-bowl drinking fountains throughout the city, so quenching your thirst on a hot summer day is just a step away.

the rest of the cast-iron neighborhood looked like.

Portland's Fountains

Fountains play a major role in Portland's charm. It seems just about everywhere you look, there are works of art and water. Fondly known locally as "Fountains as Art," you can find them prominently displayed as a centerpiece on a city block or tucked into a hidden corner off the beaten path.

The City of Portland, Bureau of Water Works, maintains 130 drinking fountains throughout the city and publishes information on their history and architecture. The water in decorative fountains is not intended for drinking. For the most part, these fountains recycle their water, which is heavily chlorinated.

Portland Parks and Recreation has information on the fountains in parks within the city. Call the Bureau of Water Works at 823-7770 or 823-6868 (TTY), or Portland Parks at 823-2223 (V/TT). For information on fountains as public art, call the Regional Art and Culture Council at 823-4196.

CAMPBELL'S FOUNTAIN
Burnside near SW 9th　　　　**DT**
This 1928 fountain is a memorial to Fire Chief David Campbell, who lost his life in the line of duty.

ELK FOUNTAIN
SW Main (between 3rd and 4th) DT
Elk Fountain, a gift from David Thompson, Portland's mayor from 1879 to 1882 and later ambassador to Turkey, was intended to commemorate the elk that once grazed in the area.

Skidmore Fountain

FORECOURT FOUNTAIN
3rd and Clay   DT

A visit to this huge (13,000 gallons of water per minute) fountain across from the Civic Auditorium is a study in how water moves. There are a variety of platforms for viewing and enjoying the water. The fountain, which is really like a series of waterfalls, takes up the entire block, and you can walk behind a waterfall, sit on a small space by a placid eddy, or just watch other people as they investigate the properties of water. This is a popular place for photos, picnic lunches, and romantic rendezvous.

REBECCA AT THE WELL
SHEMANSKI FOUNTAIN
Park Blocks between SW Salmon and Main   DT

A gift from Joseph Shemanski in 1926, the fountain was designed by Oliver Barrett and Carl Linde. The bronze and sandstone sculpture commemorates Abraham's search for a bride for Isaac. Mr. Shemanski was especially fond of dogs, so this fountain contains both high and low drinking areas—one for people and one for dogs.

SALMON STREET SPRINGS
Salmon and Front   DT

This fountain was designed with "a day in the city" in mind. The jets start off quietly in the morning, while the city is waking up, and slowly build to a crescendo of extreme activity later in the afternoon. They slow down again at the end of day and go to sleep at night. Children are encouraged to play in the water, and adults will find a cozy bench for people-watching and coffee-drinking.

SKIDMORE FOUNTAIN
SW 1st Ave. (at Ankeny)   DT

After Stephen Skidmore, one of Portland's most colorful citizens, visited the Paris Exposition in 1878, he came home with a dream. He so loved the fountains and plazas in France that he wanted to see the same in Portland. In his will, he requested that a fountain be built "for the horses, men, and dogs" of Portland. No longer used by horses and dogs, the Skidmore Fountain is a gathering place for locals and visitors alike, considered the city's most popular and oldest piece of public art. There are many legends and myths about the women depicted in the fountain, but nobody knows for sure who they are.

TRANSIT MALL ANIMAL FOUNTAIN
SW 5th and 6th between Morrison and Yamhill   DT

Beavers, seals, bear, deer, and ducks seem to spring to life in these fountains. The bronze sculptures, installed in 1989, were designed by

GREATER PORTLAND

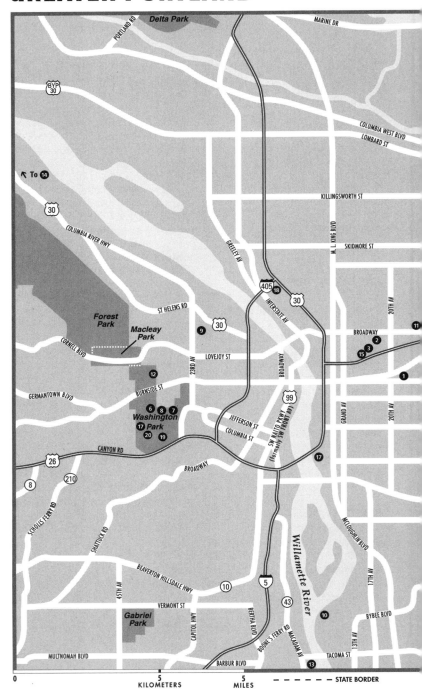

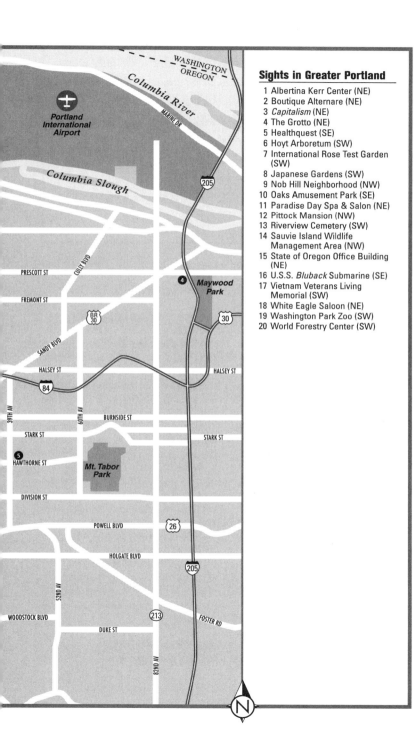

Sights in Greater Portland

1 Albertina Kerr Center (NE)
2 Boutique Alternare (NE)
3 *Capitalism* (NE)
4 The Grotto (NE)
5 Healthquest (SE)
6 Hoyt Arboretum (SW)
7 International Rose Test Garden (SW)
8 Japanese Gardens (SW)
9 Nob Hill Neighborhood (NW)
10 Oaks Amusement Park (SE)
11 Paradise Day Spa & Salon (NE)
12 Pittock Mansion (NW)
13 Riverview Cemetery (SW)
14 Sauvie Island Wildlife Management Area (NW)
15 State of Oregon Office Building (NE)
16 U.S.S. *Bluback* Submarine (SE)
17 Vietnam Veterans Living Memorial (SW)
18 White Eagle Saloon (NE)
19 Washington Park Zoo (SW)
20 World Forestry Center (SW)

Henry L. Pittock

Henry L. Pittock, who enjoyed fame and fortune in his later years, was not born with a silver spoon in his mouth. He came to Portland from Pennsylvania in 1853. Legend has it that during his struggle toward wealth, he even slept on a shelf at the Oregonian's *first print shop. According to E. Kimbark MacColl in his book* Merchants, Money & Power, *Pittock made his first real estate investment in January 1857. For the whopping sum of $74.79, he bought three wooded blocks on 10th and 11th Streets. Later, he erected the first paper mill in Oregon.*

Georgia Gerber, who inscribed them, "Mense of the wild in the midst of a busy city." These animals seem perfectly content in the city traffic and offer a bit of whimsy to passersby.

UNTITLED FOUNTAIN
SW 6th between Yamhill and Taylor **DT**
Although the fountain has no formal title, locals refer to it as "The Bathtub Fountain." Built in 1977 as part of the Transit Mall development, it is made of aluminum and stone. Here the water flows slowly and has a calming effect on the observer.

SOUTHWEST

HOYT ARBORETUM
4000 SW Fairview Blvd.
823-3655 **SW**
About 850 species of trees and shrubs and 10 miles of trails make this a hiker's paradise. It's peaceful here and smells like you are in the middle of the country, rather than right next door to a busy city. The arboretum offers guided tours April through October on Saturday and Sunday at 2 p.m. Open year-round. Free admission.

INTERNATIONAL ROSE TEST GARDEN
400 SW Kingston Ave.
823-3636 **SW**
This garden is the oldest rose test garden in the United States. Established in 1917, it has more than 7,000 roses representing 400 different varieties. The terraced garden is a popular spot for impromptu picnics, concerts, and city views. If you are an early bird, the sunrise at the Rose Garden can be stunning. In the background you will see Mt. Hood as it turns from soft gray to delicate pink to bright coral and, finally, to brilliant white as the sun rises in the sky. There's a vintage hot dog stand near the rose garden, too. Remember, it's illegal to pick the roses, but you can certainly touch and smell. Free admission.

JAPANESE GARDENS
611 SW Kingston Ave.

223-4070   **SW**

This site is known internationally as the most authentic Japanese gardens outside of Japan. Five different traditional Japanese garden styles are represented on 5.5 acres. Quiet waterways, little wooden bridges and walkways, flowers, bonsai sculpture, and grassy slopes invite visitors to spend a quiet moment in nature. Giant koi fill the ponds.

RIVERVIEW CEMETERY
8421 SW Macadam Ave.
246-4251   **SW**

Riverview is a cemetery so packed with history that it's worth a quiet visit. Along with many of Portland's founding fathers' gravesites, you'll find the final resting place of Virgil Earp. That's right, Virgil Earp, brother of the famous Wild West gunfighter Wyatt Earp. Virgil died in Nevada in 1905, but his daughter lived in Portland and brought her father's body back to the City of Roses for its final repose.

VIETNAM VETERANS LIVING MEMORIAL
4000 SW Fairview Blvd.
823-3654   **SW**

This black granite monument was put together by veterans who donated their own money, time, and equipment. Located at the south end of the Hoyt Arboretum in Washington Park, the monument makes a solemn spiral up a hill and carries the names of those reported dead or missing in action.

WASHINGTON PARK ZOO
See Chapter 6, "Kids' Stuff" and Chapter 9, "Parks and Gardens."

WORLD FORESTRY CENTER
4033 SW Canyon Rd.
228-1367   **SW**

A central African rain forest, old growth Pacific Northwest forests, and a 300-million-year-old petrified wood exhibit highlight the offerings here. Exhibits change from time to time, but the award-winning *Forests of the World* slide show is always offered to provide an informative and entertaining way to learn about the endangered wooded world around us. Open daily 9–5. Admission: $3.50 adults, $2.50 children and seniors.

NORTHWEST

NOB HILL NEIGHBORHOOD
NW 21st and 23rd Aves.
297-3454   **NW**

San Francisco might lay claim to the first Nob Hill, but it's not the only one in the country. Portland's Nob Hill is an old neighborhood filled with Victorian and Georgian mansions, turn-of-the-century apartment buildings, and shops galore. Brewpubs, coffee shops, art outlets, a cinema house, and numerous restaurants make this area a great people-watching part of town.

PITTOCK MANSION
3229 NW Pittock Dr.
823-3624   **NW**

TRIVIA

Powell's Books is the nations's largest new-and-used bookstore, with more than a million books in stock.

Henry Pittock came here in the mid-1800s as an unemployed printer looking for work in the thriving small town of Portland. From there, he went on to found the city's newspaper, *The Oregonian*, and to become one of Portland's wealthiest citizens. Pittock built this French-style chateau for his wife and, according to legend, to show the rest of the world that he had "made it." The 46-acre grounds and the mansion itself were nearly destroyed by a developer in the 1960s, but, thanks to the efforts of a group of preservationists, the property was saved. Today, the grounds are immaculate, and the chateau is restored. Of special note are the plaster work and the elegant light fixtures. The view from the hill is mesmerizing. Admission charged.

SAUVIE ISLAND WILDLIFE MANAGEMENT AREA
18330 NW Sauvie Island Rd.
Off Highway 30
621-3488   **NW**
Just north of downtown about 20 minutes is the site of Lewis and Clark's 1805 landing. Today, this rural island is a natural haven for birds and other wildlife. Along with swimming and fishing in the Columbia River, you can buy produce at fruit and vegetable stands, and pick your own berries at one of the many farms on the island.

NORTHEAST

ALBERTINA KERR CENTER
424 NE 22nd Ave.
239-8101   **NE**
The Albertina Kerr Center was founded in 1907 by William Gorden MacLaren as the Pacific Coast Rescue and Protective Society. Later, Alexander Kerr (of the Kerr canning jar family), following the deathbed request of his young wife, Albertina, donated his house to the Society as a home for abandoned children. The Old Kerr Nursery is listed on the National Register of Historic Places. Walking into the building, filled with old photos and memorabilia, is like stepping back in time. You can have lunch in Albertina's Restaurant and shop at the Kerr's Economy Jar & Gift shop, a thrift store with some rather eclectic items. The center still operates as a multiservice agency responding to critical community needs concerning children and young adults. More than 400 volunteers offer their time to keep the agency running. All proceeds from the gift shop and restaurant are used for the agency.

CAPITALISM
At the entrance to Nordstrom,
Lloyd Center   **NE**
This sculpture by Larry Kirkland, who also designed the Children's Story Garden, looks like a toppling tower of coins. Each coin is engraved with a saying or proverb about money. It's rather fitting that the sculpture stands directly in front of Nordstrom, a place where it's easy to drop many of your hard-earned coins.

THE GROTTO
National Sanctuary of Our
Sorrowful Mother
NE 85th Ave. and Sandy Blvd.
254-7371   **NE**
It's not often that a sanctuary like this is seen as a visitor attraction, but the Grotto is different. Some visitors say they think God lives there. That's for you to decide. The sanctuary sits amid towering fir trees at the base of a 110-foot cliff. Be sure to ride the elevator to the

top of the bluff to see a quiet panorama of the Columbia River Valley, Mt. St. Helens, and the Cascade Mountain Range from some comfy chairs in the meditation room. Free.

STATE OF OREGON OFFICE BUILDING
800 NE Oregon St. NE
Inside the building you will find two murals that depict Native American legends of Multnomah Falls and the Bridge of the Gods. Also inside, notice the way the light hits the floor and look for a shadow on the floor that spells "Oregon."

WHITE EAGLE SALOON
836 N. Russell St. NE
282-6810
The White Eagle has a legendary history full of shanghaied sailors, prostitutes, opium dens, and smugglers. Ghost stories abound here, too. Now the home of good old-fashioned rock 'n' roll on the weekends, the White Eagle is a Portland icon. You can belly up to the original Brunswick mahogany bar and dance on the hardwood floor, which, legend has it, came from the deck of a sunken ship.

SOUTHEAST

OAKS AMUSEMENT PARK
East end of Sellwood Bridge
233-5777 SE
The heartbeat of historic Oaks Park is the carousel, the only part of the park listed on the National Historic Register. Built in 1911 by Hershall Spellman, this American-carved carousel is called a "Noah's Ark" carousel because its animals come in pairs. Contrary to those on European carousels, the animals on this one have particularly sweet faces. Frogs, tigers, Chinese dragons, horses, and ostriches are just some of the whimsical creatures in this menagerie. Admission: $11 for five hours of unlimited rides.

USS *BLUBACK* SUBMARINE
Oregon Museum of Science and Industry (OMSI)
1945 SE Water Ave.
797-4000 SE
This warship, named for the bluback salmon, was used in the film *Hunt For Red October* and now sits as part of a permanent exhibit next to the Oregon Museum of Science and Industry. The 219-foot-long submarine was once home to 90 men, who lived under the water at depths of more than 700 feet. You'll experience close quarters and be immersed in history when you take the 40-minute tour offered. OMSI open daily 9:30–7, Thur to 8. Admission: $3.50 for submarine tour.

The Grotto

Portland Oregon Visitors Association

CITY TOURS

Items in this section are not shown on the map. Call for locations and times.

CASCADE STERNWHEELERS
1200 NW Front Ave. #110
223-3928

Paddle wheel–powered boats provide a good way to relax and enjoy views of the cityscapes from the Willamette and Columbia Rivers. The sunset dinner cruise is a favorite. Watching the colors change over the skyline while sipping some fine Oregon wine on the deck is a nice way to end the day. After dinner, the night sky and lighted bridges offer a completely different view of the city. Brunch cruises and holiday special excursions are also offered. Call for reservations and prices.

PETER'S WALKING TOURS OF PORTLAND
1563 NE Village Squire Court
Gresham
665-2558

Peter Chausse is an Antioch University instructor and ardent Portland enthusiast. A transplant from the East Coast, Peter took it upon himself to learn more about his new home, so the information he has is the information most visitors want to know. He specializes in three walking tours, two around downtown and one in Northeast Portland. His nonstop facts and trivia, knowledge of the city's history, arts, and culture, and entertaining stories are enriching and valuable. Peter will also custom-design a tour for you if you have something specific in mind. Peter's tours are handicapped accessible; just ask ahead of time, and he'll tailor the tour to your needs.

PORTLAND PARKS AND RECREATION
823-2223

Portland Parks and Rec offers a wide variety of interesting tours. Browse through their catalogue (call or stop by the office or a public library) to find a previously scheduled tour that appeals to you. Impromptu tours

---

Something's Fishy on Salmon Street

Sara Perry, whose weekly food column, "Tastemakers," can be found in the Living section of the Sunday Oregonian and whose restaurant review program can be heard on KINK radio (FM 102) Wednesday mornings, enjoys one of Portland's little-known art treasures: "Just walk across Salmon Street, by the Park Blocks behind the Heathman downtown. Once you get across the street, at the bus stop, you'll be able to see it. It's like a little hidden treasure within the city." What you'll see is a salmon on Salmon Street. But you'll have to look up.

Pittock Mansion, p. 107

Portland Oregon Visitors Association

aren't available. Although sometimes it's OK to just show up at the designated tour time and place, the bureau would prefer that you register ahead of time by phone.

PORTLAND SPIRIT
224-3900

Portland Spirit is a 150-foot yacht with three different levels. On top is an open-air observation deck for viewing the city sights. Cruising south on the Willamette River from Waterfront Park toward Lake Oswego, you'll pass marinas, floating homes, and historic houses, and you'll also see a variety of wildlife. *Portland Spirit* offers lunch, brunch, and dinner-dance cruises as well as simple sightseeing trips all year long. During the summer months, you can book a one-day cruise to Astoria. Prices vary, so it's best to call for information.

SAMTRAK EXCURSION TRAIN
653-2380

This open-air train chugs along the Willamette River and through a scenic wildlife refuge. You can catch it at OMSI, Oaks Park, or the Sellwood Bridge on Spokane Street. It operates during the good-weather months (May through October), Tuesday through Sunday. Call ahead for schedules. Admission charged.

SHARON WOOD BRIDGE TOURS & URBAN ADVENTURES
222-5535

For a bird's-eye view of riverlife, choose a walking tour high above the river on the city's historic bridges with Portland native Sharon Wood. Leading to places like Chinatown, Dan and Louis' Oyster Bar, the Children's Story Garden, and the largest collection of architecturally significant cast-iron buildings outside of New York's SoHo district, this intriguing bridge tour is a novel experience.

Other Tours of Interest

GRAPE ESCAPE WINERY TOURS
282-4262

These intimate wine tours are fun if you are alone or in a small group.

The guides are knowledgeable about the lay of the land as well as the taste of the wine.

PERSONALIZED! TOURS & TRAVEL, INC.
248-0414

If you want to create your own driving tour, this travel company can help with maps, accommodations, golf, and outdoor activities. They can also provide escorts if you prefer to have some help navigating.

DAY SPAS

Spa resorts are fast becoming the rage in cities around the country, and Portland is no exception. Though the following places are not "destination spas" (meaning they have no guest rooms), they are some of Portland's most highly prized pampering facilities. And after a day or two of touring Portland, you may want to rest your tired body and settle in for a day of relaxation, massage, healthful food, and maybe even a holistic health treatment. Here are four of Portland's best. Each one is unique. It's a good idea to phone ahead and ask questions before making your selection.

BOUTIQUE ALTERNARE
1444 NE Broadway
282-8200   NE

Boutique Alternare aims to help its clients let go of day-to-day stresses and return to their lives relaxed and rejuvented. The environment is clean, simple, and soothing. The spa offers its own line of vitamins and herbal teas, and they use all-natural skin-care products. There

are no hair or make-up services here, just "feel good" massages and body treatments, including facials, massages, herbal wraps, seaweed wraps, and exfoliating scrubs. Various packages available.

HEALTHQUEST
Center for Natural Medicine
1330 SE 39th Ave.
232-1200   SE

Holistic health is the focus here. Naturopaths and chiropractors work alongside aestheticians and masseuses. The environment is quiet, healing, relaxing, and nurturing. Facilities include a Jacuzzi and a steam room. The Center for Natural Medicine, located below the spa, has an acupuncturist available by appointment. Health-Quest specializes in romantic packages for couples as well as individual consultations.

HICKOX SALON AND SPA
711 SW Alder, 4th floor
241-7111   DT

Portland's newest addition to the spa scene is also its most luxurious. With a focus on wellness for men as well as women, John and Sharon Hickox have blended their years of international recognition in the salon industry with their innovative vision of what a spa should be. Located in the historic Alderway Building, the full-service salon not only offers hair and make-up styling, but also features packages for spa treatments. Try their Vichy shower treatment. Or any one of their herbal wraps, like the Fango or the Dead Sea Salt Glow. John and Sharon's staff is extremely professional, knowledgeable, and helpful. They'll help you custom-design a package for your individual needs.

Great food from Pazzo accompanies a day at the spa. The whole experience is truly a treat for your body, mind, and soul.

PARADISE DAY SPA & SALON
2905 NE Broadway
287-7977 **NE**
This spa is like a visit to your grandmother's house. The cozy home, built in 1918, has hardwood floors, pale peach walls, a fireplace in the waiting area, and antiques on every floor. As a warm-up before your massage, you will enjoy an aromatherapy soak in the old-fashioned claw-foot tub. Women are usually more comfortable here than men, but men are welcomed, too. The salon also offers full-service for hair and nails along with spa services.

Oaks Amusement Park

7

KIDS' STUFF

Parenting *magazine recently listed Portland as one of America's ten best family cities. There are two free monthly newspapers for families available in area libraries, bookstores, preschools, and community centers.* Portland Family Calendar *offers schedules and information.* Portland Parent *is full of suggestions for family activities (including those off the beaten path) and articles on raising kids.*

One of the first things you might want to do is check with Portland Parks and Recreation at 823-2223. Parks and Rec offers a variety of classes for kids, including arts and crafts, sports, performing arts skills, and Tot Walks. You can pick up a Portland Parks *guide at libraries, city hall, and all park facilities.*

GREATER PORTLAND

ALPENROSE DAIRY
6149 SW Shattuck Rd.
244-1133 **SW**
Alpenrose dairy is one of the oldest working dairies in Oregon. For 80 years, the dairy has been owned and operated by the same family. Summertime is the best time to visit. Kids enjoy the ducks in the pond, the play area, the old cars, and, of course, the cows. There's even a milk-cow museum that, along with

dairy-related objects, houses a collection of 4,000 dolls and music machines from the 1800s. June, July, and August bring pony rides and games for kids. The staff celebrates holidays in high style at Alpenrose, with Christmas festivities the first three weekends in December and an annual Easter egg hunt right before Easter. Alpenrose also hosts the Little Britches Rodeo the first weekend in June.

It's about a 20-minute drive from downtown Portland. Take I-5 south to the Multnomah Exit, which will lead you to 45th. Take a right to Vermont, and then a left to Shattuck. Turn right on Shattuck; the dairy is at the top of the hill.

ANNIE BLOOM'S BOOKS
7834 SW Capitol Hwy.
246-0053   SW
On Saturdays from 11 to 11:45 a.m., you'll be treated to stories, songs, and craft demonstrations at this child-friendly bookstore.

BEVERLY CLEARY
AT GRANT PARK
NE 33rd and U.S. Grant Place   NE
At this park you can see statues from

Oregon Museum of Science and Industry, p. 117

Portland Oregon Visitors Association

Beverly Cleary stories. Remember Ribsy the dog, Ramona, Henry Higgins, and Beasley? Kids love seeing the statue of Ramona Quimby in her trademark raincoat, which seems to come alive when you know that Grant Park was the setting for Beverly Cleary's stories. Go to the north end of the park near the playground.

THE CARNIVAL
2805 SW Sam Jackson Park Rd.
227-4244   SW
Kids say it's the best place for a burger and a shake. During the summer months, the kids can play outside, too. Inside the building, which looks like a big old house, you'll see a carousel horse and lots of Barnum and Bailey posters. Very child-friendly restaurant with standard fare kids will love. Open 11 a.m. to 8 p.m., closed Sundays.

CHILD'S PLAY
907 NW 23rd Ave.
224-5586   NW
Treasures for infants and toddlers. The shop is filled with high-quality European and American learning toys, like Brio sets and Toobers & Zots. Many activity books and games keep children amused. Friendly staff who, it goes without saying, love children to visit.

CHILDREN'S MUSEUM
3037 SW 2nd Ave.
823-2230   SW
Located just south of downtown

The downtown YWCA at 111 SW 10th Avenue (294-7420) offers drop-in swimming for all ages. For $2, kids can join in the community fun. An experienced coach supervises.

Portland within Lair Hill Park, the Children's Museum offers kids a learning experience and hands-on fun. They can sculpt treasures in the Clayshop, shop in the grocery store, eat a burger in a Fifties-style diner, and explore the Kid City Medical Center. The Children's Cultural Center offers changing exhibits that introduce different cultures from around the world.

The Children's Museum features many changing hands-on exhibits throughout the year. A constant feature, though, is the clientele. The museum is always filled with curious and happy kids. It's a good idea to dress your kids very casually because some of the interactive exhibits can get rather messy. Of particular interest to tots is the water exhibit *(H₂Oh!)*. Filled with valves and tanks and spigots and hoses, this exhibit takes kids on a journey through flowing water. The museum provides plastic aprons and rain boots—it's only natural that the kids will get wet, and they love every minute of it. Open daily 9–5. Admission: $4 for ages 1 and up.

A CHILDREN'S PLACE
1631 NE Broadway
284-8294 **NE**
A Children's Place often schedules readings and special events for kids. It's a friendly place full of ideas and storybooks for kids of all ages.

CHILDREN'S STORY GARDEN
Tom McCall Waterfront Park

near the Burnside Bridge **DT**
See Chapter 6, "Sights and Attractions," for description.

CHRISTMAS AT THE ZOO
118 NW 23rd Ave.
223-4048 **NW**
Great fuzzy stuffed animals like grizzly bears and giraffes (almost life-sized!). Tons of Christmas ornaments in the Old World style. This store is also home to a few good aliens. The staff is helpful.

FINNEGAN'S TOYS AND GIFTS
922 SW Yamhill
221-0306 **DT**
When you ask local adults about Finnegan's, they get a wistful look in their eyes. Although this is a toy store for kids, adults love the whimsy and bright colors, too. Kids are encouraged to "test" things in this oversized downtown toy haven, which brims with dolls and dollhouses, European building blocks, art supplies, and stuffed toys.

FRIENDLY HOUSE COMMUNITY CENTER
1737 NW 26th Ave.
228-4391 **NW**
Activities change here quarterly. The center offers summer day camps with weekly themes, cooking classes, soccer classes, play workshops, and a young children's lending library. There is a drop-in parent-child play group. Cost varies.

JEFF MORRIS FIRE MUSEUM
55 SW Ash   **DT**
See Chapter 6, "Sights and Attractions," for description.

OAKS AMUSEMENT PARK
East end of Sellwood Bridge
233-5777   **SE**
This is a great place for a bit of nostalgia. Kids will enjoy riding in the "squirrel cage" and screaming on the new Italian Pinfari roller coaster, with its 360-degree loop. Located on the east bank of the Willamette River, Oaks Park is a prime place for picnics, old-fashioned cotton candy, and the thrill of many rides. Open all year. Admission: $11 for five hours of unlimited rides.

OREGON CHILDREN'S THEATRE COMPANY
Civic Auditorium
SW 3rd and Clay
228-9571   **DT**
The Children's Theatre brings some of the most recognized classics to Portland. In seven years, more than 600,000 children have enjoyed the magic and excitement of live theater produced just for them. The sets are elaborate; the talent, superb; and the audiences, lively. Some of the highlights include a Christmas performance of a musical comedy, starring Santa, based on a story by the author of the *Wizard of Oz,* and a production of *Stuart Little*, the tale of the blue-suited mouse by *Charlotte's Web* author E. B. White. The OCTC also offers year-round acting workshops for children.

OREGON MUSEUM OF SCIENCE AND INDUSTRY (OMSI)
1945 SE Water Ave.
797-4000   **SE**
Kids are encouraged to play at the Oregon Museum of Science and Industry. They can learn about planets and stars, submarines, the properties of water, and architecture. OMSI offers a changing menu of classes and special exhibits geared to kids, so you can be assured that, no matter when you go, there will be something fun for the younger members of the family. Open daily, 9:30–7, Thur to 8. Admission: $8.50 adults, $6 seniors and children.

POWELL'S CITY OF BOOKS
1005 W. Burnside St.
228-4651   **DT**
The biggest new-and-used bookstore in the country often has special events for kids. The children's section of the bookstore is easy for all ages to access and is filled with children's books not readily found elsewhere. The staff is very helpful and friendly toward kids. Call ahead to find out if there is a storyteller coming or an author who will be reading from a new children's book. Hours: Mon–Sat 9–11, Sun 9–9.

Tune in to KOPB-FM (91.5) every Sunday at 7 p.m. to hear celebrities reading folk tales and fairy tales on *Rabbit Ears Radio*, a half-hour syndicated program.

TEARS OF JOY THEATRE
Winningstad Theatre
SW Broadway and Main
360/695-3050, 800/332-8692   **DT**
Tears of Joy Theatre performs in both Vancouver, Washington, and Portland and has been a screaming

Check with the following local libraries for storytelling times. Most of them offer children's activities on different days of the week.

Multnomah County (DT), 248-5123

Hillsdale (SW), 248-5388

Hollywood (NE), 248-5391

North Portland (NW), 248-5394

Sellwood (SE), 248-5393

success. In Portland, you can see the productions at the Portland Center for the Performing Arts' Winningstad Theatre. The bright red "Winnie," as it's known, is just right for children's plays. The art of storytelling is very much alive here. Matinees and evening performances. Call for a schedule. Admission: $12 adults, $7 children.

WASHINGTON PARK ZOO
4001 SW Canyon Ct.
226-1561   **SW**
The Washington Park Zoo offers "Camparoo," a day camp recognized as one of the best of its kind in the country. And at Halloween, families enjoy "ZooBoo," a scary train ride through the park complete with monsters and witches. Packy, the first elephant to be born at the zoo, gets a lot of attention, too, and now that he is aproaching 35 years old, his birthday is truly cause for celebration. More than a million people visit the zoo each year, and the place is always lively and entertaining. Admission: $5.50 adults, $4 seniors, $3.50 children.

Powell's City of Books, p. 117

Powell's

Washington Park Zoo

OUTSIDE PORTLAND

BONNEVILLE DAM
East of Portland on I-84
Columbia River Gorge
374-8820

Kids get a charge out of watching the Chinook salmon and steelhead climb the fish ladders in the visitor center. The center provides maps, informa- tion, and interactive exhibits. It's an educational experience that parents will enjoy, too. About a 40-minute drive from Portland, the dam is in the scenic Columbia River Gorge.

DUYCK'S PEACHY PIG FARM
34840 SW Johnson School Rd.
Cornelius
357-3570

The Rose Festival
Junior Parade and Starlight Parade

Part of the Portland International Rose Festival, the Junior Parade is the largest children's parade in the world. Lots of events during Rose Festival are fun for kids, but this parade is especially entic- ing for them.

The Starlight Parade is one of the biggest events of the Rose Festival, attracting 150,000 spectators. Children enjoy watching all the lights in the darkened downtown streets.

Sports Under the Bridges

Portland's kids, in true Oregon spirit, tend to be creative, inventive, and driven when they make up their minds. In fact, when skateboards were discouraged on city sidewalks, the kids decided they wanted a ramp where nobody would bother them. You'll find it under the Burnside Bridge, on the west side of the Willamette River. Built entirely by kids and funded by volunteer efforts, the ramp is a safe place for the younger set to enjoy their skateboards. Although it is not sanctioned by the Parks Department, it is loosely recognized as a part of Waterfront Park.

There are also lighted basketball courts under the Morrison Bridge. Safe and much-used, these courts also testify to Portland's commitment to kids.

Kids can get a real taste of farm life at Duyck's. The farm is just off Highway 26, about a 30-minute drive west of Portland. This is a working farm, where kids can see pigs in the barn (sometimes with piglets), goats in the yard, horses in the field, and other barnyard animals. At this "U-pick" farm, you can gather strawberries in the spring, blackberries in the summer, and pumpkins in the fall. Kids should wear casual clothes—they'll want to climb around on the old tractor and other farm machinery in the yard.

MALIBU GRAND PRIX
9405 SW Cascade Ave.
Beaverton
641-8122
Located just off Highway 217 across from Washington Square shopping center, the Malibu Grand Prix is a miniracetrack featuring mini-Indy-style cars. Most cars are one-passenger, but several have two seats so that a parent can accompany the child. The staff will provide plenty of safety tips and help in using helmets and safety belts. Weekend prices range from $9.95 to $18.95, depending on the number of laps. If you go on Tuesdays, you get two laps for the price of one. On Mondays, Wednesdays, and Thursdays, laps cost $1.85 each. The fee for the license is $1.

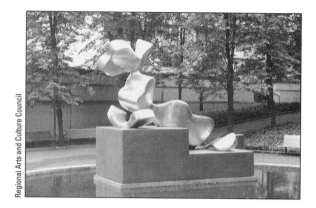

Regional Arts and Culture Council

8

MUSEUMS AND GALLERIES

Portland's museums and galleries offer a wide array of opportunity for the curious. You'll find history and art blending together in a colorful display of pure Pacific Northwest flavor.

You don't have to visit a museum or a gallery to understand why the city of Portland has been called an art form in and of itself. You'll find art on the streets in the guise of fountains, statues, architecture, and murals. But you won't want to miss the eclectic array of galleries and museums that can be found tucked into corners or consuming entire city blocks.

Visiting the Portland Art Museum can easily take up a full afternoon. It's worth the time. You can wander through numerous other eclectic galleries in an afternoon, too, or you may want to spend a day or two just taking an art and museum tour of the city.

Use the following listings as a guide, but be sure to investigate the area on your own as well. In Portland, galleries seem to spring up overnight, and you may find the right one at the right time simply by keeping your eyes and ears open. Remember, Portlanders love to talk about their city. The artists and gallery owners are no exception to that rule. If you don't see what you're looking for, just ask!

MUSEUMS

OREGON HISTORY CENTER
1200 SW Park Ave.
222-1741   **DT**
As soon as you enter the Oregon History Center, you know you're in for more than a history lesson. Incorporated in 1898, OHC takes you on a journey through Oregon's past that begins outside with two highly realistic trompe l'oeil murals. The West Mural, at the corner of Park and Madison, shows key members of

PORTLAND! *exhibit at the Oregon History Center*

the Lewis and Clark expedition. The South Mural, visible from Broadway and Jefferson Streets, relates early Oregon history by depicting its key characters: Native Americans, fur traders, and pioneer settlers.

The OHC collections contain more than 85,000 artifacts, ranging from a 12,000-year-old Fort Rock sandal to sixteenth-century maps. Also featured are contemporary exhibits of Oregon life. The manuscript collection, more than 3 million photographs, and 2,500 oral histories are some of the fascinating pieces of Oregonia you will find here. Of particular interest to visitors and newcomers is *PORTLAND!*, a permanent exhibit that walks visitors from the city's beginning to its present. From the "Portland Penny"—used in the coin toss to name the city—to interactive computer interfaces, you can track the city's progress from horses to streetcars to automobiles to the Silicon Forest of today.

The OHC museum store is a good place to find Oregon treasures and a wealth of books about the history and

people of the Pacific Northwest. Hours: Mon–Sat 10–5, Thur to 8, Sun 12–5. Admission: $6 adults, $3 students, $1.50 children 6–12; seniors free on Thursdays.

OREGON MARITIME CENTER AND MUSEUM
113 SW Front Ave.
224-7724   **DT**

Ships in bottles, scrimshaw, and various items of ship hardware are found in this museum housed in the Smith Building (built in 1872). Across the street from Waterfront Park, the museum chronicles Portland's early days as a leader in seaport and river traffic. Among many other nautical notables, you can see the flag that was flown on the battleship *Oregon* during the Spanish-American War and lots of navigation instruments dating from the 1750s to the present. Be sure to see the stern-wheeler *Portland* moored on the Willamette River, where you can view maritime artifacts on the cabin deck and glimpse what life was like aboard this much-loved vessel in 1947. The *Portland* was the last working steam-powered sternwheel tugboat to operate in an American harbor. Hours vary according to season. Admission: $4 adults, $3 seniors and children, $10 families.

OREGON MUSEUM OF SCIENCE AND INDUSTRY (OMSI)
1945 SE Water Ave.
797-4000   **SE**
One of the most popular attractions at the nation's fifth largest science museum is the earthquake experience found only at OMSI. Hang on, because this tremor registers 5.5 on the Richter scale! You can also climb aboard a submarine outside. OMSI features the OMNIMAX Theater, a five-story domed theater that gives viewers the illusion they are in the middle of the film. Murdock Sky Theater and its laser light productions are also popular. Special events and exhibits often occur at OMSI. Call 797-4588 for a listing of current events. Hours: Daily 9:30–7, Thur to 8. Admission: $8.50 adults, $6 seniors and children.

OREGON SPORTS HALL OF FAME AND MUSEUM
321 SW Salmon St.
227-7466   **DT**
It's little known, even in Portland, but if you're a sports buff, this place will interest you. More than 3,000 square feet house the history of Oregon sports. Videos, photos, uniforms, and trophies are just some of the items on display. Hours: Tues–Sun 10–6. Admission: $4 adults, $3 seniors and ages 7–21.

PORTLAND ART MUSEUM
1219 SW Park Ave.
226-2811   **DT**

The Portland Art Museum (PAM) was incorporated by a group of the city's leading citizens in December 1892. Those early visionaries were instrumental in defining PAM's mission, "to enliven and enrich people's lives through the visual and media arts." A primary focus is education and "approachable art." The museum's current home was designed by architect Pietro Belluschi. The different galleries are grouped in suites, which allows for varied displays throughout the entire building and an easy flow of traffic from gallery to gallery. The museum is spacious, airy, and full of natural light. It offers a comfortable, unassuming way in which to view art. The recently renovated gallery, held in high regard by other prominent museums across America, houses a permanent exhibit of some 32,000 works of art spanning 35 centuries. Of particular note are the Native American collection and the European Masters collection, which includes Monet's *Water Lilies* (1914) and Renoir's *The Seine at Argenteuil* (1874). Some Chinese objects from the Early Zhou Dynasty in China (c. 1027–900 B.C.) and a rare seventeenth-century Japanese screen are two highlights found in the Mark Gallery. Hours: Daily 9–7. Admission varies.

PORTLAND POLICE MUSEUM JUSTICE CENTER
1111 SW 2nd Ave.
796-3019   **DT**
In this small museum in the Justice Center, you can see early police uniforms, badges, photos, and other historical police memorabilia. Weapons also figure prominently. The museum is staffed by volunteer ex-officers. You will find willing

Hippo Hardware & Trading Co.

Hippo Hardware was started in 1977 by "two crazy guys in a pick-up," Steve Oppenheim and Steve Miller. They say they never had aspirations of being more than "junk dealers," but their business has taken them far beyond that dream.

Although Hippo Hardware is not a traditional museum, it has been classified as one because of the museum quality of some of its relics. And it's more than a secondhand store, specializing in odd old stuff like antique lighting, claw-foot tubs, brass fixtures, and stained-glass windows. A trip to Hippo Hardware is better entertainment than most movies. Roaming through the store can take hours and will certainly pique your curiosity.

The wide array (three floors) of antiques and bric-a-brac is astounding. It's like a cross between an old-fashioned hardware store and your grandparents' attic and garage. The helpful people who work here are pretty colorful themselves.

Even if you're not in the mood to buy anything, a trip to Hippo is a must. Kids enjoy it, too, and are encouraged to touch and ask questions. Dress in your grubbies because you'll want to dig around in the dusty drawers and poke your way through the basement, which is filled with all kinds of surprises. Visit Hippo Hardware & Trading Co. at 1040 E. Burnside; 231-1444.

storytellers among them, and they are eager to answer questions. Hours: Mon–Fri 10–4. Admission is free, but donations are gladly accepted.

ART GALLERIES

Portland's streets are dotted with art galleries. Many are hidden in nooks and crannies, up stairs and down alleys. Walking around the Pearl District will invariably lead you to them. If you want a map, Art Media, 902 SW Yamhill, 223-3724, offers a free pocket guide to galleries in different areas. Most museums and attractions also offer useful gallery guides and information.

AIA GALLERY
315 SW 4th Ave.
223-8757   **DT**
Unlimited variety can be found at the American Institute of Architects.

Local and international architectural work. Hours: Mon–Fri 9–5.

ART ON BROADWAY
615 SW Broadway
294-0102 **DT**
Surreal landscapes, 3-D art, photo realism, florals, and some animation cels. Hours: Mon–Sat 10–6.

ATTIC GALLERY
206 SW 1st Ave.
228-7830 **DT**
This gallery features Northwest artists working in a variety of media, including painting, sculpture, and ceramics. Exhibits change monthly. Hours: Mon–Sat 11–5:30 and by appointment.

AUGEN GALLERY
817 SW 2nd Ave.
224-8182 **DT**
Contemporary Northwest artists as well as prints and works on paper by artists such as Andy Warhol and David Hockney. Hours: Mon–Sat 10–5:30.

BEARD GALLERY
637 SW 4th Ave.
228-6250 **DT**
Prints, posters, and some original oils. Specializes in custom framing. Hours: Mon–Fri 10–7.

BLACKFISH GALLERY
420 NW 9th Ave.
224-2634 **DT**
Artist-owned gallery of diverse contemporary works. Hours: Tues–Sat 12–5 and by appointment.

BLUE SKY GALLERY
1231 NW Hoyt
225-0210 **DT**
Photography gallery specializing in both contemporary and historical work. International and regional emphases. Hours: Tues–Sat 12–5.

BUTTERS GALLERY, LTD.
223 NW 9th Ave.
248-9378 **DT**
Paintings, drawings, prints, photography, and sculpture by international and American artists. Hours: Tues–Sat 11–6.

CHETWYND STAPYLTON GALLERY
615 SW Broadway
223-4226 **DT**
Contemporary Northwest as well as national and international artists. Nineteenth-century originals and graphics. Hours: Tues–Sat 11–6.

ELIZABETH LEACH GALLERY
207 SW Pine St.
224-0521 **DT**
Contemporary fine art by Northwest and national artists. Variety of media, including bronze, paintings, photography, and prints. Hours: Mon–Sat 10:30–5:30.

FIRST AVENUE GALLERY
205 SW 1st Ave.
222-3850 **DT**
Northwest contemporary artists and some exhibits by national artists. Hours: Mon–Sat 10–5:30.

FROELICK ADELHART GALLERY
817 SW 2nd Ave.
222-1142 **DT**
Work of contemporary artists of the Northwest in a wide range of media. Hours: Tues–Fri 11–6, Sat 10–5.

GALERIE MONGEON
333 SW 5th Ave., Ste. 522
223-9093 **DT**
Two galleries, one featuring traditional sixteenth- through twentieth-

First Thursday

Webster's defines art as "the conscious production or arrangement of sounds, colors, forms, movements or other elements in a manner that affects the sense of beauty or aesthetic value." Portland artists and gallery owners seem to have taken this definition a step further, adding rugged individualism and a touch of magic to the mix they call First Thursday.

The first Thursday of every month hosts a walking tour, a kind of open house, in Portland's art world. Established ten years ago, the event was originally conceived as a way to educate the public about art and provide artists with a platform for their work and a forum for learning.

Victoria Frey, of Quartersaw Gallery, says, "We wanted to create a way to break down the barriers between artists and the general public." First Thursday is not a snooty highbrow affair, either. It's casual and interesting, designed for people who are curious about art, for those who have never even stepped into a gallery, and for serious collectors alike. Walking from gallery to gallery is an education in itself and an unassuming way to get to the heart of Portland's art.

Of the casual environment, Frey says, "We don't want the public to feel they have to buy something. It doesn't matter. We just want them to get out and see the incredible variety of work housed in Portland's galleries."

One credit to the Portland art scene is that it simply has no label. Exhibitions change, artists change, and tastes vary. You'll find romantic

century European, early American, and Oriental works in a variety of media. The other gallery features contemporary art, also in a variety of media. Hours: Mon–Fri 9–5, call for Sat hours.

GALLERY 114
1100 NW Glisan St.
243-3356 DT
Freedom of expression is empha-

sized in this cooperative gallery that showcases the work of Portland-area artists. Hours: Tues–Sat 12–6.

HENNESSY-SMITH GALLERY
74 SW 2nd Ave.
224-2088 DT
This is a working studio that features a unique mix of media and a large collection of art posters. Hours: Tues–Sat 10–5:30.

works, etchings and pastels, clay sculptures, photography, watercolors and wood, ceramics and jewelry, glass works and pottery featured in the different galleries. Frey says, "You just have to get out and see the work. After you've seen a few galleries, you'll develop a sense of what you like and what you don't like."

You'll find primitive symbolism mixed in with bold modern realism. You'll find tradition and innovation, whimsy and symmetry. But more important than categories, you'll find honest work done by independent artists whose passion and skill combine to create striking and thought-provoking works.

First Thursday is a community affair, too. Neighborhood coffee shops and bookstores stay open late for between-gallery cappuccino breaks. Thousands come to First Thursday every month. Some people purchase their first work of original art and some, who have been coming for years, do it just for the joy of viewing the different styles represented in Portland's art scene. Sometimes the artists are on hand to discuss their work, and you can always find a gallery owner to talk to. Who knows? Through viewing the diverse works, you may find something you like. You may also find something you hate. It's all OK. Art is about personal taste. And remember, there aren't any rules.

First Thursday runs from 6 to 9 p.m. To receive a guide to the galleries and a description of their works, sign up in any of the galleries or write to P.O. Box 29138, Portland, OR 97209.

AURA RUSSO GALLERY
805 NW 21st Ave.
226-2754 **NW**
This gallery features young artists and well-known Northwest contemporary artists. Hours: Tues–Fri 11–5:30, Sat 11–5.

MARGO JACOBSEN GALLERY
1039 NW Glisan St.
224-7287 **DT**

Exhibits change monthly. Include paintings, sculpture, and photography, as well as glassworks and ceramics. Hours: Tues–Fri 10–5:30, Sat 10–5.

MARK WOOLEY GALLERY
120 NW 9th Ave., Suite 210
224-5475 **DT**
Contemporary art in a variety of media from local and international

Oregon Museum of Science and Industry, p. 123

artists. Oil, watercolors, etchings, and bronzes. Hours: Tues–Sat 11–6.

**METROPOLITAN CENTER
FOR PUBLIC ART**
Portland Building
1120 SW 5th Ave., 2nd Floor
823-5388   **DT**
MCPA is administered by the Regional Arts & Culture Council. Emphasis on regional public art. Hours: Mon–Fri 8–6.

**PACIFIC NORTHWEST
COLLEGE OF ART**
Wentz Gallery
1219 SW Park Ave.
226-4391   **DT**
Contemporary works by national, regional, and local artists. College faculty work is featured as well. Mixed media including video, photography, and sculpture. Hours: Mon–Fri 8–5.

PHOTOGRAPHIC IMAGE GALLERY
240 SW 1st Ave.
224-3543   **DT**
The oldest commercial photography

gallery in the Northwest, Photographic Image specializes in traditional fine art photography and focuses on midcareer photographers working in both black and white and color. This is a good place for an emerging collector. The gallery also carries a diverse collection of posters. Hours: Mon–Sat 10–5:30.

**PULLIAM DEFFENBAUGH
GALLERY**
522 NW 12th Ave.
228-6665   **DT**
Emerging talents and masters of Northwest contemporary art. Hours: Tues–Sat 11–5:30.

QUARTERSAW GALLERY
528 NW 12th Ave.
223-2264   **DT**
Showcase for progressive art. Emphasis on abstract, expressionistic, landscape, and nonobjective work. Hours: Tues–Fri 10–6, Sat 12–5.

QUINTANA GALLERIES
501 SW Broadway
223-1729   **DT**

Known as one of the Northwest's finest Native American galleries, this is the place to go in Portland if you are interested in Southwest, Northwest Coast, or Alaskan Indian art. The gallery has paintings, wood carvings, stone sculptures, and jewelry. Hours: Tues–Sat 10:30–5:30.

S. K. JOSEFSBERG GALLERY
403 NW 11th Ave.
241-9112   **DT**
Vintage and contemporary photogra-phy and paintings from Northwest and national artists. Hours: Tues–Sat 12–5.

UMBRA PENUMBRA
316 SW 9th Ave.
223-4497   **DT**
Umbra Penumbra is the home of the quirky. Here you'll find art of a different sort by local artists on the edge. Comfortable seating in the lounge area offers you a chance to reflect while you sip an espresso. Live music

Feast on Crawfish and Art

It may not be a "real" art gallery, but Jake's Famous Crawfish, 401 SW 12th St., 226-1419, has one of Oregon's most unique art collections, along with the best seafood in town. In all the dining areas and in the bar are examples of early works by American painters such as Eliza Barchus, Updyke, Gay Doyl, F.C.R. Groth, and A. Berger. The paintings cover a range of subjects, from nudes to some of Oregon's most recognized natural scenes. You'll see places like Willamette Falls, Rooster Rock, the Columbia River Gorge, Mt. Hood, and the St. John's Bridge as they appeared in the late nineteenth century.

In the bar, you'll find especially interesting nineteenth-century barmaid paintings. Tales of unrequited love and crimes of passion accompany the paintings. Ask the bartender or your server about the bullet holes in one of them. Manager Larry Baldwin is especially knowledgeable about the paintings and will be happy to stop by your table and tell you a story.

Jake's also boasts a notable collection of museum-quality antiques. Look for the 1881 chandeliers. The oak buffets, now serving as the back bar, were shipped around Cape Horne in 1880 for a total freight cost of $10. Jake's itself has quite a colorful history, dating back to 1892, and is a true Portland tradition. It's well worth the visit, whether you're a "foodie" or an art aficionado or both.

is often featured in the evenings; you can also enjoy an occasional poetry or literary reading by some of Portland's best-known poets. Hours: Mon–Fri 8 a.m.–10 p.m., Sat 10–10, Sun 12–10.

WATERSTONE GALLERY
733 NW Everett St.
226-6196   **DT**
Northwest contemporary gallery run by the artists. Hours: Tues–Sat 12–6.

WYLAND GALLERIES
711 SW 10th Ave.
223-7692   **DT**
Environmental artist and muralist Wyland exhibits his work along with that by other local artists. Hours: Mon–Sat 10–6, Sun 12–4.

9

PARKS AND GARDENS

Portland's parks and gardens, which spill into quaint neighborhoods and parallel busy city streets, are found at nearly every corner throughout the city. Portland enjoys more parks per capita than any other city in the United States. In fact, there are 37,000 acres of parks in the metro area.

The history of the city's parks dates back to 1852, when Daniel Lownsdale and Williams Chapman set aside a parcel of their land claim that eventually turned into downtown's Park Blocks. Many of Portland's parks were designed by landscape architect John Olmsted, whose family designed Golden Gate Park in San Francisco. Today's city planners have kept the protection of open spaces a top priority.

A good beginning point for your exploration is Portland Parks and Recreation, which manages a system of more than 200 parks and recreation sites totaling almost 10,000 acres. For information, call 823-2223 (TTY). Portland Parks offers classes and recreational trips for children and adults, and also sponsors some special seniors' programs. Many of Portland Parks' programs are geared toward those with special needs. This agency can also provide you with walking maps and detailed information about its many parks and gardens.

It could take a whole book to describe the more than 700 public parks, gardens, and natural spaces in the metro area. Following are some of the highlights, but don't hesitate to venture out on your own—you will find magic in the diversity of Portland's neighborhood parks.

CRYSTAL SPRINGS RHODODENDRON GARDEN
SE 28th and Woodstock Blvd.   SE
Located near Reed College, this garden of "rhodies" (as they are fondly referred to in Portland) bursts with blooms to herald the arrival of spring. In May, the gardens come alive with colors ranging from deep reds and dark purples to delicate pinks and pristine whites. Cascading azalea trees nestle among the rhodies, producing one of Portland's most famous color-filled sights. Crystal Springs Lake provides abundant nesting areas for waterfowl; children especially enjoy feeding the ducks beside the water. A suggested donation of $2 is requested at the gate.

FOREST PARK
NW 29th and Upsher-Newberry

Fun Facts about Portland Parks

Cathedral Park, in North Portland's St. John's area, hosts a popular summertime jazz series under the historic St. John's Bridge. Food and jazz on a rolling lawn make for afternoons of splendor in the sun on the banks of the Willamette River.

Delta Park, at North Denver Avenue and Martin Luther King Boulevard, was once a city called Vanport. A flood destroyed the city, then Oregon's second largest, in 1948.

Grant Park was the setting for Beverly Cleary's children's books about Ramona and Henry. It was here that her character Henry Higgins went to dig for worms.

Leach Botanical Gardens was originally called Sleepy Hollow.

The swimming pool at Sellwood Park is the city's oldest pool. Built in 1910, it is still a favorite gathering place for families.

Butterfly Park is exactly that! Adjacent to Willamette Park, this park was expressly designed to attract butterflies. There is also a Butterfly Garden at the Washington Park Zoo.

Dunniway Park, near Terwilliger Boulevard, is famous for its lilacs in springtime. The fragrance is mesmerizing near and in this park.

Mt. Tabor Park, high above the city on the Eastside, is actually a dormant volcano. It's the only extinct volcano in the entire United States within a city's limits.

Portland Parks and Recreation

Tom McCall Waterfront Park, p. 135

Rd., between NW Skyline and St. Helens Rd. **NW**

Just two minutes from busy city streets, a lush old-growth forest offers a pleasant respite from Portland's rapid urban pulse. With 5,000 acres and more than 70 miles of walking trails, Forest Park is the largest forested municipal park in the United States. Amid swordferns and trillium, pristine waterfalls and wild animals, a pocket of natural splendor thrives in the midst of the humming city. Visitors and locals alike enjoy hiking or strolling under the shade of Douglas fir, cedar, and hemlock trees. Picnic areas, soccer fields, and secluded spots for quiet reading and reflection abound in this park.

> **T**
> **I**
> **P**
>
> Hours vary at the parks, but most Portland-area parks are open from 5 a.m. to midnight. For detailed maps and addresses, call Portland Parks Hotline at 823-2223.

MILL ENDS PARK
SW Front and Taylor **DT**

Measuring 4'x3'x6', this bit of whimsy is the world's smallest park. It was the brainchild of Dick Fagan, an imaginative journalist, who, upon returning from WWII in 1946, noted that his second-floor office afforded him a rather boring view of a busy street and a hole where a light pole was supposed to go. Fagan planted flowers in the hole, called the spot a park, and said it was a gathering place for leprechauns. Many of his *Oregon Journal* columns, titled "Mill Ends," described the life of the world's only leprechaun colony west of the Emerald Isle.

NORTH PARK BLOCKS AND
SOUTH PARK BLOCKS **DT**

Six North Park Blocks and 12 South Park Blocks stretch north and south through the heart of downtown. Walking these blocks takes you to Portland State University, Portland Art Museum, and the Oregon History Center. You also pass by impressive National Historic Sites, many historic bronze statues, and fountains. The Park Blocks remain, according to the original plan, "a cathedral of trees with a simple floor of grass." Today, they are alive with people enjoying brown bag lunches on wooden benches, musicians in impromptu jam sessions, artists with their sketchbooks, and even, during the summer months, Oregon Ballet Theatre rehearsals.

OREGON GARDEN
Across from Oregon State Office Building
800 NE Oregon St.   NE
Some 8,000 square feet of English garden–style landscaping make this little oasis adjacent to the state offices near Lloyd Center. The garden has been designed to be enjoyed year-round. It's a secret little place, not often found on tourist maps, and is a delightful sensory experience during all seasons. You can see things like Japanese Kimmia, pink wisteria, royal azaleas, and Siberian tea plants.

PENINSULA PARK
N. Albina and Portland Blvd.   NW
Peninsula Park is a treasure trove of

Zupan's Picnic Lunches

All throughout the summer months and on into Portland's famous Indian summer days, you'll find locals enjoying picnics in many of the city's parks. If you want to do the same and don't have access to a kitchen or simply don't want to cook, just head to the nearest Zupan's Marketplace. Zupan's is Portland's premier grocery market, and each location has a wonderful deli chock-full of ready-made salads, sandwiches, delicious desserts, gourmet cheeses, fresh fish, and the freshest produce in town. The staff at Zupan's is most helpful with composing picnic lunches, and if you call ahead of time, they'll even prepare one for you.

Three of Zupan's markets are conveniently located near some of Portland's favorite picnic spots:

Zupan's at 3301 SE Belmont, 239-3720, is near Laurelhurst Park, just off 39th and Belmont. Laurelhurst, one of Portland's oldest parks, is full of shade trees, water, and lots of green grass.

Zupan's at 2340 W. Burnside, 497-1088, is near Portland's 5,000, acre Forest Park, which boasts walking trails, wildlife, and natural beauty .

Zupan's at 7221 SW Macadam, 244-5666, is near Willamette Park, which offers riverside picnic spots.

floral gardens, walking paths, and recreational areas. Typical of the gracious Old World–style parks designed in the early 1900s, Peninsula Park was Portland's first community center to have a pool. Originally the site of "Liverpool Liz's Place," the park was once a roadhouse and racetrack. Two acres comprise the city's first public rose gardens, with more than 15,000 plantings. The garden is 6 feet below ground level, edged with boxwood and landscaped with walking paths and brick steps. An octagonal bandstand, built in 1913, overlooks the rose garden.

TOM McCALL WATERFRONT PARK
West bank of
Willamette River   DT
Tom McCall Waterfront Park, a 23-acre stretch along the west bank of the Willamette River adjacent to downtown, is a reclaimed expressway. Named for a former Oregon governor, the park is home to fountains, walking paths, promenades, and numerous observation points. A walk through the park will lead you to luxury condominiums, specialty stores, restaurants, hotels, and a marina. This lively and lived-in park is often referred to as "festival heaven" because visitors can find music, dance, and food festivals on any given weekend during the summer. At the north end of the park, near the Burnside Bridge, is the Children's Story Garden, an interactive sculp-

Japanese Gardens, p. 136

ture garden designed to ignite the imaginations of young and old alike. A little further down the track is a graceful and poetic memorial to the American Japanese imprisoned in internment camps during WWII. Called Gardens of Stone, the sculptures are interpretive and moving.

WASHINGTON PARK
Just off Highway 26   SW
Washington Park, located in the hills just west of downtown, is a conglomerate of activity and one of Portland's favorite parks. It's easy to spend an entire day exploring the terrain, and you're sure to find a perfect spot for a picnic lunch here. Within the park, you will find the following havens:

Hoyt Arboretum
Oaks, magnolias, maples, redwoods, and Himalayan spruce are just some of the hundreds of identified deciduous trees and conifers you will find on the trails in this 175-acre arboretum, which offers guided tours April through October on Saturday and Sunday at 2 p.m. Free. For maps, call 248-4492.

Cyclists, take note: Pedestrians have the right-of-way in Portland's parks.

International Rose Test Garden

Established in 1917, the Rose Gardens welcome thousands of visitors each year. More than 400 varieties of roses are tended by volunteers from the Portland Rose Society. Don't miss the Shakespeare Garden, in the southeast corner, which is filled with the bard's favorite flowers. Walking through the Rose Garden is a special treat filled with color and fragrance. Free admission.

Japanese Gardens

Five traditional Japanese gardens, designed by Professor P. Takum Tono, include a Sand and Stone Garden, a Tea Garden, the Strolling Pond Garden, the Flat Garden, and the Natural Garden. The tranquility of the Japanese Garden can be enjoyed all year long. Hours vary, but 10 a.m. to 4 p.m. is a safe bet. Admission: $5 adults, $2.50 students and seniors.

Washington Park Zoo

In 1887 Richard Knight, a local pharmacist with a love of animals, donated his animal collection to the city, and a zoo was born. Major exhibits include the African rain forest and savanna, the "Penguinarium," Alaskan tundra, and insects. The feline exhibit includes highly endangered Siberian tigers and endangered red pandas. Snack options at the zoo include the Afri-Cafe, a year-round cafeteria, and various summer food concession stands. Admission: $5.50 adults, $4 seniors, $3.50 children.

Pioneer Place

10

SHOPPING

SHOPPING DISTRICTS

Downtown

Shopping downtown can be a form of entertainment all its own. As you walk around the city blocks, you'll see colorful, fragrant flower carts adorning corners and kids in the street selling handmade jewelry. Spicy aromas drift from the doorways of French and Guatemalan restaurants. Street musicians provide the backbeat, and busy shoppers set the pace. Whether you're after fashion from Saks, a sketchbook from Art Media, leathers from London Underground, or exotic spices from the International Food Bazaar, you'll find it downtown.

BEE CLEANERS
939 SW 10th Ave.
227-1144 **DT**
If you need some dry cleaning done, Bee Cleaners is the place to go. Family-owned for 46 years, it's the

only place in Portland where you can pull up in front, honk your horn, and receive curbside service. They're quick and dependable for cleaning and alterations.

BRITISH TEA GARDENS
725 SW 10th Ave.
221-7817 **DT**
You'll want to stop for a respite from shopping at the British Tea Gardens. Not only will you be served the best cup of tea in Portland, but also, in true English style, authentic scones and Devonshire cream. There's plenty of tea to buy, too, if you want to take some home to brew up yourself. The British Tea Gardens also offers a wide selection of teapots, English biscuits, china cups, and cookbooks.

DAKOTA
722 SW Taylor
221-1869 **DT**
Dakota is a brightly decorated spot where you'll find Mephisto

shoes from France, clothing and accessories, and a variety of pricey, elegant home furnishings.

THE GALLERIA
921 SW Morrison
228-2748   **DT**
See lising under Portland Area Malls, page 150.

INTERNATIONAL FOOD BAZAAR
1103 SW Alder
228-1960   **DT**
This store promises sensory overload. You'll hear foreign languages and music, smell imported spices, and be offered tastes of exotic foods. Known for its Armenian, Russian, Ukrainian, Indian, Greek, and Middle Eastern foodstuffs, the Food Bazaar has it all, from barrels of spices to Turkish Delight to Cafe Najjar (Brazilian coffee with cardamom). The friendly staff will be glad to help if you don't see what you're looking for.

KATHLEEN'S OF DUBLIN
860 SW Broadway

224-4869   **DT**
Kathleen's of Dublin is a favorite for the Irish and Scottish set. Lots of imported gifts and fashions with a Celtic flair.

NIKE TOWN
930 SW 6th Ave.
221-6453   **DT**
Nike Town is a futuristic "museum" and gallery of sporting goods located at 6th and Salmon, decorated in Nike's signature flashy style. Management calls it "Nike out the yin yang."

PIONEER PLACE
700 SW 5th Ave.
228-5800   **DT**
See lising under Portland Area Malls, page 150.

PORTLAND PENDLETON SHOP
SW 4th and Salmon
242-0037   **DT**
The Pendleton Shop specializes in its own Pendleton products, including blankets, fashions, and fabric.

British Tea Gardens, p. 137

British Tea Gardens

Old Town

Portland's Old Town is known as the home to Saturday Market and a wide variety of shops and restaurants. Historic preservation is the theme, and you'll find quaint shops tucked in vintage buildings. Portland's Chinatown is part of Old Town, too. Take public transportation; parking is difficult to find in this popular area. Walking in Old Town is convenient and easy.

AUSTRALIAN ORIGINALS
Skidmore Building
SW Ankeny and 1st Ave.
228-4484   **DT**
All manner of down under products, including the dreaded Vegemite, are sold here. Didgeridoos, Tea Tree healthcare products, Driza-Bone weather gear, and Australian music share shelf space. Aboriginal art and prints, too. Authentic Aussie humor is freely dispensed by the owners.

COURTYARD LIVING GALLERY
50 SW 2nd Ave.
223-6168   **DT**
This shop specializes in garden art. Topiary animals like bears and deer live here, along with the rest of the jungle. The gallery specializes in both wholesale and retail.

IMPORT PLAZA
1 NW Couch St.
227-4040   **DT**
Stop by Import Plaza for a look at goods from all over the world.

LOCALS ONLY
61 SW 2nd Ave.
227-5000   **DT**
This is the premier Northwest music outlet for local artists and producers.

A good place to get a handle on the hot music in town.

MADE IN OREGON
10 NW 1st Ave.
273-8354   **DT**
Made in Oregon is a store filled with goodies like Pendleton blankets, Oregon art, ceramics, pottery, and Oregon foodstuffs. Stock up on souvenirs here.

NEW MARKET THEATRE BUILDING
50 SW 2nd Ave.
228-2392   **DT**
Adjacent to Portland's Saturday Market, the New Market Theatre is home to many little shops.

OLD TOWN ANTIQUE MARKET
1st Ave. and NW Couch
228-3386   **DT**
Consignment dealers gather here to show their wares. Some call it trash, some call it treasure. Depression glass, lamps, watches, wall hangings, fountain pens, and estate jewelry.

PORTLAND SATURDAY MARKET
108 W. Burnside St.
222-6072   **DT**
The nation's largest continuously operating open-air market for handcrafted goods in the United States is an experience in itself. Nearly 300 craft booths and an international food court, beer garden, and live music will keep you entertained for an entire day. The market itself has a festive air about it. Most of the time you'll find mimes, magicians, clowns, bands, and other forms of entertainment near the Skidmore Fountain. It's a great place for kids, too. The artists and craftspeople display such varied items as clothing, handmade puppets, stoneware,

bonsai trees, watercolors, wood-works, glassworks, and photography, to name only a few. There really is no limit to the sorts of things you'll find here, many of which will pique your curiosity and make you smile. Located in Old Town, the market is open on Saturdays and Sundays, March through Christmas. Parking can be problematic in the area, so it's advisable to ride MAX. Free admission. Major credit cards accepted at most booths.

THINK GOOD THOUGHTS
Skidmore Building
SW Ankeny and 1st Ave.
226-2254   **DT**
Deadhead supply shop carrying Jerry Garcia memorabilia and tie-dyed T-shirts, music, ties, and jewelry. The coffee shop next door is full of lively conversation and colorful people.

Northwest 23RD

The Northwest section of town, sometimes referred to as Uptown or Nob Hill, has become a shopping mecca for both locals and visitors. Trendy and sophisticated, the tree-lined streets are filled with shops selling everything from imported Italian pottery to antique table-cloths and African ceremonial masks. You can browse through shops that specialize in handmade artifacts right next door to a lace and lingerie shop.

"Northwest 23rd" refers to the neighborhood as much as the avenue itself. Wandering off of 23rd, up toward 24th or down toward 21st, leads to even more shopping. Eclectic hair design shops, shoe shops, and old-fashioned pharmacies are just some of the establishments you'll see tucked in among vintage apartment buildings and Victorian homes.

Along with upscale restaurants, hamburger joints, coffee shops, and gourmet pizza parlors, you will find art shops, bookstores, and a smattering of record stores. Wear sturdy walking shoes—you'll walk more than you anticipate, and nothing kills the thrill of the retail hunt like throbbing feet.

Portland Saturday Market

Portland Oregon Visitors Association

Store hours vary, but most are open daily 10 a.m. to 6 p.m. Here are just a few of the highlights.

BELLA LUNA
610 NW 23rd Ave.
248-0191   **NW**
Unique designs in women's clothing. Funky defines it. Nice staff and comfortable surroundings.

CHILD'S PLAY
907 NW 23rd Ave.
224-5586   **NW**
See Chapter 6, "Kids' Stuff."

CHRISTMAS AT THE ZOO
118 NW 23rd Ave.
223-4048   **NW**
See Chapter 6, "Kids' Stuff."

THE COMPLEAT BED AND BREAKFAST
615 NW 23rd Ave.
221-0193   **NW**
Everything to help make your home cozy. European linens, candles, hair-brushes, soaps; plus thick, stylish bath-robes, towels, and down products.

CP SHADES
513 NW 23rd Ave.
241-7838   **NW**
California found a home in Portland. This is a store for women who want comfortable clothing at reasonable prices. Lots of different colors in all-natural fabrics.

DAZZLE
704 NW 23rd Ave.
224-1294   **NW**
Look for the wooden horse outside at the front door. This shop is aptly named—the array of items will dazzle you. It's always busy here. Lots of eclectic clocks and watches, picture frames, candle holders, and a wide variety of Mexican art.

ESCENTIAL LOTIONS AND OILS
710 NW 23rd Ave.
248-9748   **NW**
It smells like it sounds. Sandalwood and lavender mix with gardenia oil and Victorian vanilla bath beads. The staff will custom mix a fragrance for you, and you are more than welcome to try before you buy. Great selection of greeting cards, too. Not so pricey as name-brand perfumes and lotions but every bit as good in quality.

HANSON'S FINE BOOKS
814 NW 23rd Ave.
223-7610   **NW**
This is a quality bookstore with very helpful staff. If you're looking to widen your reading horizons, this is the place to stop. The store is housed in a beautifully refinished Victorian painted in purple, cantaloupe, and teal.

IMBA FINE ARTS GALLERY
818 NW 23rd Ave.
295-2973   **NW**
Downstairs you'll find serpentine sculptures, oils from Africa, and a large selection of African jewelry and artifacts. You can also sign up for conga lessons here if the spirit moves you.

IN THE BAG
708 NW 23rd Ave.
223-3262   **NW**
All kinds of greeting cards, stationery, gift wrap, and whimsical gifts. From the risqué to the romantic, the hilarious to serious, you'll find the right message "in the bag."

JANE'S OBSESSION
728 NW 23rd Ave.

The didgeridoo collection at Austrialian Originals, p. 139

221-1490   **NW**
This is the place for romantic and frisky thoughts. Fine European lingerie.

KITCHEN KABOODLE
404 NW 23rd Ave.
241-4040   **NW**
Every cook's dream, Kitchen Kaboodle offers upscale kitchen and home goods. Wild print tablecloths, designer cookware, furniture, and books for cooks. It's all here, and to top it off, the staff tends to be extremely friendly and sometimes will even make you laugh.

LA BOTTEGA DI MAMMARO
940 NW 23rd Ave.
241-4960   **NW**
Handmade Italian ceramics and accessories for the table. From European elm cutting boards to hand-woven cotton tablecloths and rustic tableware, MammaRo is filled with wonderful choices for the gourmet cook—or the cook who wants to look gourmet!

MUSIC MILLENIUM
801 NW 23rd Ave.
248-0163   **NW**
This is the place to go for music in Portland. The staff prides itself on its knowledge of music, from classical to hip-hop, jazz to opera. Large selection of CDs and tapes.

MYRA'S
712 NW 23rd Ave.
227-5454   **NW**
Myra's is a colorful place. Chock-full of linens, cottons, and lots of clothing. Smart staff, eager to help.

NORTHWEST GARDEN AND TOPIARY
805 NW 23rd Ave.
222-9939   **NW**
If you don't have acres for a garden, this is the place to find pots and decorative tiles for your patio. Exotic plants and vines along with a variety of hanging baskets. Helpful advice and instructions from the staff, too.

PAINT THE SKY KITES
828 NW 23rd Ave.
222-5096 **NW**

One of the most colorful shops in Portland. Where else can you purchase a flying pig or a floating wizard? From kites to fly to windsocks for the patio, this store is filled with goods to lift the spirits.

PLANET X
406 NW 23rd Ave.
241-4724 **NW**

Planet X is wild. Though it's not a place for kids, adults will find action figures, Star Wars memorabilia, books, magnets, cards, and toys of a different sort. Some X-rated comics here, too.

POTTERY BARN
310 NW 23rd Ave.
525-0280 **NW**

Excellent help from the proprietors here. You'll find designer furniture, accessories, and a wide variety of pottery.

RESTORATION HARDWARE
315 NW 23rd Ave.
228-6226 **NW**

Here you'll find all kinds of stuff you simply must have, just because it's there. Lovely couches and other furniture; cabinets, unique drawer and cabinet pulls, housewares. And lots and lots of light fixtures. Restoration Hardware can take awhile to see because there are so many things to choose from.

RETRO VIVA
816 NW 23rd Ave.
227-5105 **NW**

Upstairs from Hanson's Fine Books, you'll find retro-style clothing in all sizes and colors. Everything from a miniskirt that looks like quilted

aluminum to red plastic trousers and yellow platform shoes.

RICH'S CIGAR STORE
706 NW 23rd Ave.
227-6907 **NW**

With the current cigar rage, if you are looking for cigars, this is the place to go. Ample choices and a wide range of prices offered. Also on hand are exotic pipes, chessboards, European cigarettes, and lighters. Rich's is also known for its great selection of international magazines. There's a downtown store at 820 SW Alder Street, so if it's not in stock in the NW store, they'll be glad to phone downtown.

THE SALT BOX COLLECTION
525 NW 23rd Ave.
295-1102 **NW**

A collection of everything from antique snowshoes to velvet accent pillows. Beeswax candles, English baskets, and antique quilts. Lots of ideas for home decorating.

SHOE REPAIR
921 NW 23rd Ave. **NW**

There's no name on the outside, just a sign that says "Shoe Repair." It's an established shoe shop where you can get those heels fixed or buy some new clogs or sheepskin slippers.

SHOGUN'S GALLERY
206 NW 23rd Ave.
224-0328 **NW**

You'll find all things Oriental here. Rich wood smells capture your imagination as you explore exotic tables, mirrors, and cabinets. There are some refurbished items as well as kimonos, china plates, and vases.

SIGNATURE IMPORTS
920 NW 23rd Ave.

The Galleria, p. 150

274-0217   **NW**
Sweaters from Nepal and Nepalese ceremonial masks, Indonesian art frames and clothing, Mexican masks and blankets. Large collection of Guatemalan beads and handmade jewelry.

TORREFAZIONE
838 NW 23rd Ave.
228-2528   **NW**
In the true spirit of the Northwest, you might want to stop first at Torrefazione, an Italian coffee store where the cappuccino, poured into Italian ceramic cups, is excellent and the ambiance reflects the area. You'll overhear artists talking about their work alongside developers planning their next urban renewal project. The *baristas* at Torrefazione look like they came directly from Italy, and for those who crave even more authenticity, some even speak Italian.

URBINO
521 NW 23rd Ave.

220-0053   **NW**
The narrow aisles overflow with hand-milled soaps from Provence, Italian pottery, essential oils, books, buckwheat pillows, handblown glassworks, and more. There's an artsy collection of greeting cards back in the corner.

WHAM
617 NW 23rd Ave.
222-4992   **NW**
Kind of a gag shop, it's filled with pop art, retro kitsch, and cheap Asian toys. A fun place to browse.

WILD WEST CLOTHING
740 NW 23rd Ave.
222-6666   **NW**
Leather vests, wool shirts, and red silk evening wear combine to make Wild West Clothing a shop in which you never quite know what you'll find. Upstairs in the old gray house, you'll find What's Upstairs, a women's consignment clothing store full of good clothes at good prices. Wild West is located right downstairs from NW Futon.

Hawthorne Boulevard

Cross the Hawthorne Bridge from downtown and continue straight on Hawthorne Boulevard to 30th Avenue. From 30th to about 39th, you'll find shopping of a different sort. This is a "working artist" sort of area filled with antique shops, vintage clothing stores, art shops, great restaurants, and bookstores, all within easy walking distance of each other. The climate is decidedly different from that of NW 23rd. It's friendly and funky, rather than upscale and trendy, less hectic and much more colorful for people-watching. Among the more inter-

esting shops in the Hawthorne District are the following.

BLUE BUTTERFLY IMPORTS
3646 SE Hawthorne Blvd.
238-6639 **SE**
Colorful import store worth a visit, especially if you're looking for decorating ideas or something new and unusual.

GRAND CENTRAL
BAKING COMPANY
2230 SE Hawthorne Blvd.
232-0575 **SE**
You really shouldn't miss this rustic bakery. Old World–style breads abound. Try the yeasted corn bread and the Como loaf. Nice place for a snack, too, with great homemade cookies, lemon bars, and other desserts. It's a funky concrete place, where the casual service is friendly and informative. You can watch the guys in the back bake the bread while you wait for your latte. Loud music sometimes.

GREG'S ECLECTIC MIX ANTIQUES
3707 SE Hawthorne Blvd.
235-1257 **SE**
Eclectic is the word. Music stands, antique brass, china, and furniture mix it up with toys, wall plaques, and linens.

NAKED CITY
3730 SE Hawthorne Blvd.
239-3837 **SE**
OK. This is the place for funky. European funky. The shop specializes in European vintage clothing at extremely reasonable prices. You'll find Swedish army coats, French policemen's leather jackets, German satin pajamas from the Forties, and much more. The stock changes frequently, but there is

always something colorful, odd, and suprising.

THE PASTAWORKS
3735 SE Hawthorne Blvd.
232-1010 **SE**
It's all here for the kitchen. Cookbooks, fine food, candles, wrapping paper, gourmet kitchen items. A superior selection of Italian products and some truly fine wines. The fresh flower market just outside the store is open year-round and offers some of the best fresh flowers in Portland for very reasonable prices. You can compose your own bouquet to add just the right touch to the table.

RUBY'S ANTIQUES, FINE GIFTS, AND INTERIORS
3590 SE Hawthorne Blvd.
239-9867 **SE**
This huge store literally overflows with antiques and bric-a-brac. You'll find everything from fine furniture to lace handkerchiefs, baby clothes, lamps, and teapots.

WILDFLOWERS ON HAWTHORNE
3202 SE Hawthorne Blvd.
230-9485 **SE**
Just like it sounds. Lots of gardening goods, dried flowers in bouquets, and other arrangements. Helpful advice and humor.

Antique Row
"Antiquers" are a breed unto themselves. If you consider yourself a member of that breed, Portland will make you feel like you've died and gone to heaven. There are antique malls and shops scattered throughout the city, but true antique lovers won't want to miss Sellwood.

Sellwood is a "hometown" kind of place. Just across the Willamette via the Sellwood Bridge, you'll

General Store

find vintage houses, antiques stores, and restaurants in a community that prides itself on historic preservation. In the old days, the Sellwood Ferry was the mode of transportation across the river. Even today, it's not hard to imagine ferries on the river and horse-drawn wagons traveling down what is now Tacoma Street.

Sellwood is known as "Antique Row," and whether you're looking for ivory lace or a Fabergé egg, you'll find it here. You might want to drop the kids off at Oaks Amusement Park, just a few blocks away (see Chapter 7, "Kids' Stuff"), for a couple of hours while you browse through the area.

Shopping is made easy in Sellwood. Most of the stores are located on SE 13th and Milwaukie Avenue, just north of Tacoma Street, the street you end up on if you cross the Sellwood Bridge. Though the stores vary in merchandise, you can rest assured you'll find something of interest in nearly every nook and cranny. A few highlights of the area are listed below.

CALAMITY JANE INC.
7908 SE 13th Ave.
235-3467   SE
You won't find antiques here, but you will find lots of "comfy-funky" clothing, from flannel nightshirts to silk dressing gowns and even designer dresses. Service sometimes verges on the nonexistent here.

DEN OF ANTIQUITY
8012 SE 13th Ave.
233-7334   SE
The very friendly proprietors carry lots of furniture and antique curios.

GENERAL STORE
7987 SE 13th Ave.
233-1321   SE
This is not a true general store, but the merchandise is wide and varied. Just look for the big red boxcar that says "Spokane, Portland & Seattle Railway."

GOLDEN GIRLS ANTIQUES
7834 SE 13th Ave.
233-2160   SE
Silver tea services and lace doilies, perfume bottles, and some furniture.

THE RAVEN
7805 SE 13th Ave.
233-8075 **SE**
Military memorabilia and collectibles.

RS SPENCER'S ANTIQUES
8130 SE 13th Ave.
238-1737 **SE**
The building alone is worth a visit. It's the site of the old Isthmus Theatre, built in 1926 and now full of relics and antiques.

SCHONDECKEN COFFEE ROASTER
6720 SE 16th Ave.
236-8234 **SE**
OK, so it's not an antique store. But you'll miss a real treat if you don't stop in at this old house filled with herbal teas and coffee freshly roasted on-site. They also carry potpourri and spices from around the world.

SELLWOOD ANTIQUE MALL
7875 SE 13th Ave.
232-3755 **SE**
Lots of stalls and lots of choices can be found in the old Wall's Hardware Store. You will find Formica tables from the Fifties and other retro-style furniture next to kachina dolls from Phoenix. It's an eclectic mix, and it takes a while to see it all.

SOUTHERN ACCENTS
7730 SE 13th Ave.
231-5508 **SE**
If the Old South interests you, this store will whet your appetite. Old quilts, table linens, rugs, and furniture with a Southern flavor abound here.

BOOKS AND MAGAZINES

Portland is known nationwide as a city of readers. There are bookstores all over town. Portlanders tend to support independent bookstores rather than large chains. A few of the highlights include the following.

CAMERON'S BOOKS AND MAGAZINES
336 SW 3rd Ave.
228-2391 **DT**
This is Portland's oldest used bookstore. You'll find lots of paperbacks at bargain prices and an especially varied selection of vintage magazines.

LAUGHING HORSE BOOKS
3652 SE Division
236-2893 **SE**
Some say it's a radical bookstore. Others say it's the best place to find progressive environmental and political books, as well as feminist and multicultural works and books by Northwest authors. Lectures are often scheduled here on a range of topics that has included pirate radio, women's issues, health concerns, and other social issues. It's a community-oriented, funky, downhome kind of place, with an eager-to-be-of-service staff. If you ask.

MURDER BY THE BOOK
3210 SE Hawthorne Blvd.
232-9995 **SE**
Murder mystery fans unite! This is it, if you're into whodunits. This store is proud of its selection of Northwest authors. You can trade in or sell your already-solved mysteries at the store.

NEW RENAISSANCE BOOKSHOP
1338 NW 23rd Ave.
224-4929 **NW**
Spirituality and self-improvement are the mainstays here. Housed in an old

Top Ten Places to Shop for Your Home

Ken Hoyt, of Ken Hoyt Style, has spent 20 years developing his discerning eye. As an interior designer, he is sought after by some of Portland's best-known homeowners. Below, Ken shares some of his favorite spots to shop for the home.

1. **The Blue Pear**, 1313 NW Glisan, 227-0057. Clean lines and unfussy detail typify the offerings at designer Jenise Adams' signature store.

2. **Carl Greve Jewelers**, 731 SW Morrison, 223-7121. The second floor, called On Two, is filled with the best china, crystal, and linens in town. In Portland, sending a gift in their unique gift wrap is the last word in Social Security.

3. **City of Paris**, 1425 NE Broadway, 284-3720. Tim O'Hearn has collected a large assortment of lovely candles, soaps, and small gifts with an Old World flair.

4. **Doma**, 2310 NE Broadway, 288-9123. From dinnerware to sofas, Robert Swortfiguer defines his collection with fresh color, clean lines, and a sense of what's now.

5. **Geraldine's**, 2772 NW Thurman, 295-5911. Local designers constantly prowl here to see what antiques and elegant trims Geri has brought back from distant corners of the world.

6. **Greg's**, 3707 SE Hawthorne, 235-1257. From small decorative items to exquisite soaps and candles, this is a great place for gifts at very reasonable prices.

7. **P.H. Reed**, 1100 NW Glisan, 274-7080. The best contemporary furniture and lighting store in the city. Here, freshness alternates between the sublime and the daring.

8. **Portland Antique Company**, 1211 NW Glisan, 223-0999, and 2601 SE Clinton, 239-5124. The antiques range from pedigreed to "uncertain birth," all at great prices.

9. **Rejuvenation House Parts**, 1100 SE Grand, 238-1900. This store began its life recycling old houses and has expanded to its current full shopping experience with Stickley furniture and its own line of reproduction light fixtures.

10. **The Whole Nine Yards**, 1023 NW Glisan, 223-2880. Amy Estrin has collected an enormous array of interior fabrics at prices below what decorators must pay. Contemporary fabrics are the specialty.

Victorian mansion, the bottom floor is chock-full of personal growth and self-transformation books. Upstairs, there is a meditation room along with some used books. You can schedule a tarot reading or an "intuitive" counseling session, listen to some New Age music, or browse the abundant supply of drums, incense, herbs, and crystals.

PERIODICALS PARADISE
3366 SE Powell
236-8370 **SE**
If you're looking for an old issue of a certain magazine, chances are you'll find it among the half-million used periodicals on sale here. Once you see the daunting variety of publications here, you'll believe that number.

POWELL'S CITY OF BOOKS
1005 W. Burnside St.
228-4651 **DT**
Powell's Books is the granddaddy of 'em all. With more than a million books filling a building that consumes an entire city block, it's hard, if not impossible, not to find what you're looking for. You'll want to get a map at the entrance to find your way through the maze. There's a rare book room tucked back in the corner in the Anne Hughes Coffee Room, which is a great place to review your purchases while you sip a cappuccino. Powell's staff is reliable and helpful. Author readings are popular here, too. Just ask at the information counter for a schedule. Hours: Mon–Sat 9–11, Sun 9–9.

Powell's Technical Books is around the corner. Here you'll find every book you need on computers and engineering.

POWELL'S BOOKS FOR COOKS
3747 SE Hawthorne Blvd.
235-3802 **SE**
If you like to cook, you'll drool over the huge selection of cookbooks from all over the world at this bookstore. The staff is knowledgeable and eager to help. Conveniently located next door is a gourmet food shop carrying all the ingredients you'll need to whip up those exotic dishes from Russia, Indonesia, or Africa.

TITLE WAVE BOOKSTORE
216 NE Knott St.
248-5021 **NE**
The Multnomah County Library "recycles" its books here. Title Wave has a huge selection of used books at incredibly low prices. And there are plenty of magazines, too. Sometimes, when the library gets too many copies of a particular title, you can scoop up a hot new release at a bargain-basement price.

DEPARTMENT STORES

MEIER AND FRANK
621 SW 5th Ave.
223-0512 **DT**
Oregon's oldest and largest department store and one of Portland's locally owned hallmarks, Meier and Frank began operating in 1898. Similar to "Nordie's" in apparel carried, it offers a wide selection of home goods, too.

NORDSTROM
701 SW Broadway
224-6666 **DT**
The cornerstone of Portland's downtown shopping is the Nordstrom store, which takes up a whole city block. If you are not familiar with Nordstrom, take some time to

browse through this elegant clothing store. Known for its high-quality customer service, Nordstrom can be spendy, but satisfaction is guaranteed. Nordie's is also know for its wide selection of shoes in all sizes. They even carry women's size 11, which, if you've got big feet, is nirvana in a shoebox.

PORTLAND AREA MALLS

CLACKAMAS TOWN CENTER
12000 SE 82nd Ave.
653-6913 **SE**
Usually full of kids hanging out, but if big-time mall shopping is your bag, this is it. Approximately 200 shops.

THE GALLERIA
921 SW Morrison
228-2748 **DT**
The Galleria is a registered National Historic Landmark in the heart of downtown that houses "Northwest flavor" shops. The building was originally the site of the first department store west of the Mississippi, Olds, Wortman & King. It was one of the first of Portland's historic buildings to undergo renovation in the Seventies. Today, the three-story building contains a variety of restaurants and eclectic shops including Made in Oregon, Jantzen, Jay Jacobs, and Marios. The 75-foot atrium makes it airy, light, and comfortable for lunch, shopping, or people-watching. Currently undergoing renovation.

LLOYD CENTER MALL
9th and Halsey
282-2511 **NE**
This is probably Portland's best-known shopping center and recently most notable as the place

where Tonya Harding practiced her ice moves. But you won't find Tonya here anymore, much to the delight of most locals. It's recently been remodeled but still maintains some of its Sixties look. There are 175 retail shops (including Nordstrom and Marshall's) on three levels.

MALL 205
9900 SE Washington
255-5805 **SE**
It's way out there in Clackamas County, just off of I-205. This is a non-descript place, but if you're in the area, it's worth stopping to check out some of the 80 stores here.

PIONEER PLACE
700 SW 5th Ave.
228-5800 **DT**
Pioneer Place is a shopping extravaganza, containing almost 80 stores on four floors. The Northwest's only Saks Fifth Avenue is part of this mall. Among other fine stores at Pioneer Place, you'll find Ann Taylor, Crabtree & Evelyn, Banana Republic, Eddie Bauer, Williams-Sonoma, Pottery Barn, The Gap, Coach Leather, Nine West, Talbot's, the Sharper Image, the Nature Company, and Structure. Parking is available in the garage or in the lot on SW 4th just across the street. Pioneer Place is also near a MAX stop, so getting there is convenient.

WASHINGTON SQUARE
Exit Greenburg Road off Hwy. 217
639-8860 **SW**
Five department stores and about 120 retail specialty stores are housed in Washington Square. Expect lots of traffic. Unless you're going to be in the Beaverton area anyway, there's not much reason to go out of your way to shop here.

FACTORY OUTLETS

COLUMBIA GORGE FACTORY STORES
450 NW 257th (off Highway 84)
Troutdale
669-8060

Drive about 20 minutes to the eastern suburb of Troutdale, and you'll find yourself in outlet shopping heaven. Discounted merchandise from Adidas, Bass, Geoffrey Beene, Izod, Norm Thompson, Hanes, Levi's, and Van Heusen is available here. Other vendors in this concrete "no-frills" setting include children's, leather goods, and home furnishings outlets. There are lots of fast-food restaurants, too.

H.K. LIMITED
1827 NW 15th Ave.
223-3131   **NW**

This outlet store has the sleek line of Danish furniture and knotty pine pieces that H.K. is noted for. Pieces and selections change, and most (which can be slightly damaged or discontinued) are sold at 25 to 30 percent less than retail.

11

SPORTS AND RECREATION

Sporting enthusiasts will find ample opportunity to find their niche in the Portland sporting scene. Whether you are a participant or an observer, there's no shortage of things to do and see. From a simple walk in the park to windsurfing in the Gorge, there's plenty to do within the city limits and just beyond. Since Portland is a wet town, water sports are especially popular.

RECREATIONAL ACTIVITIES

Bicycling

Cyclists enjoy a friendly environment in Portland. You can even combine a commute by bus or MAX with biking. Portland is the first city in the United States to provide bike racks on buses. The City of Portland, Bureau of Traffic Management, has a bicycle program that includes bike parking, rental lockers, and events such as BikeFest and Bicycle Commute Day. To learn about bikes on buses, call the hotline at 239-3044. Before putting your bike on a bus, you must purchase a permit for $5 from Tri-Met (a short training session is required,

too). You are responsible for loading, securing, and removing your own bike from the rack.

Bikes are not allowed on MAX during Rose Festival from 3 p.m. to end of service on the day of the fireworks display, on the Starlight Parade Day, or on the Grand Floral Parade Day. They are also prohibited during snowy weather or icy conditions for safety reasons.

Cyclists are required to ride "as close as practical to the right curb of the roadway," except when:
• Traveling at normal speed of traffic
• Avoiding hazardous conditions
• Traveling on a too-narrow roadway

A Multnomah County bike map and brochure is free through Multnomah County, 248-5050. For information on bicycling in Portland, call 823-7082 or 823-7083.

• Preparing to make a left turn

All cyclists under 16 are required by law to wear a bicycle helmet on public property. Failure to do so may result in a fine. Cyclists are not allowed to ride on sidewalks in the downtown area.

For maps and information, call or write the following:

BIKES ON TRI-MET
4012 SE 17th Ave.   **SE**

CITY OF PORTLAND BICYCLE PROGRAM
1120 SW 5th Ave., Room 730
823-7082   **DT**

TRI-MET PIONEER SQUARE 701
SW 6th Ave.
239-3044   **DT**

Bowling

GRAND CENTRAL BOWLING
808 SE Morrison St.
232-5166   **SE**
Just across the Morrison Bridge is Portland's only 24-hour bowling alley. Twenty-eight lanes, pool tables, video games, and a 24-hour restaurant make it a popular spot for late night activities. Microbrews are served in the pub. Day prices are $1.95 per game, 95¢ for kids; night prices are $2.75 per game.

HOLLYWOOD BOWL
4030 NE Halsey
288-9237   **NE**
Hollywood Bowl has been around since the Sixties and still maintains that rockin' flavor. On Saturdays, you can enjoy Rock & Bowl from 10 p.m. to 2 a.m. for $1.50 per game. They turn off all the approach lights, turn the music way up, and let you go at it. Also, Saturdays at 7 p.m. feature Monte Carlo Night, where you bowl with colored pins for money. Cost is $12 per person.

Fishing

It may surprise you to learn that there is world-class walleye fishing near Portland. Fishing on the Columbia and Willamette Rivers is a popular pastime, and often the rewards are plentiful. A 5-pound walleye is standard, and there have been many 10-pounders caught just 20 minutes from the city.

Sauvie Island, at the junction of the Willamette and Columbia Rivers, is a popular spot to fish. Fishing from slough and pond banks can yield catfish, perch, and crappie. You must

TRIVIA

Terwilliger Boulevard is perhaps the most scenic urban on-street bikeway in the country. Four continuous miles of bike lanes through the hills of southwest Portland connect downtown to the Tryon Creek Trail and Lake Oswego.

Bicycling outside the city

purchase and display an annual or daily parking permit while on the island. For information on fishing or to obtain a permit, contact the Oregon Department of Fish and Wildlife, 2501 SW 1st Avenue, Portland, OR 97207; 229-5403. (503) 872 5268

Fitness Clubs

Both of the following fitness clubs offer passes by the day or week.

GOLD'S GYM
1210 NW Johnson
222-1210 DT
Day pass $10, weekly pass $25. Open Mon–Fri 5 a.m. to midnight, Sat–Sun 7 a.m. to 8 p.m.

NAUTILUS
110 SW Yamhill
222-3030 DT
Day pass $10, weekly pass $20. Open Mon–Fri 5 a.m. to 9 p.m., Sat–Sun 8–5.

Golf

Golf has a long history in Portland.

Among the most famous of Portland's courses is Eastmoreland Municipal Golf Course. This course, opened in 1918, is Portland's oldest and one of its most beautiful. Its gently rolling hills and steep slopes are kept in immaculate shape all year long. *Golf Digest* has ranked Eastmoreland among the top 25 public courses in the United States.

Architect Robert Trent Jones Jr. used an impressive combination of water, sand, and natural obstructions when he designed the city-owned Heron Lakes Golf Course. These three nines are hazardous and not for the faint at heart. The first 18 holes alone claim 86 sand bunkers and six ponds.

EASTMORELAND GOLF COURSE
2425 SE Bybee Blvd.
775-2900 SE
Dawn to dusk year-round.

HERON LAKES GOLF COURSE
3500 N. Victory Blvd.
289-1818 NW
Dawn to dusk year-round.

Ice Skating

Tonya Harding notwithstanding, there is ample opportunity for ice skating in Portland. The following places are popular. Call ahead for information about hours.

DOROTHY HAMILL SKATING CENTER
Clackamas Town Center
12000 SE 82nd Ave.
786-6000   **SE**
Lessons and ice games are available on this 185' x 85' rink. Admission: $5.50 includes two skate rentals. Call ahead for times. Closed mornings; afternoon hours vary.

LLOYD CENTER ICE CHALET
953 Lloyd Center
288-6073   **NE**
Lessons are available on this 175' x 75' rink. Morning and evening hours vary, but the rink is always open afternoons. Admission: $5 adult, $4 youth; $2 skate rental.

Kayaks and Canoes

During the summer months, the Willamette River is home to kayaks and canoes as well as fishing boats and racing sculls. Whether you're a beginner or a seasoned professional, you can rent a kayak for an hour or a day, take a kayaking lesson on the water, or canoe your way over to Ross Island, a blue heron refuge in the middle of the Willamette on Portland's south end, near the Ross Island Bridge. Water-skiing is also popular on the Willamette, equally enjoyable from the banks of the river or the back of a boat. During Rose Festival, you will see colorful Chinese dragon boats racing on the river, too. In every season, the Willamette River provides a backdrop to all kinds of sports. You can rent kayaks and take lessons from the experts at:

EBB & FLOW PADDLESPORTS
604 SW Nebraska
245-1756   **SW**

River kayaking

Roller Skating

OAKS AMUSEMENT PARK
East end of Sellwood Bridge
236-5722 **SE**

Oaks Park boasts one of the oldest continually operating roller rinks in the U.S. and the only one with live Wurlitzer organ music. Built in 1905, the rink has a unique wave motion at the end of the floor. Skaters come from around the world because of the floor, the music, and the rink's history. The rink is open year-round and is especially popular for parties. Rates vary according to season and time. Call ahead for information.

Skiing

Groomed cross-country trails and spectacular downhill ski areas are within a little over an hour's drive west of Portland. Mt. Hood Meadows, Ski Bowl, and Timberline are all part of the world-famous skiing to be found on Mt. Hood. Open year-round. Mt. Hood is the summer home of the U.S. Olympic Ski Team.

MT. HOOD MEADOWS
Highway 35
Mt. Hood, OR 97041
337-2222

Recreational slopes for all levels, open 9 a.m. to 4 p.m. and some evenings.

MOUNT HOOD SKI BOWL
87000 E. Highway 26
Government Camp, OR 97028
222-2695

America's largest night ski area, open most days until 11 p.m.

TIMBERLINE SKI AREA
Timberline Lodge, OR 97028
231-7979

Cross-country skiing

Bend Chamber of Commerce

Summertime ski season hours are 7 a.m. to 1:30 p.m.

Swimming

The City of Portland Parks and Recreation Department offers swimming at several parks in Portland. The local Y offers a variety of swimming programs, too.

BUCKMAN POOL
320 SE 16th
823-3668 **SE**

DISHMAN COMMUNITY CENTER & POOL
77 NE Knott St.
823-3673 **NE**

METROPOLITAN LEARNING CENTER
2033 NW Glisan St.
823-3671 **DT**

YWCA FITNESS & SWIM CENTER
1111 SW 10th Ave. **DT**

Open swim in the mornings and after-

TIP

If you see a brightly painted yellow bike anywhere in Portland, you can safely assume it's a community bike. That's right, a bike for you to use! Just hop on it and leave it at your destination for the next rider to use.

noons (times vary day by day); women-only hours every afternoon and evening. Admission: $5 for non-members. Pool is 25 yards long.

Walking and Hiking

Portland is known as one of the most pedestrian-friendly cities in the United States. Cars actually stop for walkers and runners here. Pedestrian right-of-way is taken seriously on the city streets and country back roads. You can find wilderness trails in the city, paved jogging paths along the river, and historic walks through downtown. At any time of the day, you'll be in the company of many other walkers, hikers, and runners who find Portland's mild climate and groomed paths to be enticing partners in their daily exercise rituals. You might also choose to take part in a walking tour of Portland's bridges, where you will learn about the city's history and its built environment while enjoying fresh air and exercise.

Maps of walking trails and city sites are available by contacting Portland Parks and Recreation, 1120 SW 5th Avenue, Portland, OR 97204, 823-2223.

The Portland metro area is filled with parks, gardens, and hiking trails. Some are easy strolls, others are arduous adventures. For general information, call METRO at 22-GREEN. The Portland Parks bureau also provides maps outlining park trails. U.S. Forest Service Maps are available at 333 SW 1st Avenue or by calling 326-2877.

CHINOOK WINDS LLAMA TREKS
658-6600

Enjoy an interesting day "Lunching with a Llama" in the Mt. Hood Wilderness. Along with bountiful natural settings, you are treated to a gourmet lunch. Cost varies.

SPECTATOR SPORTS

Auto Racing

PORTLAND INTERNATIONAL RACEWAY
West Delta Park
1940 N. Victory Blvd.
285-6635   **NW**

This raceway is built on the site of the former WWII city of Vanport, which was destroyed by a flood in 1948. The first drag races were held at PIR in 1965. There is a professional driving school on site. Events vary, as do hours and admissions, so it's best to call ahead.

PORTLAND SPEEDWAY AUTO RACING
9727 N. MLK Jr. Blvd.
285-2883   **NW**

The speedway, one of the oldest continuously operated racetracks in the nation, is the oldest in Oregon. Six different racing divisions, including

Portland Rockies Baseball

NASCAR and stock-car racing, are featured here. Admission varies; call ahead for information.

Greyhound Racing

MULTNOMAH KENNEL CLUB
944 NE 223rd
Wood Village, OR 97060
667-7700   **NE**
Greyhounds chase a little mechanical rabbit around a 770-yard track. Races are held May through September, Wednesday through Saturday, with matinees on Sunday afternoon. Children under 12 not allowed during evening races. Admission: $1.50.

Horse Racing

PORTLAND MEADOWS
1001 N. Schmeer Rd.
285-9144   **NW**
Horse racing enjoys a long history in Portland. Records of racehorse breeding in Oregon stem back to the late 1800s. Portland Meadows opened for its first night of racing in

September 1946, with a crowd of 10,000, who wagered a whopping $140,000 in eight races. Today, races are run every Friday, Saturday, and Sunday.

PROFESSIONAL SPORTS

Baseball

PORTLAND ROCKIES
Civic Stadium
1844 SW Morrison St.
223-2837   **SW**
Baseball has a long history in Portland. Portland's early baseball teams spent the first half of the century playing in the historic Vaughn Street stadium. A bleacher seat cost 25¢ and a covered grandstand seat, 50¢. In 1901 Portland won a pennant in its first professional season. In 1904 Walter McCredie, a former Brooklyn Dodger, took over as player-manager, and his father, Judge W. W. McCredie, became owner and team president. Together, the

McCredies took the team to a PCL flag in 1906, 1910, 1911, 1913, and 1914. Although there have been periods of no baseball and long losing streaks, the Portland Rockies now enjoy big crowds, avid fans, and a good playing record. The games are held in the Civic Stadium. Call ahead for schedules.

Basketball

PORTLAND TRAILBLAZERS
Rose Garden
1 Center Court
TicketMaster, 224-4400   **NE**
The Portland Trailblazers fill up the new Rose Garden on a regular basis. They have an ardent local following, but if you call ahead, you should be able to get tickets. (For details on the Rose Garden, see Chapter 12, "Performing Arts.")

Hockey

PORTLAND RAGE ROLLER HOCKEY
Memorial Coliseum
1 Center Court
236-7243   **NE**

In addition to watching the roller hockey interleague tournaments and games, you can take lessons and enroll in special clinics. Rage Roller Hockey prides itself on providing family-oriented entertainment.

WINTER HAWKS
Western Hockey League
Memorial Coliseum
1 Center Court
238-6366   **NE**
The Portland Winter Hawks are fast becoming one of the city's favorite teams. Fast-paced and thrilling, ice hockey is a great source of family entertainment.

Soccer

PORTLAND PRIDE INDOOR SOCCER
Memorial Coliseum
1 Center Court
244-2378   **NE**
It's professional soccer during the summer months at Memorial Coliseum. Kids love to attend. The music is loud, the fans are excitable, and the tickets are affordable.

Bruce Forster

12

PERFORMING ARTS

Performing art seems to happen naturally in Portland. From street musicians and jugglers to symphony and opera, you'll easily be entertained when visiting the city.

Portland has a reputation for supporting its artists in a way uncommon to other cities of its size. Broadway shows sell out, concerts in the parks abound, and crowds gather at Saturday Market to watch Peruvian musicians and French mimes entertain for tips.

Whether your taste runs toward an extravagant production, such as that offered by the Portland Opera and the Oregon Ballet, or to an intimate black box theater with seating for 20, you'll find it in Portland.

PERFORMING ARTS VENUES

MEMORIAL COLISEUM
1 Center Court
797-9617   NE
The older brother of the Rose Garden was opened in November 1960. It's a smaller version of the Rose Garden and hosts various events. You can't miss it. It's the smaller "big" building in the complex, and you can't mistake its Sixties look. Acoustics for concerts are not the best at Memorial Coliseum, but it's an OK venue for trade shows and

smaller events. Basketball seating capacity is roughly half of the Rose Quarter's, and parking is the same nightmare as at the Rose Garden. Take the bus or MAX.

OREGON CONVENTION CENTER
777 NE MLK Jr. Blvd.
235-7575   NE
On the east bank of the Willamette River, just over Steel Bridge, the teal-colored twin glass spires of the Oregon Convention Center soar 250 feet above the surrounding buildings, drawing dancing light downward into

this unusually elegant complex. Whether artificially illuminated at night or filled with natural daylight, these glass pyramidal skylights are visible from all over the Rose City.

The intriguing artwork displayed throughout the Convention Center, which opened in 1990, reflects regional tastes with international accents. A 40-foot-long red and blue Chinese dragon boat hangs in suspended animation in the south tower, seemingly waiting for the race to begin. A 750-pound hollow brass pendulum swings high above the north tower floor; it hangs from a nearly invisible wire and changes its circular slow-motion sway according to the Earth's rotation. An eclectic collection of sculpture, painting, woodwork, and decorative art weaves its way throughout one of Portland's primary symbols of civic pride.

PORTLAND CENTER FOR THE PERFORMING ARTS
SW Broadway and Main
248-4335   **DT**

The Portland Center for the Performing Arts (PCPA) is housed in three separate buildings that accommodate four different theaters. The facilities include the Portland Civic Auditorium, the Arlene Schnitzer Concert Hall, and the New Theatre Building. The PCPA's theaters bustle with activity all year long, and, for its diverse range of performance art possibilities, Portland has become something of a mecca. Whether it's drama, Broadway shows, opera, science and technology lectures, classical concerts, pop or rock music, or puppetry, more than a million patrons attend some 900 entertainment events each year.

The box office, open Monday through Saturday 10 a.m. to 5 p.m., sells tickets to all four theaters, the Civic Stadium, and most Coliseum events as well. Tickets can also be obtained from TicketMaster and Fastixx (numbers below).

New Theatre Building

The New Theatre Building has won several design-excellence awards and is known as a state-of-the-art facility. The building houses the Intermediate and Dolores Winningstad Theatres, each with its own distinct personality. Also within the New Theatre Building is Jake's Backstage, where you can enjoy a preconcert drink or dinner, or stop by after the show for espresso or dessert.

The New Theatre's Winningstad Theatre is modeled after the theaters of Elizabethan England. The interior of the "Winnie" is finished in warm red tones and is never completely

Portland Center for the Performing Arts

darkened, so the audience enjoys a communal theater experience similar to that common in Shakespeare's day. Resident companies are Tygres Heart Shakespeare Company and the Tears of Joy Puppet Theatre.

The Intermediate Theatre is the biggest of the two theaters in the New Theatre Building. It's a luxurious and intimate place, with plush velour seats and balconies that curve close to the stage in a horseshoe pattern. Warm, rich cherry wood is featured throughout this Edwardian-style theater. The domed ceiling, studded with brass stars and planets, recalls the outdoor feeling of true Edwardian theater. Resident companies include Portland Center Stage and the Musical Company.

T i P Several Portland cinemas present performance art as well as film. For a listing of these, see Chapter 13, "Nightlife."

The New Theatre Building and the Arlene Schnitzer Concert Hall are adjoined by the Main Street Mall, a plaza of checkerboard bricks, which makes walking from theater to theater a snap. During performances, the mall is closed to car traffic. Look for visual art on Main Street, too, where three of Portland's finest artists—Walton Fosque, Kim Hoffman, and Angelita Surman—donated their time and talent to produce three colorful paintings that tell a story in symbols of dance, theater, and music. Three other paintings, on Salmon Street, are more abstract expressions of the artists' views of music, theater, and dance.

Portland Civic Auditorium

Built in 1917, the Portland Civic Auditorium was originally known as Municipal Auditorium. The building was completely renovated in 1968. The hall is known for its excellent acoustics and its technically sophisticated stage area. Ballet, opera, and national touring shows, including

The Schnitz

Vaudeville chorus girls performing at the theater now known as "the Schnitz" stayed at the Heathman Hotel next door and used the alley between the two buildings to enter the theater. Legend has it, however, that in the interest of saving time, the dancers stretched ladders from the hotel windows to the theater dressing room, giving them a quick, but rather perilous, shortcut.

Surprise, the marble statue of the nude goddess of music found in the Arlene Schnitzer Concert Hall, originally stood in a fountain. In July 1928, when the movie The Wheel of Chance was playing at the Paramount, a bit player, Robert Nolan, came to see himself on film. After the movie, Nolan stole the day's receipts and, while attempting to flee, was caught in a gun battle. Two of Surprise's fingers were shot off during the ruckus. Nolan got away to spend his money on a drinking spree, and Surprise's fingers are still missing.

The Arlene Schnitzer Concert Hall is equipped with an infrared listening system for the benefit of hearing-impaired patrons. With the aid of a wireless headset, they can enjoy performances from any seat in the house.

When the theater opened in 1928, it claimed to have the longest projection throw north of Los Angeles, 154 feet to the stage.

The star dressing rooms and the dressing room of conductor James DePreist of the Oregon Symphony are said to be top-of-the-line in furnishings and decor. The first people to use the renovated dressing rooms were Steve Lawrence and Eydie Gorme, on opening night in 1984. Since then Mikhail Baryshnikov, Harry Belafonte, Madonna, and Yo Yo Ma have used the rooms.

In 1988 the world's largest electronic organ, according to the Guinness Book of World Records, was installed in the Schnitzer Hall. Originally built for New York's Carnegie Hall by the Rodgers Organ Company of Oregon in the Seventies, the organ was put in storage in New York after the Carnegie Hall renovation left no space for such a huge instrument. It took two trucks to bring the organ back home to Oregon and two weeks to install.

Broadway productions, are at home in the Civic Auditorium. The resident companies in this hall include Portland Opera Association, Oregon Ballet Theater, Oregon Children's Theater Company, and Portland Community Concert Association. Bonnie Raitt and the Doobie Brothers feel equally as comfortable here as Broadway shows like *Cats* and *Phantom of the Opera.*

Schnitzer Concert Hall

Schnitzer Hall, once called the Paramount Theatre, was built in 1928. It's noted for its Italian Rococo Revival architecture and was completely restored in 1984. You'll recognize it on Broadway by the 65-foot-tall "Portland" sign with 6,000 flashing lights. Its chandeliers, artwork, spiral staircases, ornate plasterwork, and heavy velvet drapes give this concert hall a truly Old World feel. And, what's more, there's not a bad seat in the house, although seating on the orchestra level is preferable. The hall seats nearly 2,800 people and is home to the Oregon Symphony.

ROSE QUARTER
1 Center Court
235-8771
231-3211 events hotline   NE
The Rose Quarter is the newest addition to the entertainment venues in the City of Roses. More than just an arena, the Rose Quarter is a sports and entertainment complex encompassing more than 37 acres. Included in the Rose Quarter are the Rose Garden, Memorial Coliseum, the Commons at Rose Quarter (an outdoor area for food festivals and concerts), One Center Court (restaurants, box office), Post Up Productions (pre- and post-production video and audio studios), and the Rose Quarter Transit Mall.

Located on the Eastside near Martin Luther King Boulevard, you can't miss the huge arena called the Rose Garden, which opened in the fall of 1995. Equipped with state-of-the-art technologies, the Rose Garden is free of that big hollow echo so common in the traditional arena. Its gargantuan scale makes it hard to believe, but it's actually kind of cozy in here—except in the "nosebleed

Artists Repertory Theatre's 1998 production of Jean Cocteau's Indiscretions, *p.167*

© Owen Carey/Artists Repertory Theatre

TRIVIA

section." Those seats are way up there. The consolation is that they go for only $5 at a Blazers game. Prices are otherwise pretty stiff for these games, but you can get a good seat for about $40.

Even the concession menus here are high-tech: the "boards" are colorful video monitors. Gourmet food is available as well as the standard hot-dog fare. All 32 public restrooms have piped-in radio for play-by-play updates. A system of panels on the ceiling, called an "acoustic cloud," can be adjusted to provide the best sound for specific events and concerts. There's even an in-house video-production center here. The Rose Garden is the only arena with a television studio built into it. There are more than 700 televisions in the Rose Garden's concourses, restaurants, clubs, suites, and back-of-house areas.

The Rose Garden hosts a variety of events and is home to the Portland Trailblazers. Total capacity for NBA basketball is 21,300. Other events hosted here include college basketball, professional hockey, in-door soccer, indoor track and field, gymnastics, major concerts, monster truck rallies, rodeo and bull riding, circuses, ice shows, boxing, professional wrestling, and convention and trade shows. In short, if it's big, it's in the Rose Garden.

Parking: Although there is ample parking for most events, it's much easier to ride MAX. The space for parking isn't a problem, but the traffic in and out is. It's a slow-motion nightmare, especially if you don't know your way around. Riding MAX is quick and relatively worry-free. The Rose Quarter Transit Center is located on Multnomah Street near the Garden's front doors and is served by Tri-Met buses and MAX.

Bikes and walking: The Rose Quarter is pedestrian- and bicycle-friendly. Twelve-foot sidewalks and 5-foot dedicated bike lanes on major streets, along with improved access on and off the Steel and Broadway Bridges, make for easy foot and bike traffic. There are more than 155 bike parking spaces in the parking garages and on the Commons.

You can access the ever-changing calendar of events (including free events such as the Brown Bag Lunch Series) through the Friends of the Performing Arts Center. Call the Friends at 248-4335 or visit their site on the Internet at http://www.eek.com/friends.

Artists Repertory Theatre (A.R.T.)

Joe Cronin, a recognized Portland stage, television, and movie actor, helped establish Artists Repertory Theatre in 1982. Artists Rep, or A.R.T., as it is affectionately known, recently celebrated its 15th anniversary and has moved to a new and wonderful space. If you love strong performances and innovative direction, A.R.T. is the theater to attend. It focuses on premiere productions as well as recognized works by such playwrights as Edward Albee. Cronin offers the following perspective:

"In this time of vacillating support for theater, Artists Rep has kept not only its financial feet but its artistic vision as well. Live theater in Portland has had a bumpy history over the past 25 years. Small and vibrant groups have sprung up regularly and have died just as regularly. Artists Rep, which was founded as a cooperative in 1982 by a group of seven Portland actors, has grown steadily, from its first production in the Wilson Center at the YWCA to the opening of its grand new space at 1516 SW Alder in 1997.

"The actors and crew who put together the first show—Butley, by Simon Grey—worked for love and $35 for the entire 20-performance run. Today, A.R.T. is operating under a small professional theater contract with Actors Equity Association and regularly mounts performances with budgets in the five figures.

"From the beginning, A.R.T. found its niche in the community by presenting intimate theater, focusing on contemporary playwrights and powerful issues, while emphasizing the relationship between the actors and the audience. A.R.T.'s new theater is a comfortable combination of black box intimacy and the open flexibility of a modern arena stage. Its acoustic ambiance has been well engineered to give the audience an easy time. The back rows are close to the action, ensuring that all who attend will catch even the most subtle dramatic moment. Artists Repertory Theatre is one of the longest surviving of Portland's small theaters and promises to hold true to its vision into the twenty-first century."

Oregon Ballet Theatre

CLASSICAL MUSIC AND OPERA

OREGON SYMPHONY ORCHESTRA
Arlene Schnitzer Concert Hall
SW Broadway and Main
228-1353   **DT**
The OSO gives 130 concerts per season (classical, pops, Symphony Sunday, kids' concerts, special events).

PORTLAND OPERA ASSOCIATION
Civic Auditorium
SW 3rd and Clay
241-1802   **DT**
The Portland Opera Association produces five operas annually and gives four performances of each.

DANCE

OREGON BALLET THEATRE
Civic Auditorium
SW 3rd and Clay
222-5538   **DT**
Oregon Ballet Theatre stages four productions each year and gives four to six performances of each. They present 28 performances of the *Nutcracker.* The ballet's spring recital is held at the Intermediate Theatre.

THEATER

ARTISTS REPERTORY THEATRE
1516 SW Alder
241-1278   **SW**
Located just two minutes from downtown, Artists Repertory Theatre is one of Portland's favorite intimate theaters. Productions range from recognized national works to premiere productions by emerging playwrights. A.R.T. offers matinees as well as evening performances. Call ahead for tickets.

MUSICAL THEATRE COMPANY
East Side Performance Center
SE 14th Ave. off Stark
224-5411   **SE**
This company stages three productions during its June through October season.

OREGON CHILDREN'S THEATRE COMPANY
Civic Auditorium
SW 3rd and Clay
228-9571   **DT**
Two school/public productions are offered each season. See Chapter 7, "Kids' Stuff," for more information.

PORTLAND CENTER STAGE
Intermediate Theatre
SW Broadway and Main
274-6588   **DT**
Thirty performances of five different productions are staged during the October through April season.

PORTLAND'S BROADWAY THEATRE SERIES
Civic Auditorium
SW 3rd and Clay
241-1802   **DT**
Four national touring Broadway productions are presented per season; eight performances each.

PORTLAND YOUTH PHILHARMONIC
Arlene Schnitzer Concert Hall
SW Broadway and Main
Fastixx, 224-8499   **DT**
In addition to school performances, the Portland Youth Philharmonic presents four public performances each year.

TEARS OF JOY THEATRE
Winningstad Theatre
SW Broadway and Main
248-0557   **DT**

Tears of Joy presents three productions, plus school performances, each year. See Chapter 7, "Kids' Stuff," for more information.

TYGRES HEART SHAKESPEARE COMPANY
Winningstad Theatre
SW Broadway and Main
222-9220   **DT**
During the company's October through May season, three productions, with 25 to 30 performances each, are staged.

WEST ONE BANK BROADWAY SERIES
Civic Auditorium
SW 3rd and Clay
TicketMaster, 224-4400   **DT**
The series offers five national touring shows per season; eight performances each.

MORE PERFORMANCE ART

A more diverse, eclectic array of venues and artists thrives on the Eastside. The art and entertainment here tends to be an interpretation from one particular artist's view. The individual expressions found on the Eastside are, in the words of Susan Banyas of Dreams Well Studio, "like personal pieces of the big puzzle we call 'performance art.'"

In the category of performance art, you will find conceptual art and

---

For tickets, call either Fastixx, 224-8499, or TicketMaster, 224-4400.

PICA:
Portland Institute for Contemporary Art

If you want to learn something about the state of contemporary art, PICA, 720 SW Washington #745, 242-1419, is the place for you. Formed in the fall of 1995, PICA is the brainchild of excurator of Art on the Edge at the Portland Art Museum, Kristy Edmunds. Edmunds' belief in progressive art and her strong relationship with Portland's supportive audiences have proven to be a winning combination. PICA's season includes dance, theater, music, and some types of performance that defy definition. Drag queen troupes, operatic tenors, freestyle jazz musicians, and stand-up comedians, among other experimental artists, all play an important role in what Edmunds calls "a very ambitious program." PICA's programs focus on current trends in contemporary art with an emphasis on the open-ended.

You never know quite what they're up to at PICA, but it's always good, surprising, and worth seeing. Give them a call, and they'll give you an update on current exhibitions, residencies, and educational forums. And don't hesitate to ask questions if you don't quite "get it." "Contemporary art" can be a confusing term; that's why part of Edmunds' mission is to offer arts education for the public.

dance, spoken word, visual theater, and cultural celebrations. Dramas, musicals, and film are as much a part of this scene as are concerts, street performances, and vaudeville performances.

There's no central ticketing office, and the scene changes, so call the venues to find out what's happening. Some of the interesting art houses and production companies include the following:

CAFE LENA
2239 SE Hawthorne Blvd.
238-7087 **SE**

Started by poets, for poets, this little corner cafe is a popular spot for locals. Dedicated to freedom of expression, Cafe Lena prides itself on providing good food and open-mic poetry jams on Tuesdays and music throughout the week.

DREAMS WELL STUDIO
2857 SE Stark
231-1108 **SE**

The owners call it a "laboratory for experimentation." The storefront studio is wide-open and warm. Here you can see dance, performance art, music, and theater based on the philosophy that performance can be powerful and transforming when it is intimate and direct.

ECHO THEATRE
1515 SE 37th Ave.
231-1232 SE
Echo Theatre houses Do Jump Movement Theatre and hosts a variety of performances. Dance acrobatics, trapeze, and mime all find their way to the stage here. You can see a range of musicians, dancers, and comedians, both local and national at Echo. Howie Baggadonutz Presents, a production company, sometimes presents shows here, too.

IMAGO
17 SE 8th Ave.
231-3959 SE
This theater company has an international following. After touring different corners of the world, Imago comes home to Portland, where their innovative experimental theater works appeal to all ages and all kinds of audiences. Known for physical im-possibilities and visual illusion, Imago's productions are truly a joy to watch.

INTERSTATE FIREHOUSE CULTURAL CENTER (IFCC)
5340 N. Interstate Ave.
823-2000 NW
The IFCC is a community-based center that houses a gallery and a theatrical company, the Oregon Stage Company. Emphasis is on ethnic and cultural art. IFCC gets its name from the old firehouse it calls home.

LA LUNA
215 SE 9th Ave.
235-9696 SE
La Luna could be considered an

For more information on performance art in and around Portland, contact the Portland International Performance Festival at 725-5389.

"alternative center" for the Southeast area. It's a live music venue that also sponsors spoken word presentations on occasion. You can sip a micro, listen to some great music, play a game of pool, and even order a burrito, all in the same building.

MIRACLE THEATRE GROUP
525 SE Stark
236-7253 SE
The Miracle Theatre group is the largest Northwest Hispanic arts and culture organization. Visual and performing arts by Latinos and other people of color are offered here.

OREGON STAGE COMPANY
5340 N. Interstate Ave.
289-5450 NW
Traditional and contemporary dramas, comedies, and light musicals of special interest to the multicultural community.

PAULA PRODUCTIONS/ STAGE 4 THEATRE
527 SE Pine
238-9692 SE
Cabaret seating for 30 and a black box area for 49 people. It's small, intimate, and not necessarily for the "commercial" set. Performances are affordable, sometimes morose, and always challenging.

PORTLAND INTERNATIONAL PERFORMANCE FESTIVAL
School of Extended Studies at Portland State University
724 SW Harrison
725-5389 **DT**

For a good idea of what's hot throughout the metro area in the summer months, you can call the Portland International Performance Festival, which presents innovative and provocative international and intercultural performances in theater, performance art, and puppetry.

STARK RAVING THEATER
Theater! Theatre! Building
3430 SE Belmont
232-7072 **SE**

This is an 80-seat thrust-stage theater. Here you'll see revisionings of dramatic classics as well as new works by a range of actors, writers, and directors.

Tri-Met

13

NIGHTLIFE

Nightlife in Portland is diverse, to say the least. Depending on your taste, you can enjoy late-night poetry in a coffeehouse; quiet cocktails, romantic jazz, and stunning vistas from atop the US Bancorp Building; wild samba dancing at a Latin club; country swing at a truck stop; or a Guinness accompanied by some Celtic sounds at a neighborhood restaurant.

Portland is nationally recognized as a hub of good music. The city also lays claim to some of the country's most interesting vintage movie theaters, where folks can enjoy a micro (a locally brewed beer) with a movie.

Don't expect nightlife in Portland to be organized at all times. If you walk along the Willamette River at night, you'll often hear music in the park. Sometimes you can hear a melody wafting across the water from a slow-moving sternwheeler.

It's not hard to find entertainment at night in Portland. Just look around the next corner, and you'll probably find what you're looking for.

DANCE CLUBS

ANDREA'S CHA CHA CLUB
832 SE Grand Ave.
230-1166   **SE**
Underneath the Grand Cafe on (where else?) Grand Avenue you can dance to recorded salsa music Wednesday through Saturday nights. If you don't know the steps, it's OK. The DJs are also instructors and will

frequently walk people (even those without partners) through the basic steps. It's great fun and can get pretty rowdy on the dance floor.

CHAMPIONS
Portland Marriott Hotel
1401 SW Front Ave.
226-7600   **DT**
Steve and Matt, two of Portland's favorite DJs, play a variety of music

here, but their main focus is on current tunes. Champions is a sports bar by day, but evening transforms it into a lively nightclub.

CRYSTAL BALLROOM
1332 W. Burnside
225-0047 or 778-5625 DT

It's been said that dancing at the Crystal is like dancing on a cloud. The mechanical floor of the ballroom literally "floats" while you move. The Crystal Ballroom is another of the McMenamin properties that feature microbrews, food, and great music. Recently restored, the original ballroom was built in 1914 and has a history from big band to Ike and Tina Turner to Eric Burdon. Today, the Crystal brings national acts and local bands to an enthusiastic crowd. You can even take tango lessons on Sunday afternoons. Look up their Web page at www.mcmenamins.com for a complete rundown.

EMBERS AVENUE
110 NW Broadway
222-3082 DT

Disco city! Not much techno but a lot of mainstream dance music. The bar shuts down at 2:30 a.m., but the dancing goes on almost 'til dawn—4 a.m., to be exact. After dancing 'til 4, lots of tired feet find their way to Grand Central Bowl (across the river), where a 24-hour restaurant awaits them.

LOTUS ROOM
CARDROOM & CAFE
932 SW 3rd Ave.
227-6185 DT

The old-fashioned bar and the underground music here provide a high-energy atmosphere for the hip crowd. There's no dress code. Often you'll find a line waiting to get in, but it's worth the wait. The pool tables in the middle of the three-sectioned bar are crowded and lively. The Lotus Room is known for its plentiful and cheap appetizers and the "cool" crowd that goes there.

QUEST
126 SW 2nd Ave.
497-9113 DT

It's the place to be seen, especially for the young set, but the music is pretty generic. Furnished in retro diner, Quest has two different dance floors, video games, and a no-alcohol bar. All ages welcome.

THE RED SEA
318 SW 3rd Ave.
241-5450 DT

Friday and Saturday nights turn this Ethiopian restaurant into a calypso and reggae dance club. Sometimes there's live music, sometimes there's a DJ, but the back room literally howls with world-beat rhythms.

SANDOVAL'S
133 SW 2nd Ave.
223-7020 DT

Latin dance is serious business here. Live music includes some of the best salsa bands around the Pacific Northwest. If you don't know how to do the rumba, watch the sweaty couples gliding around the floor in a flurry of color to learn the basics. It can get crowded, so be prepared to stand in line.

JAZZ CLUBS

ATWATER'S
US Bancorp Building, 30th Floor
111 SW 5th Ave.

275-3600 **DT**

Actually known as "The Bar," this is *the* place for jazz. You can sip a martini or order your favorite single-malt while you gaze at the best view in town. You'll hear Leroy Vinnegar and Mel Brown here, along with other local jazz greats like Craig Carothers, who plays on Thursdays. Getting a window table can be a problem, but the nighttime view of the bridges and the river is worth the wait.

BENSON HOTEL
309 SW Broadway
228-9611 **DT**

This is the place to go for that after-dinner drink in a cozy but elegant surroundings. The lobby at the Benson features warm Russian walnut walls and a waitstaff that is second to none. Fluid jazz is a perfect accompaniment to the comfy chairs and rich, relaxing environment.

BRASSERIE MONTMARTRE
626 SW Park Ave.
224-5552 **DT**

The French bistro menu and decor, the practiced "cool" of the crowd, and the haunting jazz will make you think you've just stepped into a Paris cafe. Live jazz every night.

HEATHMAN HOTEL
1001 SW Broadway
241-4100 **DT**

There are actually three bars here. The Marble Bar can be cold in the winter, but it's a chic place to be seen before or after the theater. The Lobby Lounge is more formal, with wood walls, a crystal chandelier, and a grand piano. Upstairs, the Mezzanine Bar features local art and a view of the downstairs crowd from tiny tables. It's one of the few places where you can smoke, eat, and drink while

you listen to jazz and watch the crowd.

JAZZ DE OPUS
33 NW 2nd Ave.
222-6077 **DT**

Here's where you can hear local saxophonist Patrick Lamb perform his magic. Dan Balmer plays here, too. It's a warm, cozy, laid-back environment and one of Portland's best restaurants.

PARCHMAN FARM
1204 SE Clay St.
235-7831 **SE**

Don't judge a book by its cover, nor a club by its exterior. It looks like, but is not, a brass-and-fern bar. But it's actually a smoky, sexy lounge where jazz and cigarettes go hand in hand. Some of the best acts in town play late nights on a postage-stamp-size stage, sometimes rounding up members of the audience for an impromptu jam session. The menu at Parchman Farm isn't as fine as the music, so it's a good idea to eat beforehand.

ROCK AND BLUES CLUBS

BERBATI'S PAN
231 SW Ankeny St.

226-2122 **DT**

It's hard to categorize Berbati's: you might hear spoken word or blues or rumba music, depending on which night you attend. Berbati's has become a favorite spot for the mysterious artsy crowd. It's lounge act meets born-again beatnik here, a mecca for creative types. Calamari and other Greek delights are also served here.

BUFFALO GAP
6835 SW Macadam
244-7111 **SW**

Live acoustic music inside during the winter and outside on the back patio during the summer. This is a funky place with irreverent bartenders who love to chat with their customers, always leaving them with a great story or two. Or at least a question in mind. Comfy big booths, great burgers.

CAFE LENA
2239 SE Hawthorne Blvd.
238-7087 **SE**

Catch Leroy Vinnegar and other jazz greats at Atwater's, p. 173

Atwater's

Intimate surroundings in split-level style, so you don't really feel like you're in a bar. Cafe Lena boasts everything from open-mic poetry to power ballads and brunch with roots rock guitarist Billy Kennedy.

KEY LARGO
31 NW 1st Ave.
223-9919 **DT**

The Democratic Party uses this club as its watering hole, and so do local rhythm and blues aficionados. It's a well-known spot on the blues circuit. Curtis Salgado calls the Key Largo home, and Linda Hornbuckle belts out the blues here, too.

LA LUNA
215 SE Pine St.
241-5862 **SE**

You can lounge on a couch, play a game of pool, drink a beer, and listen to live music here. It's a subculture kind of place featuring live music of all sorts. Registered as a historic site, the place is worth checking out because of the diverse crowd; as Henry Rollins says, it's one of the few early punk rooms still thriving. If decibels get too high, earplugs are available for 50 cents. Music ranges from Nick Lowe to McKinley to Australian and English bands.

COUNTRY MUSIC CLUBS

THE DRUM
14601 SE Division
760-1400 **SE**

Line dancing and two-step thrive here. It's always crowded and you never have to feel self-conscious if you don't know all the steps. Pool tables, too.

MONTANA'S

590 SW Taylor St.
222-5309 DT

This club is right downtown and alcohol-free—so alcohol-free, in fact, that if you've been drinking beforehand, you'll be turned away at the door. DJs teach and talk to a varied crowd, mostly dressed in country style. There's even a practice room at the back if you want to rehearse or synchronize your steps before you make your line-dance debut. It used to be a bus station, so it's unusually large and rather ugly, but the dancers make the place.

PONDEROSA LOUNGE AT JUBITZ TRUCK STOP
10130 N. Vancouver Way
283-1111 NW

You can hear live country music every night of the week at this Oregon-flavored truck stop. As you might guess, the place crawls with truck drivers, cowboys, and the women who want to get to know them.

CELTIC SOUNDS

Portland has become a center for all things Gaelic. If you are a Celtic music fan, look in the Willamette Week *paper for listings. If you want a pint of Guiness and a bit of Irish humor, try these pubs and restaurants.*

BIDDY MCGRAW'S
3518 SE Hawthorne Blvd.
233-1178 SE

There's a real Biddy at Biddy's. Locals flock here for her Irish food and quick wit. Most of the time you'll find great music, and you'll always find an abundance of Irish irreverence. It's a working class pub where the Guinness always pours well.

HORSE BRASS PUB
4534 SE Belmont
232-2202 SE

The Horse Brass is about as authentic an English pub as you'll find this side of London, but there's a strong Irish influence felt here, too. Dark ceiling beams, traditional English

Neil Gilpin's Belmont St. Octet at Laurelthirst Public House

Julie Keefe

fare (like Scotch eggs and trifle), and one of Portland's largest selections of beers make it a favorite watering hole.

KELL'S IRISH RESTAURANT AND PUB
112 SW 2nd Ave.
227-4057   **DT**
Upscale and entertaining, Kell's features one of Portland's most popular St. Patrick's Day festivals. All year you can catch Celtic sounds and enjoy great beer accompanied by a bit of Irish sass at Kell's.

OTHER GOOD PLACES

LAURELTHIRST PUBLIC HOUSE
2958 NE Glisan St.
232-1504   **NE**
A neighborhood bar with exceptional music. The antique bar is a visual feast in itself. The tiny stage recalls vaudeville, and the micros flow freely to an eclectic crowd. Occasional dancing (if you can find the room, it's OK with the management) to music as varied as the audience. The Laurelthirst prides itself on supporting local musicians, and you're likely to hear some of the best music around in an understated, comfortable environment. Eavesdropping is great here. The conversations are often tinged with French and English accents, and the intellectual subject matter borders on the anarchistic.

MUMMY'S
622 SW Columbia Ave.
224-7465   **DT**
As you might guess, this is an Egyptian-themed club that features Middle Eastern music. Etched glass and wooden mummies decorate this below-street-

level establishment. It's like stepping into an Egyptian tomb. Sort of.

RIALTO POOLROOM, BAR AND CAFÉ
529 SW 4th Ave.
228-7605   **DT**
Off-track betting, video games, and 15 Brunswick pool tables combine to make this an exciting place to be. The "all-in-black" crowd favors this spot for late-night drinking. The fabulous jukebox features tunes ranging from Johnny Cash to Johnny Ramone and Elvis Costello.

ROSELAND THEATRE
10 NW 6th Ave.
224-2038   **DT**
For years this club was known as the Starry Night. It's dark and dank, but the alternative crowd loves its heavy metal and smoke atmosphere. Occasional softer music, too.

SATYRICON
125 NW 6th Ave.
243-2380   **DT**
Underground music and black lights make this an alternative mecca. The crowd looks rough, but they're really just kids having a good time. For the most part, anyway. Satyricon is one of America's oldest underground clubs and a favorite haunt of Portland grunge fans.

SAUCEBOX
218 SW Broadway

241-3393 **DT**

Downtown hip meets shadowed cool. It's one of Portland's newest hot spots and has quickly become a mainstay for the modern set. Saucebox features pan-Asian cuisine; DJs after 10 p.m.

COMEDY CLUBS

COMEDY SPORTZ
Moyer's Little Roxy Theatre
1953 NW Kearney St.
236-8888 **NW**

A smoke-free, alcohol-free environment for all ages. Comedy Sportz likes to take donations for the Oregon Food Bank, so bring a can of food with you, and you'll get $1 off the $8 admission. Improv comedy is featured.

DARCELLE XV
208 NW 3rd Ave.
222-5338 **DT**

Two words describe this club: female impersonators. Lip synching and sharp wit share the stage with burlesque dancing and risqué double entendres. Darcelle's is a Rose City classic, and Darcelle herself, one of Portland's favorite personalities.

HARVEY'S COMEDY CLUB
436 NW 6th Ave.
241-0338 **DT**

National acts and local favorites perform at Harvey's. It's a fairly big place and seems to have become the king of comedy clubs in Portland.

NOTABLE MOVIE THEATERS

ACT III THEATRES

With more than 20 movie theaters all over the city, ACT III is the supermarket of movie houses. Daily showtimes and theater addresses are listed in the *Oregonian* and *Willamette Week*. Early shows, which run $3.75, are indicated by brackets in the ads. Evening shows are $7. First-run films.

The Mission Theatre and Pub, p. 180

McMenamin's

On Location in Portland

David Woolson, executive director of the Oregon Film and Video Office in Portland, is the eyes and ears of Oregon's emerging film industry. In the last four years, his office has generated more than $100 million in revenue for the city through feature films, commercials, and TV productions. Projections for the future are even higher.

"Portland offers a variety of location advantages," says Woolson. "There is a thriving film and video community permanently based here. We have a wealth of talent in all the categories that it takes to produce quality film." A number of Hollywood companies, he says, are impressed with the level of local talent and the quality of life Portland has to offer. Some are even considering relocating here.

"Along with the talent, Portland has a unique sense of place," adds Woolson. "The variety of scenery within the city creates a wide array of possibilities." Brick warehouses, plenty of waterways, a colorful Chinatown, ample forested spaces, and gleaming skyscrapers are just some of the backdrops that spark the imaginations of film producers and directors.

Woolson says that Portland is on the cutting edge in this sophisticated and fast-moving industry. "We see Portland becoming a center for the emerging digital media technology. We have high-tech companies here, first-class creative talent, and a cooperative community. That combination comes together in Portland in a way that is unusual for the film industry."

THE BAGDAD THEATRE
3708–26 SE Hawthorne Blvd.
230-0895 **SE**
Built in 1927 and owned by the Mc-Menamin brothers today, the Bagdad Theatre recalls the elaborately decorated theaters of the glitzy Twenties. Outside the theater, you'll first see the massive sparkling marquee with neon lights in the shape of stars

and the moon with the name "Bagdad" spelled out and outlined in neon. The theater's signature red tile roof and exotic style is a feast for the eyes. Upon entering the 700-foot lobby, you can't help but notice the Byzantine feel of the place. Vaulted ramps, filigree light fixtures, and stenciled motifs of animals and mythological creatures grace the interior. Note the trompe l'oeil tiles and arches, too.

And then there are the movies. Featuring second-run films in a casual environment, the Bagdad is a favorite destination in the Hawthorne District. You can order pizza, sip a microbrew, watch a good movie, and taste a bit of history at the same time. Admission is only $1, but you must be 21 to attend.

CINEMA 21
616 NW 21st Ave.
223-4515   **NW**
One of the last bastions of union-operated movie houses, Cinema 21 is very much a presence in Portland's art-cinema scene in the hip Northwest section of town. Here you might catch a foreign film, a film noir, or a twisted animated flick. Unlike the modern multiplexes, this theater has big comfy seats with plenty of leg room. And, if you never sat in the loge and smooched with your sweetheart, you'll want to check out the loge at Cinema 21. There aren't many smoochers nowadays, but the theater balcony is filled with amorous memories.

CLINTON STREET THEATRE
2522 SE Clinton St.
238-8899   **SE**
This turn-of-the-century theater serves a variety of purposes that include performing arts, spoken word, and independent film, so call ahead to see what's shakin'. It's a homey, funky kind of place with an avant-garde bent. And it's the only place in Portland where you can see *The Rocky Horror Picture Show*. It shows at midnight every Saturday, and the theater management encourages patrons to bring their own props for this famous cult movie, where the audience is as much a part of the show as what's on the screen. Tickets are $4, and the doors open at 11:30.

MISSION THEATRE AND PUB
1624 NW Glisan St.
223-4031   **NW**
Once the Swedish Evangelical Mis-

Feature Films Shot in or near Portland

Assassins
Body of Evidence
Claire of the Moon
Drugstore Cowboy
Foxfire

Free Willy
Gathering Evidence
Imaginary Crimes
Maverick
Mr. Holland's Opus

sion Covenant Church of Portland (or the Swedish Tabernacle) and later a union hall, the McMenamin brothers have turned this two-story sturdy brick building into a movie house and pub. According to legend, one of the considerations in building the Tabernacle on this site was the fact that there were many single females in the area who could walk to church from their jobs as maids and governesses in the well-heeled community of Nob Hill. Once known as a center of worship, missionary work, and social service, the Mission Theatre is now a hub for fellowship of a different sort. No-frills food and micros can be ordered during the second-run movies. You must be 21 to attend.

THE MOVIE HOUSE
1220 SW Taylor
225-5555, ext. 4609   **DT**
There's no other place in town where you can visit a historic build-

ing, play a game of chess in the parlor, and watch a movie when you're done. In 1922 the Portland Woman's Club commissioned this building, and it has remained an active part of the community ever since. During WWII, the Club made bandages for the soldiers here. The interior hasn't changed much since then, and it's not hard to imagine the role these women played in the war effort. Upstairs, in the parlor and seating room, there is still ample space for reading or chatting with friends in comfortable furniture before showtime. The Portland Woman's Club leases the building to ACT III Theatres, but the Club still meets here twice a month for business and social activities. The room with the movie screen used to be home to dances and other community events, including movies. Notice, in particular, the art deco style.

Portland Oregon Visitors Association

14
DAY TRIPS FROM PORTLAND

DAY TRIP: The Columbia River Gorge

No trip to Oregon is complete without a drive up the Columbia River Gorge, a land of superlatives and surprises. Oregon's only National Scenic Area, the Gorge holds a permanent place in many hearts as the favorite sight in Oregon and has been called "a poem in stone." You can spend a couple hours in the Gorge, or you can make a two-day trip of it if you choose to stay in Hood River.

Born of fiery volcanoes, lava flows, and Ice Age floodwaters, the Columbia Gorge provides the only sea-level passage through the Cascade Mountain Range. First navigated by the Lewis and Clark Expedition in 1804–05, the Columbia River surges through the Gorge beside snow-capped mountains and through prospering cities and fertile farmlands as it pushes its way toward the Pacific Ocean. A historic highway winds through the canyon just above Interstate 84; be sure to drive it. Follow the signs on I-84.

From a breathy whisper to a thundering roar, waterfalls with names like Horsetail Falls and Bridal Veil cascade over the rugged basaltic cliffs. A steep and winding trail through the misty woods leads to the top of Multnomah Falls, where it is said an Indian princess jumped to her death to ease her broken heart. Her visage may still be seen in the mist of the falls.

Beacon Rock, a towering 800-foot sheer-walled monolith, on the north side of the Columbia, is the largest formation of its kind in the United States. Back on the Oregon side, the commanding vista from Crown Point, high above the Columbia River, stuns photographers and inspires writers. Known for its stone Vista House, built in 1917, Crown Point stands today as one of Oregon's most cherished landmarks.

Known as the "Windsurfing Capital of the World," the Columbia River thrills windsurfers with raging winds of up to 35 mph. Seven months out of the year, the river also hosts fluorescent sailboards and their determined riders, who live to ricochet across the water near the historic town of Hood River. The tumbling currents of the Columbia provide a ride unlike any found this side of Aruba.

While in Hood River, treat yourself to a train ride through the valley on the Mt. Hood Scenic Railroad (386-3556). Whether you're a railroad buff or not, you will find yourself transported to another century when the steam engine's whistle blasts the final "all aboard" signal and begins to push its way up the first 3 miles of this steep ride into the heart of the Columbia Gorge. Chugging along tracks laid in 1906, this restored passenger train meanders through the Oregon Cascades, making its way past orchards, forests, rivers, and canyons. The also-refurbished Mt. Hood Railroad Depot, built in 1911, has been designated a National Historic Site.

Hood River boasts one of Oregon's most elegant hotels. The Columbia Gorge Hotel (386-5566), built in 1921, has entertained guests like Rudolph Valentino, Clara Bow, and Myrna Loy. Listed on the National Historic Register, the hotel serves a farm-style breakfast in a dining room with a commanding view of the Columbia River.

Multnomah Falls

Portland Oregon Visitors Association

DAY TRIP: Astoria

Going west from the city along Highway 30, the Columbia River rolls its way west through the Gorge and finally empties into the Pacific at Astoria, about a 90-minute drive from Portland. The mouth of the Columbia was explored and claimed in 1792 by Capt. Robert Gray in his ship the

TRIVIA

Multnomah Falls, in the Columbia Gorge, is the second highest waterfall in the United States, tumbling 620 feet.

PORTLAND REGION

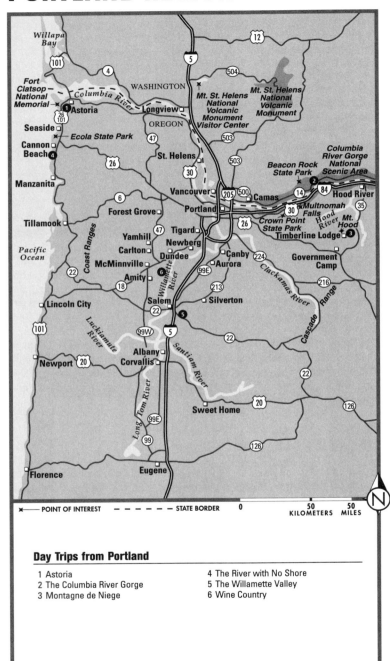

Willapa Bay

101

12

5

4

504

WASHINGTON

Mt. St. Helens National Volcanic Monument Visitor Center ✕

Mt. St. Helens National Volcanic Monument

Fort Clatsop National Memorial ✕

Columbia River

26 101

✕ 1 Astoria

Longview

OREGON

Seaside

✕ Ecola State Park

47

503

Columbia River Gorge National Scenic Area

Cannon Beach 4

St. Helens

503

Beacon Rock State Park ✕

26

30

2

84 Hood River

Manzanita

Vancouver

205 500

14

35

Tillamook

6

Forest Grove

Portland

Camas

30

Multnomah Falls ✕

Crown Point State Park ✕

Hood River

Mt. Hood

Pacific Ocean

Coast Ranges

Yamhill

47

Tigard

26

Timberline Lodge 3

Carlton

Newberg

224

Government Camp

McMinnville

Dundee

Amity

6

99E

Aurora

Clackamas River

216

Cascade Range

18

Willamette River

Canby

213

Lincoln City

Salem

22

Silverton

22

101

Luckiamute River

5

22

Newport

20

99W

Albany

Santiam River

22

Corvallis

Long Tom River

Sweet Home

20

126

99E

99

126

Florence

Eugene

✕⟶ POINT OF INTEREST   – – – – STATE BORDER

0   50   50
         KILOMETERS MILES

N

Day Trips from Portland

1 Astoria
2 The Columbia River Gorge
3 Montagne de Niege

4 The River with No Shore
5 The Willamette Valley
6 Wine Country

Columbia Redidiva, as he sailed up the Pacific Coast. Since then, more than 200 ships and 2,000 small craft have been lost at or near this river's dangerous mouth. Known as the "Graveyard of the Pacific," this area still suffers from a grim reputation among fishermen, sailors, and ship captains. Today's navigators maintain a healthy respect for the Columbia River Bar when crossing into the Pacific Ocean.

One of the most visible wrecks in the United States can be seen on the beach near Astoria. On October 25, 1906, the *Peter Iredale,* a 2,000-ton cargo ship, ran into dense fog and zero visibility. Driving winds snapped the ship's masts as the helpless freighter was tossed about and ultimately driven ashore. Today, clinging for survival to the restless sandy shore, the rusted iron frame of the *Peter Iredale* is all that remains of this once magnificent vessel.

Astoria's rich history includes people like Lewis and Clark and their guide, Sacajawea; the wealthy fur merchant John Jacob Astor; and Jane Barnes. Jane Barnes? Yes, Jane Barnes. The one from Portsmouth, England, who was the first white woman to set foot in Astoria, 30 years before the covered wagons arrived. She is still celebrated today on Jane Barnes Day, one of Astoria's favorite celebrations.

Oregon's oldest town, Astoria today is a colorful river town. Its personality is revealed in its restored Victorian homes, its bookstores and restaurants, its fishermen and artists. Astoria enjoys a reputation as a working seaport village, a historic center, and a recreational haven for sports enthusiasts and vacationers.

In Astoria, the steep wooded hills rise and fall much like San Francisco's. In fact, it's so steep that some streets just wouldn't stay where they were put. So, instead of rebuilding and reinforcing stubborn sliding blacktop, the city maintains a series of walking paths that connect neighborhoods. These paths wind in and around Astoria and even lead explorers through an ancient forest and down to the piers on the waterfront. This is a pedestrian town, where traversing the hills leads visitors to believe they've discovered something that's supposed to be hidden.

For more information, contact the Astoria Warrenton Chamber of Commerce, 111 West Marine Drive, Astoria, OR 97103; 325-6311.

Bed and Breakfasts

Ornate Victorian architecture abounds in this scenic port town. Each home has its own personality, history, and unique environment. Some, like those below, are open to the public as bed-and-breakfast inns.

The Martin and Lilli Foard House (325-1892) is run today by the great-granddaughter of Mr. and Mrs. Foard. Original woodwork, wainscoting, pocket doors, chandeliers, and even some of Mrs. Foard's vintage 1900 dresses grace this 1892 Queen Anne–style Victorian home. Winner of the Edward Harvey Historic Preservation Award, this bright bed and breakfast is open on weekends only.

The elegantly appointed Rosebriar Inn (325-7427), built in 1902, was

Fort Clatsop National Memorial

once a convent. Today, vintage rugs, brass chandeliers, lace curtains, and family heirlooms decorate this warm restored home. Travel-weary guests enjoy a welcoming reception and full breakfasts as part of their comfortable stay.

Guests can relax in a claw-foot tub in the Astor Suite at the Franklin Street Station (325-4313) or curl up in a cozy room filled with elegant Victorian furniture. Rich woodwork, local art, and fine breakfasts combine to provide a quiet respite in this friendly family-owned B&B.

Also worth noting is Clementine's Bed and Breakfast (325-2005). Sitting high on a hill, Clementine's offers the best view in Astoria. The adjacent coffee shop, Lagniappe (Creole for "something extra"), is an experience in itself. Lagniappe serves the best cappuccino and homemade scones in Astoria.

Other Sights and Activities

The Columbia River Maritime Museum (325-2323) houses superb displays depicting legendary shipwrecks, lighthouses, and fishing and naval history. Architecturally designed to recall the feel of a soaring waveform, this museum brings together education, conservation, and research facilities for its visitors. More than 200 years of rich maritime history are represented here. Among the favored artifacts are rare documents, paintings, sailboats, and clipper ship replicas.

The Flavel House, once home to bar pilot Capt. George Flavel, has been restored to its original splendor. Built in 1885, the exotic home is filled with antiques, storytellers, and photographs.

The Astor Street Opry Co. produces lively family events all year. Vaudeville entertainment, live theater, and original productions provide an evening of local color, history, and insight. If you see *Shanghaied in Astoria,* you will learn much about Astoria's colorful history of dance halls, surly sailors, and shanghai as it really happened.

For a real history lesson, sail up the Columbia with Capt. Jim Van Cleeve and Columbia River Scenic Cruises and Fishing Expeditions. You'll see a variety of wildlife, including eagles, seals, and nesting herons. Captain Jim's lively repartee entertains and informs.

Fort Clatsop National Memorial is an authentic reproduction of the place where Lewis and Clark spent the winter of 1805–06. Costumed guides walk you through history as they demonstrate cooking skills, black powder weapons, tanning methods, and other frontier skills needed for survival in the wild. Inside the visitor center, you can see maps and copies of the journals and watch a lively movie about the Lewis and Clark Expedition. The center is open daily year-round. For more information, contact Fort Clatsop National Memorial, Route 3, Box 604-FC, Astoria, OR 97103; 861-2471.

Where to Eat

House of Chan is owned by Ronnie Ma, whose exotic dishes are made from fresh ingredients. If you go fishing, he'll even cook your fish for you in a meal you'll long remember. This is a local gathering place for sailors and sea captains, so it's a good place to soak up the local color.

Uriah Hulsey, owner and chef of the small, eclectic Columbia Cafe, provides as much entertainment as he does good food. It's on the spicy side, and what is served is what chef wants to cook! Hours vary, so it's a good idea to call ahead.

DAY TRIP: Montagne de Niege

Mt. Hood, or *Wy'east*, as the Indians knew it, was respected and feared by the Native Americans. They believed it was home to both good and bad spirits. It was also believed to be a single spirit in and of itself, not merely a mountain, but a chief and the son of the Great Spirit. French trappers knew it as *Montagne de Niege*, or "Mountain of Snow," and explorers knew it as "an old acquaintance." Today, this old friend looms over the landscape, as if protecting the very heart of Oregon. It's only about a 90-minute drive from Portland, through wooded valleys and steep inclines.

Mt. Hood, named after Samuel Viscount Hood, an English admiral of the West Indies, stands at 11,235 feet. It is actually the remains of the

TRIVIA

Estacada, at the gateway to Mt. Hood National Forest, is the Christmas tree capital of the world.

TRIVIA

original north wall and rim of a once-volatile crater. Although the peak no longer spews ash or spits fire, volcanic activity in the area has not ceased. Washington's Mt. St. Helens, a brother to Wy'east, powerfully erupted on May 18, 1980.

The Mt. Hood of the Nineties is sprinkled with ranger stations, ski runs, hiking trails, and little villages like ZigZag, Government Camp, Frog Lake, and Little John Snowplay.

Activity on "The Mountain" (as it's called by locals) is diverse. Picking huckleberries, digging mushrooms, and fishing for trout are favored relaxing pastimes. Blackberries and fiddlehead ferns find their way from the mountainsides to some of the area's most elegant tables.

Whether you like shooshing downhill or traversing a quiet trail, skiing on Mt. Hood is an experience not to be missed. Year-round downhill skiing is a popular activity, even when the summer heat's in the valley.

Cross-country skiers can study history and enjoy scenery and exercise at the same time. Several ski trails in the area follow the Oregon Trail. The Barlow Trail, named after Oregon pioneer Sam Barlow, winds between Government Camp and Trillium Lake. The trail passes a spot where pioneers camped and could obtain supplies, or be guided up the mountain on the Oregon Trail. Barlow Trail winds around Devil's Half Acre and provides access to the grave site of Pioneer Woman, a place still honored by visitors today.

Climbing Mt. Hood is no easy feat. Although it is one of the world's most popular mountains to climb, it is a technical climb and requires special equipment. Thousands of climbers per year register for the climb at the Wy'east Daylodge at Timberline. The right gear, plenty of layered clothing, and knowledge of the changing and sometimes hazardous weather conditions are prerequisites for any climb on this powerful mountain.

On the mountain's north side, the Hood River Valley is Oregon's largest fruit-growing district. Almost 15,000 acres of apple, pear, and cherry orchards thrive in this fertile valley. More than 185,000 tons of fruit are produced here annually.

In the springtime, the entire valley dances with color, and, if drivers slow down and open the window, they will be mesmerized by the thick, sweet fragrance of pear and apple blossoms. The Mt. Hood Railroad, built in 1906, still takes passengers up impressive grades, through blooming orchards, and into steep canyons, for a relaxing and enjoyable ride in restored vintage railroad cars. Autumn lures fruit-pickers and gourmet cooks from around the area looking for just the right pear for chutney or butter.

The scenic 40-mile Mt. Hood Loop meanders around the base of The

Oregon Coast

Mountain and provides a rich playground for all five senses. Orchards and bridges, waterfalls and campgrounds, ski areas and country inns, fish hatcheries and breweries, sternwheelers and state parks make it difficult to drive in one day. It's not that the drive is so arduous—that's actually the easy part. It's the sensory overload that's the challenge.

Situated just up the road from Government Camp, you'll find Timberline Lodge, which was built during the Great Depression as part of the WPA and Civilian Conservation Corp. It's still popular as a year-round ski lodge and restaurant. The original workmanship of the weavers, stonemasons, iron workers, painters, carpenters, and architects has been thoughtfully preserved. Timberline Lodge is a National Historic Landmark and is part of the National Scenic Byway system.

For more information, contact the Mt. Hood Area Chamber of Commerce, P.O. Box 185, Government Camp, OR 97028; 272-3403.

Where to Stay

COLUMBIA GORGE HOTEL
4000 Westcliff Dr.
Hood River, OR 97031
800/345-1921 or 386-5566
$$$$
Rudolph Valentino, Clara Bow, Jane Powel, and Shirley Temple all stayed here. Built in 1921, the hotel has been restored to its original splendor complete with gardens, pathways, and gorgeous rooms. The food is spectacular, and the rooms are decorated in vintage style. It's a place for romance and special getaways.

FALCON'S CREST INN
87287 Government Camp Loop Hwy.
Government Camp, OR 97028
272-3403
$$$$

This 5,000-square-foot chalet is full of surprises. Four-poster beds, Chinese rugs, and Queen Anne–style chairs furnish the bed and breakfast. Gourmet dinners are served in style here. A common loft area is also a plus. You can listen to CDs (choose from a huge collection), read, stargaze through a telescope, or play board games while enjoying the view.

TIMBERLINE LODGE
Timberline Lodge, OR 97028
231-7979
$$$$

Timberline Lodge on Mt. Hood was built during the Great Depression and is a National Historic Landmark. The wood and iron work and the historic architecture provide a one-of-a-kind Oregon experience. The rooms are sparsely furnished with an authentic "cabin" feel. Families especially enjoy the ambiance here, in part because some of the ski slopes are open year-round on Mt. Hood. Even if you don't ski, Timberline Lodge is a must-see.

DAY TRIP: The River with No Shore

Devil's Punch Bowl. Cape Perpetua. Cape Foulweather. Deception Bay. With names like these, it's not difficult to imagine why the headlands along Oregon's coast have lured curious visitors for centuries. The Pacific Ocean, often called "the Grandfather of all Oceans," carves high drama into this rugged shoreline.

One legend, that of the Clatsop Indians, says this rough-hewn coastline was created by Talapus, or Coyote, the trickster god, who stood at the top of Neahkahnie Mountain and threw chunks of molten rock into the water below. Today, Oregon's rugged shoreline waters continue to boil and churn as testament to ancient lore.

The Plains Indians, never having seen the ocean, referred to it in legend as "the river with no shore." When Sacajawea, Lewis and Clark's Shoshone guide, first laid eyes on the Pacific Ocean, she vowed to tell her people of the plains that their legend was indeed true.

In 1913 Governor George Oswald declared Oregon's beaches public property. Nowhere else can visitors explore nearly 400 miles of open beach with such varying terrain. From misty cliffs and wind-carved spruce trees to lazy sand dunes in the sun, the Oregon coastline embraces the unique.

To get to the Oregon Coast, take Highway 26 west out of Portland. You'll want to visit towns like Cannon Beach, a thriving community filled with shopping, arts, restaurants, hotels, and one of Oregon's most outstanding beaches. Cannon Beach is about a 90-minute drive through Oregon's Coastal Range.

While in Cannon Beach, be sure to find Ecola State Park on the north end of town. The park has winding trails leading to some of the most stunning scenery in North America. From the top of the park, you can watch the sun sink into the Pacific while seals play on the rocks below. Picnic areas and convenient restrooms make this an especially nice place to enjoy lunch or a quiet read on a sunny afternoon.

About 15 minutes south of Cannon Beach lies the sleepy little village of Manzanita. Known for its quiet beach and small town atmosphere, it's a perfect place to get away from it all. There's not much going on in Manzanita, but you can be sure to find good food at a couple of restaurants.

Where to Stay

STEPHANIE INN
2740 S. Pacific
Cannon Beach, OR 97110
436-2221
$$$$
The Stephanie Inn is romance defined. Rooms have four poster beds, Jacuzzis, ample seating areas, and amenities galore. The lobby is a work of art, with its stone and wood accents. The restaurant has an excellent wine list, courteous service, and food that reflects the true flavors of the Pacific Northwest.

SURFSAND RESORT
P.O. Box 219
Cannon Beach, OR 97110
800/547-6100 or 436-2274
$$$$
Surfsand Resort is an oceanfront family resort. A wide variety of options is available to suit all kinds of needs, including 14 types of rooms—accommodating two to six people—all with kitchens or wet bar areas. There's even a large house to rent. Amenities include a Jacuzzi, an indoor swimming pool, and the Wayfarer Restaurant. The resort is within walking distance of the heart of Cannon Beach.

DAY TRIP: The Willamette Valley

The Willamette Valley, stretching south of Portland to Eugene, is known as "The Bread Basket of the West." The valley is roughly 60 miles wide and 100 miles long. Settled by Oregon Trail pioneers, it was once called the Promised Land. The fields of the valley produce much of the food, agricultural seed products, grass sod, Christmas trees, and flower bulbs for the entire nation. Mint, corn hops, hazelnuts, wheat, and fruit orchards line the country roads in the Willamette Valley.

Although the valley is generally temperate year-round, springtime is an especially colorful time to visit. That's when the iris and tulip farms are in full bloom. The fields come alive as garnet red and coral hues, light and sassy yellows, regal violet and tender pinks splash the roadside along the Northern Willamette Valley near Salem and Canby. Willamette Valley iris farms dot the lush terrain, offering an uncommon vista of blooms as you cruise south from Portland on Interstate 5. Herb gardens, historical colonies, and nurseries also punctuate the area amid the valley's rolling fields and stately forests.

Traveling by car isn't the only way to go, either. Literally hundreds of miles of bike paths lead through this scenic area, so, if you are a cyclist, the flat roads and winding trails will entice and entertain you.

Sights Along the Way

Open mid-May through the first week in June, the 200-acre Schreiner's Iris Gardens has been in the same Oregon family for almost 70 years. Mr. Francis X. Schreiner, a Swiss American, turned his iris hobby into a thriving catalogue business in 1928. Located just north of Salem, the Schreiner's garden invites visitors to walk through the fields, choose their favorite flowers in colors and styles to fit their imaginations, then place orders for their own impressive gardens back home.

Each year around May 20, Cooley's Gardens celebrates its anniversary by hosting ten days of special events centered around a cut flower show featuring more than 300 varieties of bearded blooms. Located near Silverton (15 miles east of Salem), Cooley's Gardens was planted by Rholin Cooley, whose interest in growing iris was sparked by the family physician in the 1920s. Dr. Richard Kleinsorge's hobby was the hybridization of iris and is believed to have been the catalyst for many of today's vibrant varieties found in faraway European gardens and American country homes.

Through his private love affair with rhododendrons, Cecil Smith has been credited with many of the modern hybrid plants found in the world today. The quiet Cecil and Molly Smith Garden displays not only its famous rhododendrons, but encourages its visitors to meander along its many pathways through less recognized botanic marvels, like licorice fern, huckleberry bushes, and fragile bleeding heart, which is often found entwined with moist moss-laden logs. This garden is open from March to May.

The historic Aurora Colony, formerly home to 600 German settlers, was founded in 1856. Aurora is alive with history, dozens of antique shops, and quaint restaurants. It's a sleepy little community and hasn't yet become a tourist trap. You can still walk through some of the colony's original and restored buildings, including a log cabin built in 1876, and wander through the museum, where historic exhibits tell the story of this self-sufficient settlement. The museum's guides are especially knowledgeable. They

TIP

Oregon winery events and festivals are popular in the summer. They range from food festivals to jazz concerts to wine-tasting events and are always fun to attend. To get a schedule of events, call the *Oregon Wine Newspaper* at 232-7607. This valuable resource is chock-full of information. A complete guide to wineries in Oregon is available from the Portland Oregon Visitors Association, Three World Trade Center, 26 SW Salmon St., Portland; OR 97204, 800/345-3214 or 222-2223.

haven't become jaded yet, and their enthusiasm for the area is contagious. The Willamette Valley Herb Society tends and manages a charming herb garden in the colony as well. A festival celebrating Aurora's history and culture takes place annually in August. For further information, contact the Aurora Chamber of Commerce, P.O. Box 86, Aurora, OR 97002; 623-2564.

DAY TRIP: Wine Country

The fertile Willamette Valley, which lies protected between the Coast Range and the high Cascade Mountains, provides a temperate climate for some of the world's great wines. Long summer days and mild winters allow for a range of wine varieties. Oregon wineries have won such awards as the coveted Olypiades of the Wines of the World, in Paris, and the Brouhin Tasting, in Burgundy.

Oregon is especially known for its award-winning pinot noir wines. Other major varieties produced include Chardonnay, Riesling, pinot gris, Cabernet Sauvignon, Muller-Thurgau, Gerwurztraminer, Sauvignon Blanc, Merlot, and zinfandel. Some wineries even produce fortified dessert wines and iced wines.

It's fairly safe to say that a drive through the Willamette Valley will inevitably lead you to a winery. Wineries in Oregon are noted by dark blue roadside signs with the name of the winery and arrows pointing the way.

One of the easiest drives is down Highway 99W. Take Exit 294 off I-5 just south of Portland proper. Follow the winding road through the small town of Tigard and on to Newberg and Dundee.

Some of the most notable wineries are along the way. Here's a small sampling of what you'll find while spending the day in the Willamette Valley.

ARGYLE
691 Highway 99W
Dundee, OR 97115
538-8520
Argyle produces some of the top sparking wines in the country. The winery itself is in a former hazelnut processing plant. The tasting room is in a restored Victorian farmhouse. Australian vintner Brian Croser and Oregon

vintner Cal Knudsen are the winery's co-owners and are both long associated with wine-making.

CHATEAU BENOIT
6580 NE Mineral Springs Rd.
Carlton, OR 97111
864-2991
Chateau Benoit, in keeping with its very French name, boasts a French-style chateau that can be rented for special occasions. A hilltop winery, its view of Yamhill County below is one to enjoy with a picnic lunch. Try its Sauvignon Blanc or the pinot noir. Wheelchair-accessible.

KRISTIN HILL WINERY
3330 SE Amity-Dayton Hwy.

Oregon's Wineries

Susan Sokol Blosser and her husband, Bill, whose winery celebrated its 20th anniversary in 1997, are considered pioneers in Oregon's wine history. Susan offers the following historic perspective:

"It's been quite an adventure. When Bill and I cleared an old prune orchard in 1971 to plant wine grapes, we never imagined that today we would be surrounded by vineyards and wineries and that our wines and those of our neighbors would be served at the best restaurants in the country.

"Even the landscape has changed. Hillsides that were once covered with prune, cherry, and nut orchards are now lush with vineyards. Wineries of all sizes are tucked in their midst and overlook the Willamette Valley.

"Most of Oregon wineries are still small family businesses and are located within an hour's drive of Portland. Many of us have tasting rooms and picnic areas with panoramic views of the countryside. The vintners are friendly and approachable, and, of course, the wines are delicious. At Sokol Blosser, we welcome visitors daily at our tasting room and our walk-through showcase vineyard. Come see us, ask questions, and taste our wines. It's a wonderful way to spend a day."

Amity, OR 97101
835-0850
It's a family affair at this winery. The first vineyard was planted in 1985, with the help of friends and family, and the tasting room opened in 1992. The specialty at Kristin Hill is Methode Champenoise sparkling wine. Visitors are usually welcome, but winter hours are a little shorter. You can always call for an appointment.

PANTHER CREEK CELLARS
455 N. Irvine
McMinnville, OR 97128
472-8080
Panther Creek is one of the nation's few producers of Melon, made from the Muscadet grape. Visitors are welcome daily by appointment. Panther Creek hosts an open house on Thanksgiving and one during Memorial Day weekend.

REX HILL WINERY
30835 N. Highway 99W
Newberg, OR 97132
538-0666
Rex Hill Winery has some of the oldest vineyards in Yamhill County. Antiques and oriental rugs grace the elegant tasting room, where you can try Rex Hill pinot noir or any of the several other wines produced. If you'd like to bring your lunch along, you can enjoy a picnic on a terrace surrounded by extensive landscaping. Hours vary; call ahead.

SOKOL BLOSSER WINERY
5000 Sokol Blosser Lane
Dundee, OR 97115
800/582-6668 or 864-2282
The Sokol Blosser label is probably one of the most recognized. The winery sits at the top of a hill with a commanding view of the Willamette Valley. Sokol Blosser's walk-through showcase vineyard is a self-guided tour. The tasting room is open daily year-round and is filled with fun wine gifts. Sokol Blosser is one of Oregon's oldest and largest wineries, established in 1977. Summertime concerts on its rolling hills are popular in wine country. Call ahead for a schedule of events.

Side Trip in Wine Country

MOMOKAWA SAKE BREWERY
920 Elm St.
Forest Grove, OR 97116
357-7056

If sake is your fancy, be sure to check out the Momokawa Sake Brewery in Forest Grove. Already famous in Japan, Momokawa Sake is now produced in the United States, too. At the tasting room you can learn about the old tradition of fine rice wines and taste while you compare a variety of imported sakes.

Where to Stay

FLYING M RANCH
23029 NW Flying M Rd.
Yamhill, OR 97148
662-3222
The Flying M Ranch sits in a valley that was once filled with wheat fields, stagecoach lines, and train tracks. For more than 100 years, travelers have rested at this quaint little spot. Though the Flying M was born in 1970, it is rich in history and tradition. Here you'll find a mixture of cabins, camping spots, and a Bunk House motel. You can dine by a huge native stone fireplace while you watch the sparkling clear waters of the North Yamhill River. Stagecoach and trail rides, horseback trips and tennis are just some of the activities available at the Flying M. Prices range from $10 for a campsite to $175 for a huge cabin with a fireplace.

YOUNGBERG HILL FARM INN & VINEYARD
10660 Youngberg Hill Rd.
McMinnville, OR 97128
472-2727
From the top of the 700-foot Youngberg Hill, you can see Mt. Hood, Mt. Jefferson, and on sunny days, even the Three Sisters mountains in Central Oregon. The inn is surrounded by working farms and has an old country feel to it. Meals are reminiscent of Austria or Germany and are made with only Oregon-grown products.

Where to Eat

JOEL PALMER HOUSE RESTAURANT
600 Ferry St., Dayton
864-2995
The Joel Palmer House is an historic Southern Revival–style home. Jack and Heidi Czarnecki recently moved from Pennsylvania to Oregon's wine country, where they serve some delightful food. Jack is a renowned cookbook author, and his specialty is mushrooms, which abound in the Pacific Northwest. In the summer, you can eat outdoors on the wide and wonderful patio and choose from eclectic dishes, most of which focus on mushrooms, and all of which feature fresh Northwestern products. Open for dinner Tuesday through Saturday. Call ahead for reservations.

APPENDIX: CITY•SMART BASICS

IMPORTANT PHONE NUMBERS

Emergencies—911

PORTLAND POLICE BUREAU
1111 SW 2nd Ave.
823-3333

PORTLAND FIRE BUREAU
55 SW Ash
823-3700

HOSPITALS

LEGACY EMANUEL HOSPITAL
2801 N. Gantenbein Ave.
413-2200

LEGACY GOOD SAMARITAN HOSPITAL
1015 NW 22nd Ave.
229-7711

OREGON HEALTH SCIENCES UNIVERSITY
3181 SW Sam Jackson Park Rd.
494-8311

PROVIDENCE PORTLAND MEDICAL CENTER
4805 NE Glisan St.
215-1111

PROVIDENCE ST. VINCENT MEDICAL CENTER
9205 SW Barnes Rd.
216-2115

OTHER USEFUL NUMBERS

Time & Temperature
225-5555

Road Conditions
222-6721

CITY MEDIA

Newspapers

DAILY JOURNAL OF COMMERCE
2840 NW 35th Ave.
226-1311

THE OREGONIAN
1320 SW Broadway
221-8327

WILLAMETTE WEEK
822 SW 10th Ave.
243-2122

Radio

This is a partial listing of the most recognized stations. KOPB (91.5), Oregon's Public Broadcasting station, is one of the most varied and informative regarding national and local news and notes. KBPS is unique in that it is run by Benson Public Schools. The PM station (89.9) is classical while the AM station (1450) is student-run.

KBBT-AM 970
222-9700
Alternative/progressive

KBNP-AM 1410
223-6769
News

KBOO-FM 90.7
231-8032
Community-sponsored radio;
full service

KBPS-AM 1450, FM 89.9
916-5828
Benson Public School. AM Student-run; FM: Classical

KEX-AM 1190
225-1190
Full service

KFXX-AM 1520
223-1441
Sports, news, talk

KGON-FM 92.3
223-1441
Album-oriented rock

KINK-FM 102
226-5080
Adult contemporary

KKEY-AM 1150
222-1150
Talk, mutual broad-casting system

KKJZ-FM 106.7
223-0300
Smooth jazz

KKRZ-FM 100.3
226-0100
Contemporary hits

KKSN-AM 910, FM 97.1
226-9791
Big band/nostalgia, oldies

KMXI-FM 106.7
245-1433
Oldies

KNRK-FM 94.7
223-1441
Alternative, progressive

KOPB-FM 91.5
293-1905
Oregon Public Broadcasting; mix of talk and varied music

KPDQ-AM 800
244-9900
Religious

KRRC-FM 104.1
771-2180
Reed College station;
alternative/progressive

KUFO-FM 101.1
222-1011
Album-oriented rock

KUPL-FM 98.5
223-0300
Contemporary country

KWJJ-AM 1080, FM 99.5
228-4393
Contemporary country

KXL-AM 750, FM 95.5
231-0750
AM: Talk, news; FM: Adult contemporary

KXYQ-FM 105.1
226-6731
Contemporary hits

Television Stations

ABC
KATU-TV CHANNEL 2
2153 NE Sandy Blvd.
231-4222

CBS
KOIN-TV CHANNEL 6
222 SW Columbia
464-0600

FOX
KPDX-TV CHANNEL 49
910 NE MLK Blvd.
239-4949

NBC
KGW-TV CHANNEL 8
1501 SW Jefferson
226-5000

PBS
KOPB-TV CHANNEL 10
7140 SW Macadam Ave.
244-9900

VISITOR INFORMATION

AAA
600 SW Market St.
Portland, OR 97201
222-6734
Automobile Club; emergency road
service and travel-related services.

**PORTLAND METROPOLITAN
CHAMBER OF COMMERCE**
221 NW 2nd Ave.
Portland, OR 97209
228-9411

**PORTLAND OREGON VISITORS
ASSOCIATION**
3 World Trade Center
26 SW Salmon St.
Portland, OR 97204
800/345-3214 or 222-2223

BANKING

**BANK OF AMERICA
FINANCIAL CENTER**
121 SW Morrison
275-2222

BANK OF TOKYO, LTD.
1211 SW 5th Ave.
222-3661

FEDERAL RESERVE BANK
915 SW Stark
221-5913

KEY BANK OF OREGON
1222 SW 6th Ave.
790-7699

US BANK
321 SW 6th Ave.
275-7345

WASHINGTON MUTUAL
811 SW 6th Ave.
238-3100

POST OFFICES

AIRPORT
7640 NE Airport Way
800/275-8777 or 335-7920

EAST PORTLAND
1020 SE 7th Ave.
800/275-8777

FOREST PARK
1706 NW 24th Ave.
800/275-8777

MULTNOMAH
7805 SW 40th Ave.
800/275-8777

PORTLAND MAIN OFFICE
715 NW Hoyt St.
800/275-8777

SELLWOOD
6723 SE 16th Ave.
800/275-8777

UNIVERSITY STATION
1505 SW 6th Ave.
800/275-8777

DAY CARE

Finding temporary day care while visiting can be a bit difficult. The first thing to do is check with your hotel for referrals. You might also check with community centers and churches.

AUNTIE FAY AGENCY
10725 SW Barbur Blvd.
293-6252
This agency uses only nannies or child-care providers who have extensive experience and excellent references. Agency-only references and criminal histories are thoroughly checked. Fees start at $7/ hour, four-hour minimum.

COMMUNITY CHILD CARE
5431 NE 20th Ave.
287-4959
Part-time and full-time child care

HELPING HAND CHILDCARE
1032 N. Sumner
281-1511
Drop-in day care

METRO CHILDCARE RESOURCE AND REFERRAL
253-5000
This is strictly a resource and referral agency. They don't employ their own child-care providers but have an extensive list of those who are. Call well

ahead of time; it can take a while for them to return the call.

NORTHWEST NANNIES INSTITUTE
11830 SW Kerr Parkway #100
Lake Oswego, OR 97035
245-5288
Most of the nannies have gone through a seven-month training program. Those who haven't have been professional nannies for a long time. The institute checks criminal history, driving records, and references. Nannies are all ages, starting at 18 on up to grandmotherly types. Temporary care $9 hour, four-hour minimum.

PROVIDENCE WEE CARE
842 NE 47th Ave.
215-6832
Part-time and full-time child care, affiliated with Providence Hospitals

MULTICULTURAL RESOURCES

CHINESE SOCIAL SERVICE CENTER
4937 SE Woodstock Blvd.
Portland, OR 97206
771-7977

COAST LANGUAGE ACADEMY
200 SW Market St. #111
Portland, OR 97201
224-1960

HISPANIC METROPOLITAN CHAMBER OF COMMERCE
222-0280

I HAVE A DREAM FOUNDATION
4919 NE 9th Ave.
Portland, OR 97211
287-7203

**JAPAN-AMERICA SOCIETY
OF OREGON**
221 NW 2nd Ave.
Portland, OR 97209
228-9411

**LESBIAN AND GAY
PROGRAM/AFSC**
2249 E. Burnside
Portland, OR 97214
230-9430

**MITTLEMAN JEWISH
COMMUNITY CENTER**
6651 SW Capitol Hwy.
Portland, OR 97219
244-0111

**OFFICE FOR HISPANIC
MINISTRIES**
2838 E. Burnside
Portland, OR 97214
233-8324

**SONS OF NORWAY GRIEG LODGE
NO. 15**
111 NE 11th Ave.
Portland, OR 97232
236-3401

**SOUTHEAST ASIAN APOSTOLATE
CENTER**
5404 NE Alameda Dr.
Portland, OR 97213
249-5892

URBAN LEAGUE OF PORTLAND
10 N. Russell
Portland, OR 97227
280-2600

INDEX

accommodations, 43–57; Downtown, 45–49; Southwest, 49–52; Northwest, 52–53; Northeast, 53–56; Southeast, 56–57
airport shuttle service, 37, 40
airports, 38–42
Alameda, 16
Albertina Kerr Center, 108
Alpenrose Dairy, 114–115
animals, 108, 114, 118–120
Ankeny's New Market Block, 101
Antique Row, 145–147
architecture, 97
ART, the Cultural Bus, 34
Artists Repertory Theatre, 166, 167
Astoria, 183–187
auto racing, 157–158

Bank of California Building, 99
banks, 199
baseball, 158
basketball, 158
Bathtub Fountain, 106
beer, 84–91
Benson Bubblers, 102
Beverly Cleary at Grant Park, 115
biking, 35–36, 37, 152–153
Bishop's House, 92
Blagden Block, 92
boats, 38, 110, 111
Bonneville Dam, 119
bookstores, 98, 115, 117, 147–149
bowling, 153
bridges, 2, 111
bus service, 32, 42

Cafe Lena, 169
Cambell's Fountain, 102
canoeing, 155
Capitalism, 108
Cascade Sternwheelers, 110
Celtic music, 176–177
Charles F. Berg Building, 99
chefs, 82
child care, 200
children's activities, 114–120
Children's Museum, 115–116
Children's Story Garden, 92–93
Chinatown, 93
Church of Elvis, 93
city layout, 29–30

Civic Stadium, 158
classical music, 167
Columbia River Gorge, 182–183
comedy, 178
Corbett/Terwilliger, 10
Council, 8–9
country music, 175-176
Crystal Springs Rhododendron Garden, 132

dance, 167
dance clubs, 172–173
day spas, 112–113
department stores, 149–150
Downtown shopping, 137–140
Dreams Well Studio, 169–170
driving, 32–34
Duyck's Peachy Pig Farm, 119–120

Eastmoreland, 15–16
Eastside, 1–2, 12–16
Echo Theatre, 170
economy, 26–28
Elk Fountain, 102
Erickson's Saloon, 93
events, 19–26

factory outlets, 151
Fareless Square, 33
First Congregational Church, 95
First Thursday, 126–127
fishing, 153–154
fitness clubs, 154
food, *see* restaurants
Forecourt Fountain, 103
fountains, 102–106
Friendly House Community Center, 116

Galleria, the, 150
galleries, 124–130
gardens, 106–107, 132, 134, 135–136
Glazed Terra Cotta Historic District, 98–100
golf, 154
Grape Escape Winery Tours, 111–112
greyhound racing, 158
Grotto, the, 108–109

Hallock and McMillian Building, 101
Hawthorne Boulevard shopping, 144–145

hiking, 157
Hippo Hardware & Trading Co., 124
history, 2–4, 6–7, 121–122
hockey, 158–159
horse racing, 158
hospitals, 197
hotels, *see* accommodations
Hoyt Arboretum, 106, 135

ice skating, 155
Imago, 170
Intermediate Theatre, 161–162
International Rose Test Garden, 106, 136
Interstate Firehouse Cultural Center, 170

Jake's Famous Crawfish, 65, 129
Japanese American Historical Plaza, 95
Japanese Gardens, 106–107, 136
jazz, 173–174
Jeff Morrison Fire Museum, 95

kayaking, 155

La Luna, 170
Ladd's Addition, 14–15
Lewis and Clark, 2–3, 121–122
lodging, *see* accommodations
Lovejoy, Asa, 3

Malibu Grand Prix, 120
malls, 150
MAX, 31–32
Meier and Frank, 149
Memorial Coliseum, 158, 159, 160, 164
Merchant's Hotel, 96
microbreweries, 84–91
Mill Ends Park, 133
Miracle Theatre Group, 170
Morgan Building, 100
movies, 178–181
Mt. Hood, 187–190
Mt. Tabor, 13–14
multicultural resources, 200–201
Multnomah, 10–11
museums, 115–116, 121–124
music clubs, 173–178
Musical Theatre Company, 167

neighborhoods, 1, 5–16
New Market Theater Building, 101
New Theatre Building, 161–162
newspapers, local, 197
Nob Hill, 11–12, 107

Nordstrom, 149
North Park Blocks, 133–134
Northwest 23rd shopping, 140–144
Northwestern National Bank Building, 100

Oaks Amusement Park, 109, 117
Old Town Historic District, 100–102
Old Town shopping, 139–140
OMSI, *see* Oregon Museum of Science and Industry
opera, 167
Oregon Ballet Theatre, 167
Oregon Children's Theatre Company, 117, 168
Oregon Coast, 190–191
Oregon Convention Center, 160–161
Oregon Garden, 134
Oregon History Center, 3, 121–122
Oregon Maritime Center and Museum, 96, 122–123
Oregon Museum of Science and Industry, 109, 117, 123
Oregon Sports Hall of Fame, 123
Oregon Stage Company, 170
Oregon Symphony Orchestra, 167
Oregon Trail, 3

Pacific Telephone and Telegraph Company Building, 100
parking, 34
parks, 131–136
Paula Productions/Stage 4 Theatre, 170
Pearl District
Peninsula Park, 134–135
people, 4–5
Personalized! Tours & Travel, Inc., 112
Peter's Walking Tours, 110
Pettygrove, Francis, 3
PICA, *see* Portland Institute for Contemporary Art
picnics, 134
Pioneer Courthouse Square, 96
Pioneer Place, 150
Pittock, Henry L., 106, 107–108
Pittock Mansion, 107–108
population, 3–4
Portland Art Museum, 96, 123
Portland Center for the Performing Arts, 161–164
Portland Center Stage, 168
Portland Civic Auditorium, 162–164
Portland Guides, 31

Portland Heights, 9
Portland Institute for Contemporary Art, 169
Portland International Airport, 38–41
Portland International Performance Festival, 171
Portland International Rose Festival, 22, 119
Portland Mounted Patrol, 4
Portland Opera Association, 167
Portland Parks and Recreation, 110
Portland Police Museum and Justice Center, 123–124
Portland Pride Indoor Soccer, 159
Portland Rage Roller Hockey, 158
Portland Rockies, 158
Portland Spirit, 111
Portland Town mural, 98
Portland Trail Blazers, 158
Portland Youth Philharmonic, 168
Portland's Broadway Theatre Series, 168
Portlandia, 96–98
post offices, 199–200
Powell's City of Books, 98, 117, 149
public transportation, 30–32, 33

radio stations, 197–198
rain, *see* weather
real estate, 27–28
Rebecca at the Well Shemanski Fountain, 103
restaurants, 58–83; by cuisine type, 59–60; Downtown, 60–70; Southwest, 70–72; Northwest, 72–76; Northeast, 76–78; Southeast, 78–83
Riverview Cemetery, 107
rock and blues, 174–175
roller skating, 156
rose festival, 22, 119
Rose Garden, 158, 164–165
rose gardens, 106, 136
Rose Quarter, 164–165

Salmon Street Springs, 103
Samtrak Excursion Train, 111
Saturday Market, 98, 139–140
Sauvie Island Wildlife Management Area, 108
Schnitzer Concert Hall, 163, 164
Sellwood, 12–13
Sharon Wood Bridge Tours & Urban Adventures, 111

shopping, 137–151
Skidmore Fountain, 103
skiing, 156
slang, local, 20
Smith Block, 101
soccer, 159
South Park Blocks, 133–134
sports, 120, 123, 152–159
Stark Raving Theater, 171
State of Oregon Office Building, 109
submarine, 109
swimming, 156–157

taxes, 26, 28
taxis, 36–38
Tears of Joy Theatre, 117–118, 168
television stations, 198–199
theater, 117, 117–118, 167–171
Tom McCall Waterfront Park, 135
tours, 110–112
toys, 115, 116
trains, 30–32, 42, 111
Transit Mall Animal Fountain, 103–104
Tri Met, 30–32, 34
trolleys, 38, 98
Tygres Heart Shakespeare Company, 168

Union Station, 42
US National Bank Building, 100
USS *Bluback*, 109

Vietnam Veterans Living Memorial, 107
visitor information, 199

Washington Park, 135–136
Washington Park Zoo, 118, 136
weather, 16–18
Wells Fargo Building, 100
West One Bank Broadway Series, 168
Westover, 11
Westside, 1, 8–12
White Eagle Saloon, 109
Wilcox Building, 100
Willamette River, 1, 2
Willamette Valley, 191–193
wineries, 111–112, 193–196
Winningstad Theatre, 161–162
Winter Hawks, 158–159
World Forestry Center, 107

zoo, 118, 136

ABOUT THE AUTHORS

Linda Nygaard, a Portland freelance writer, is a regular contributor to *The Oregonian*. Her work has also appeared in the *Chicago Tribune* and *Walking, American Brewer, Seattle*, and *Vacations* magazines, as well as on-line at abcnews.com. She undertook the task of getting to know Portland when she moved to the city in 1988 after leaving a successful sales and marketing career in Colorado. A rancher's daughter from Montana, Linda's career has led her throughout United States, Canada, Central American, Europe, and Australia. Even though her wanderlust paves a trail through continent after continent, she says her favorite place is still Portland. Linda is a member of the American Society of Journalists and Authors as well as a board member of Oregon Writers Colony and of Bones and Brew (a benefit for the Oregon Food Bank). She is also hard at work on a novel.

Susan Wickstrom is a long-time regular contributor to *Willamette Week*, Portland's alternative news weekly, and an associate editor for the *Bear Essential* magazine. In addition to her job at the Oregon Council for Humanities, she sits on the board of Portland's Community Music Center and is an avid volunteer in the Oregon Children's Foundation's Start Making a Reader Today (SMART) program. She has an M.A. in communications from Stanford Univeristy. During college and graduate school, she worked in the trenches of the restaurant industry as a waitress. Her aching feet finally demanded that she write about food rather than serve it.

JOHN MUIR PUBLICATIONS
and its City•Smart Guidebook authors are dedicated to building community awareness within City•Smart cities. We are proud to work with Oregon Literacy as we publish this guide to Portland.

Oregon Literacy was founded over 30 years ago as a nonprofit organization dedicated to promoting free tutoring for adult learners. Their primary focus is to provide advice and technical support to local and statewide literacy efforts. They also offer information and referral services to organizations, volunteers, and students through the Literacy Line, a toll-free hotline. Oregon Literacy is based in Portland and maintains collaborative relationships with affiliated literacy groups throughout the state.

For more information, please contact:
Oregon Literacy, Inc.
9806 SW Boones Ferry Rd.
Portland, OR 97219
Phone: 503/244-3898
Fax: 503/244-9147
Literacy Line: 800/322-8715